STAGE FRIGHT

40 STARS TELL YOU
HOW THEY BEAT
AMERICA'S #1
FEAR

MICK BERRY, MFA

MICHAEL R. EDELSTEIN, PHD

SEE SHARP PRESS • TUCSON, ARIZONA

See Sharp Press
P.O. Box 1731
Tucson, AZ 85702-1731

www.seesharppress.com

Berry, Mick.
   Stage fright / by Mick Berry, MFA, and Michael R. Edelstein, Ph.D. ; introduction by Nando Pelusi,
Ph.D. -- Tucson, Ariz. : See Sharp Press, 2009.
   250 p. ; 23 cm.
   Includes bibliographical references.
   ISBN: 9781884365461

Contents: Introduction -- Preface -- 1. How you can beat stage fright. 2. Carlos Alazraqui --
3. Jason Alexander -- 4. Mose Allison -- 5. Maya Angelou -- 6. Lawrence P. Beron -- 7. Mark Bittner --
8. Walter Block -- 9. Jim Bouton -- 10. David Brenner -- 11. Larry "Bubbles" Brown --
12. David Burns -- 13. Tony Castle -- 14. Peter Coyote -- 15. Phyllis Diller -- 16. Olympia Dukakis --
17. Will Durst -- 18. Albert Ellis -- 19. Melissa Etheridge -- 20. Tony Freeman -- 21. Dave Goelz --
22. Bonnie Hayes -- 23. Dan Hicks -- 24. Mickey Joseph -- 25. Kevin Kataoka -- 26. Jerome Kelly --
27. Richard Lewis -- 28. Paul Lyons -- 29. Maria Mason -- 30. Meehan Brothers -- 31. Larry Miller --
32. David A. Moss -- 33. Frank Oz -- 34. Ron Paul -- 35. Mark Pitta -- 36. Simon Phillips --
37. Kevin Rooney -- 38. Bob Sarlatte -- 39. Mark Schiff -- 40. Ben Sidran -- 41. Robin Williams.

Summary: Stage Fright is a collection of interviews with 40 prominent public figures, including famous
actors, comedians, musicians, and a former presidential candidate. It includes a lengthy chapter which
describes several proven-effective Rational Emotive Behavior Therapy (the original form of cognitive-
behavioral therapy) self-help techniques useful in overcoming stage fright.

1. Stage fright. 2. Performance -- Psychological aspects. 3. Public
speaking. I. Title. II. Edelstein, Michael R.
         158.27

Contents

For the countless potential stars who experience frustration and failure along the way, yet persist in following their passion

The co-authors of this book are available to conduct "Beat Stage Fright" workshops and seminars. For more information, go to

www.howtobeatstagefright.com
or write to
info@howtobeatstagefright.com

Introduction

About a decade ago, the co-author of this book, Michael Edelstein, and I were giving a presentation to the National Association of Cognitive Behavior Therapists, of which we're both on the Board of Advisors. And, wouldn't you know it, my co-presenter interrupted and corrected me. Sure, I balked a little, but I knew I'd better listen, as he is a master. He didn't let the point go—he was more concerned with the truth than my possibly bruised feelings. So we debated, and eventually I conceded his point, very publicly.

It's a good thing that our discussion was about how not to disturb oneself. I got a lesson on practicing self-mastery in public by the co-author of this very book on practicing self-mastery. Boy, is he good.

Dr. Edelstein and Mick Berry have synthesized in the most elegant and simple way the principles used by many popular performers to overcome their own stage fright. Taking the tenets of Rational Emotive Behavior Therapy, a powerful and focused type of cognitive-behavioral therapy developed by Dr. Albert Ellis, they present step-by-step exercises designed to help anyone overcome stage fright.

They interview many incredible performers in this book, including Phyllis Diller, Melissa Etheridge, Robin Williams, Maya Angelou, Olympia Dukakis, Frank Oz ("Miss Piggy" of the Muppets), Richard Lewis, David Brenner, and Jason Alexander (George Costanza from "Seinfeld"). These performers present their own techniques for overcoming stage fright, and many of their techniques are similar to those outlined in more detail by the co-authors of this book in the first chapter.

In my many years of practice, I've come to respect the subtlety and power of many of these methods, and how they work to change lives for the better. My practice and thinking on these matters show me endless variation in human desires, but definite patterns in disturbances such as fear of public speaking, social phobia, and stage fright. Our tendency to take preferences for public approval and escalate them into demands is at the root of stage fright, and Edelstein and Berry clearly identify the three main ways in which to overcome it.

First, they'll have you identify and dispute your demands on yourself and your performance. That sounds daunting, but it's like removing a tarp on a baseball field: it reveals many possibilities. Second, they'll have you assess your implicit and explicit demands on others, and the ways these demands can lead to anger and resentments. Addressing these demands will do wonders for your relationships with others, and will make ensemble performing easier. Third, they'll have you explore the demands that you may unconsciously be placing on performance conditions — and how quickly you can find excuses to quit or to not even try.

Dr. Michael Edelstein is often my go-to guy for the finer points of theory and practice. He knows his stuff inside and out—and that's reflected here in a clarity and focus rarely found in self-help books. If Michael Edelstein agrees or disagrees with me, I listen. His co-author, Mick Berry, is an energetic, witty, and insightful entertainer who has mastered the methods described here, and is a great complement to Dr. Edelstein. Their collaboration has really borne fruit.

This book will help you get better, not just feel better. In my years of practice, writing on and reading literature on human change, I can say that the most effective methods of overcoming stage fright are distilled in this very readable book by two skilled and dedicated change-agents.

I can promise that you'll have fun getting better, too. Study this gem and gain mastery over yourself. Then, go out, take the stage, and gain mastery over your audience!

—Nando Pelusi, PhD, Contributing Editor, *Psychology Today*

Preface

When we began working on this book, we reasoned that most people suffering from stage fright would not buy it simply because of its title and the insights it offers. We aren't household names (yet). So, we decided to ask celebrities about their struggles with stage fright—what works for them and what doesn't. This approach succeeded beyond our hopes. Readers will be touched by the intimate struggles and triumphs of the stars they love and, as a wonderful bonus, will see validation of our recommendations on dealing with stage fright.

You'll find the essence of our approach to this very common problem detailed in the first chapter. It presents proven anti-anxiety strategies from Rational Emotive Behavior Therapy (REBT), developed by pioneering psychologist Albert Ellis. (As a bonus, Dr. Ellis passionately spells out his concepts and strategies in our interview with him.) These strategies will allow you—through persistence and hard work—to greatly diminish or perhaps entirely overcome your stage fright.

Contrary to common sense, an illustrious career, celebrity status, great wealth, or other success as a performer will not cure your stage fright. Phyllis Diller told us: "I know of entertainers, in long, long careers, who never got over it, to the point of throwing up before every performance. . . . And they were big, big stars." (p. 96–97)

Entertainers of all stripes overcome stage fright by changing how they think: a change in thinking causes a change in feeling and behavior. As Robin Williams incisively notes: "Obviously, thinking is what creates the anxiety. And also, thinking diminishes it." (p. 246)

Even though many of those interviewed here appear to not fully appreciate this fact, they all, commendably, have devised their own strategies for dealing with stage fright. Some of these parallel one of our recommendations—using rational self-statements to put stage fright into perspective. We heard, over and over, the interviewees say that a bad performance is "not the end of the world." Many of the interviewees reveal other personal strategies that may prove useful to readers.

We recommend that after reading the first chapter you study the interview with Dr. Ellis. He's the master. Then, enjoy whichever interviews particularly interest you. But please don't neglect the rest. All of the interviewees have helpful insights, and you'll likely mine a few gems from the interviews with performers you've never heard of.

We believe that this book provides you the best means available to beat stage fright. Consistently apply the strategies described in Chapter 1, and in the engrossing interviews, and you'll be well on your way to overcoming America's #1 fear.

—Mick Berry, MFA
—Michael R. Edelstein, PhD

Acknowledgments

We are indebted to many. First, we wish to thank all the interviewees. They generously gave their valuable time to share their wisdom and experience, with the hope of aiding other performers. In particular, Dr. Maya Angelou deserves special credit. She agreed to be interviewed before any other celebrities had participated, taking a leap of faith that we wouldn't waste her valuable time. Her kindness, along with that of all the other performers, enabled us to interview an impressive group of artists; as one came aboard, others seemed to follow more readily.

We would also like to thank our publisher, Chaz Bufe, who encouraged us to write this book. Countless other people deserve our special gratitude, including Charlotte Behre, Daniel Behre, Debbie Behre, Leah Behre Miskimen, Patricia Behre, Walter Block, Jon Boyle, Pat Bruens, Burton Butler, Janice Edelstein, Steve Farber, Ross Grossman, Claribel Meserve, Marty Nemko, Nando Pelusi, Roberta Rosen, David Ramsay Steele, Jerome Tarshis, and Emmett Velten. Finally, and most significantly, we would like to thank our mentor Albert Ellis, the genius behind the advice we give here. Dr. Ellis and his wife, Debbie Joffe Ellis, generously agreed to our interviewing him in the last days of his inspiring life. May his trail blazing teachings benefit struggling artists forever.

* * *

Thank you to the editors and board members of the **Albert Ellis Tribute Book Series** for selecting *Stage Fright* as a Series title. (The editors and board members are listed on the following page.)

General Editors: Albert Ellis Tribute Book Series

Bill Knaus, EdD, Founder of Rational Emotive Education. Former Director of Training, Institute for Advanced Study in Rational Emotive Therapy.

Jon Carlson, PsyD, EdD, ABPP Distinguished Professor, Governors State University and a proponent of Adlerian psychotherapy.

Elliot D. Cohen, PhD, Professor, Indian River State College; Adjunct Professor, Florida State University College of Medicine; and founder, Logic-Based Therapy.

Albert Ellis Tribute Book Series Honorary Board

Irwin Altrows, PhD • Guy Azoula , PhD • Joel Block, PhD • Walter Block, PhD
Giulo Bortolozzo, MS • Chuck Carins, PhD • Nick Cummings, PhD
Rev. Thomas Downes, PhD • Michael R. Edelstein, PhD
Debbie Joffe-Ellis, LMHC, REBT Fellow • David Ellis, JD
Susan Ellis, PhD • Frank Farley, PhD • Pam Garcey, PhD • Edward Garcia, MA
H. Jon Geis, PhD • Joe Gerstein, MD • Russ Greiger, PhD
Nancy Haberstroh, MBA, PhD • Steven C. Hayes, PhD • Gerald Koocher, PhD,
ABPP • Howard Kassinove, PhD, ABPP • Sam Klarreich., PhD
Paul Kurtz, PhD • Arnie Lazarus, PhD, ABPP • Barry Lubetkin, PhD
John Minor, PhD • John C. Norcross, PhD • Christine A. Padesky, PhD
Vince Parr, PhD • Leon Pomeroy, PhD • Aldo R. Pucci, PsyD
Roberta Richardson, PhD • Will Ross, Webmaster, REBTnetwork.org
Gayle, Rosillini, MA • Nosheen Kahn Rahman, PhD
Richard S. Schneiman, PhD • Sanjay Singh, MD, DNB, PhD
Deborah Steinberg, MSW • Thomas Szasz, MD Danny Wedding, PhD, MPH
Richard Wessler, PhD • Janet L. Wolfe, PhD

A Final Word from Dr. Debbie Joffe Ellis—Wife of Dr. Albert Ellis

Early one Saturday morning, in May 2006, my husband was rushed to the emergency room of a major New York hospital with severe pneumonia—only hours after giving his famous Friday Night Workshop. Doctors attempted to prepare me for his imminent death, but through determination he survived for more than a year and two months after that prediction. Doctors constantly expressed amazement and admiration for Al's fighting spirit. Throughout that time Al was in and out of hospital, and in a facility for rehabilitation in between the hospital stays. While he was becoming increasingly frail, and health complications kept arising, he was determined to work and to help others until he absolutely could not. And that is what he did.

It was during this period that he answered the questions of Mick Berry and Dr. Michael Edelstein for this interview, and he continued to contribute to the well-being of people in other ways as well. Students would come to his bedside, and he would conduct workshops. He would speak to journalists. He attended to correspondence by dictating letters for me to send. He was an outstanding model of applying his approach and philosophy in order to not succumb to obstacles—and hence he kept on living a courageous, constructive and contributing life till his severely failing health was at a level that prevented that.

Countless people continue to fight and eliminate their fears, and in so doing experience happier and healthier lives, by applying Rational Emotive Behavior Therapy and remembering the example of the remarkable Dr. Albert Ellis. That is what he would want.

The Authors

Mick Berry, MFA

Cited by the *San Francisco Chronicle* as a "local phenom," Mick Berry has been performing for over 40 years. He has worked as an actor and teacher with The San Francisco Shakespeare Festival, The California Shakespeare Festival, The San Francisco Mime Troupe, Marin Shakespeare Festival, George Coates Performance Works, and California Conservatory Theatre. He has performed stand-up comedy and three critically acclaimed one-man shows across the United States and Canada. With nearly four decades of drumming experience, he has accompanied musicians such as Paul Jackson, Henry Butler, Michael Wolff, and Eddie Henderson, and currently plays regularly in the SF Bay Area while maintaining a weekly teaching schedule of over 30 students. He is now working on a new one-man show on rock drumming legend Keith Moon. He is the co-author of two other books: *The Drummer's Bible* (with Jason Gianni) and *The Bassist's Bible* (with Tim Boomer). He holds a Master of Fine Arts in acting from the University of North Carolina.

Mick's web site is www.mickberry.com.

Michael R. Edelstein, PhD

Dr. Edelstein has an in-person and telephone therapy practice in San Francisco. He is the author (with David Ramsay Steele) of *Three Minute Therapy*, a self-help book for overcoming common emotional and behavioral problems. The book was a Quality Paperback Book Club/Book-of-the-Month Club Selection, a Behavioral Sciences Book Service Book Club Selection, and an Albert Ellis Institute Selection.

Dr. Edelstein specializes in the treatment of anxiety, depression, relationship problems, and addictions. He is also the San Francisco SMART Recovery Professional Advisor.

Dr. Edelstein lectures nationally and internationally, appears on radio and television, and is published in psychological journals. He was a Training Supervisor and Fellow of the Albert Ellis Institute. He holds a diplomate in Cognitive-Behavioral Therapy from, and is on the Board of Advisors of, the National Association of Cognitive-Behavioral Therapists. He is Past President of the Association for Behavioral and Cognitive Therapy. He is a Certified Sex Therapist and has served as a Consulting Psychologist for the National Save-A-Life League, Inc., the oldest suicide prevention center in the United States.

Dr. Edelstein's web site is www.threeminutetherapy.com.

How You Can Beat Stage Fright

Stage fright is America's #1 fear, greater than the fear of death. Virtually everyone who has spoken or performed in public has felt it. Many others avoid public performing—or asking a question at a lecture or in a classroom—to avoid it. Jumpiness, fidgeting, profuse sweating, gut-wrenching bouts of self-doubt, acute self-consciousness, nausea, vomiting, and nervous, botched performances are some of its symptoms. Comedian Mark Schiff describes one of his worst bouts with it (at Caesar's Palace): "My brain went dead. I got frozen, and I started hyperventilating. . . . I almost bolted off the stage."

Fortunately there are effective ways to beat stage fright. Foremost is the cognitive-behavioral approach to banishing anxiety problems. Albert Ellis's Rational Emotive Behavior Therapy (REBT), the precursor to all other cognitive-behavioral therapies, is our foundation in this chapter.

Briefly stated, stage fright is not produced by public speaking or public performing. Speaking or performing do not have the power to frighten you. Circumstances do not make you anxious. Rather, you induce stage fright in yourself with the thoughts, beliefs, and ideas in your very own head.

How to Give Yourself Stage Fright

Stage fright-inducing self-messages have several common features:

• **They almost always emanate from *musts***: "I *must* do well or I'm no good." "The audience *must* like me, otherwise I'm a hopeless loser." "I *must* not feel anxious; if I do feel anxious I won't be able to stand it." "I *must* not appear anxious or go blank. If I do, I'll be a laughing stock." "I absolutely *must* perform well, or my life will be ruined." These are absolutistic, take-no-prisoners demands (and mostly self-demands). Since we're all fallible humans who make mistakes and easily worry, *musts* are quite common. Yet they are a recipe for self-induced anxiety; and that anxiety contributes to poor performance.

• **Musts** **are often coupled with** *awfulizing*: "I *must* do well. It would be *awful* if I don't." "It would be *terrible* if the audience doesn't like me." "It would be *horrible* if I appear anxious." In other words, it would be hellish if things don't go as they must. This failure to see things in perspective, to exaggerate the consequences of doing poorly to infinity, lies at the core of your anxiety.

• **Demanding acceptance** by an audience. You tell yourself: "I *must* be liked by the audience. It will be *awful* if I'm not. If they don't like me, it'll prove I'm a total failure." Notice that these thoughts make your self-worth dependent on an external factor. Equating your value as a person with your performance and/or acceptance by an audience increases pressure dramatically, thus amplifying the anxiety produced via *musts* and *awfulizing*.

• **Perfectionism** rubs salt in the wounds: "I *must* do well or even outstandingly well. In fact, I *must* do as well as possible—*perfectly*. It'll be *awful* if I don't. And if I don't perform perfectly, I'll be a loser." While setting high goals—even impossibly high goals—can prove motivating, perfectionism involves setting impossibly high goals for yourself coupled with the demand that you reach them.

• **Self-rating and self-downing** are almost invariably the result of demands, awfulizing and, often, perfectionism: "I must do well; I must do as well as is possible; I must do perfectly. It'll be awful, terrible, horrible, and I'll be lower than a worm if I don't." Notice that these thoughts make your self-worth dependent on how well you perform.

• **Anxiety about anxiety** is the cherry atop the sundae. It's what often leads to full-blown panic attacks. Performers notice that they're anxious or that they may become anxious, and then compound their anxiety by making themselves anxious about being anxious. They tell themselves that they must not be anxious; that they're no good for being anxious, it's awful if they're anxious, and they can't stand it. This last statement is an expression of Low Frustration Tolerance (LFT), the refusal to accept, and thus tolerate, frustrating or anxiety-laden experiences.

Several of the performers interviewed in this book recognize this problem of anxiety about anxiety—and how to beat it through self-acceptance. Maya Angelou puts it beautifully:

> "Accept it; don't fight it." My mother used to tell me, "If you're afraid, tell yourself you're afraid." She said, "When a snake approaches a bird, the bird—if it knew it was afraid—could fly above the snake in a second. But the bird doesn't say to itself, 'I'm afraid.' It just allows itself to be paralyzed."
>
> I think this is true for a performer. What he or she should do is say, "I'm nervous as the dickens. I'm as nervous as I can be. And I'm going to say this piece." That's better than trying to ignore it.

Olympia Dukakis puts the matter more succinctly: "I don't fight it [the nervousness] anymore. I let it happen. If that's who I am, that's who I am."

* * *

Thus far, we've considered stage fright as it applies to all performers. There are additional factors, especially when considering performers in ensembles.

• **Anger**. Performing with others is sometimes intensely frustrating. Then, along with or distinct from placing absolutistic demands on yourself, you may place them on others: "They *must* do well. And they must treat me well. If they don't, it'll be *awful*. They'll be jerks who deserve punishment. And I *can't stand it*." This is a recipe for resentment, hostility, and anger directed at your fellow performers.

• **Anxiety about acceptance** by your fellow performers often compounds problems in ensemble performing. Similar to anxiety over audience acceptance, here you may raise the stakes by overvaluing the opinions of your fellow performers, thinking they presumably are more important judges of your performance than the audience.

Stage Fright—The Damage It Does

Performance anxiety interferes with attaining your basic goals, and hence blocks your happiness in several ways.

• **Common human goals** include: survival / physical health; good social connections—with friends, lovers, co-workers, family; mastery of one's work, a craft, or an avocation; vital absorbing interests—in one's work, one's art, in a cause, or in spirituality.

Stage fright tends to interfere with all of these, and hence with your happiness.

• **Survival/health**. Anxiety has a well-documented adverse effect on both physical and mental health. The Rand Corporation states: "the impact of an anxiety disorder is roughly equivalent to that of irritable bowel syndrome, a serious chronic condition."
(www.rand.org/pubs/research_briefs/2006/RAND_RB9173.pdf)

• **Social connections**. The worse one's stage fright, the worse its impact tends to be on one's social connections. The more individuals are preoccupied with themselves, the less attention they have for others. Further, if they're making absolutistic demands on others, e.g., "they *must* perform well," the attention the demand-maker pays to them will be negative—impatience, resentment, anger—and will likely alienate them or completely drive them away.

• **Mastery**. At least one common American belief is actually true: the more effortless a performance appears, the better it will be. Those suffering from stage fright tend toward preoccupation with themselves, rather than clearly focusing on the task at hand; their attention is divided and they're likely to also suffer physiological reactions from stage fright, such as tightness, sweating and shaking, that detract from their performance.

• **Vital, absorbing interests**. When individuals are focused on themselves, their energies are divided and they cannot pay full attention to their interests.

Beating Stage Fright—Traditional Strategies

• **Hard work**. In the course of conducting the interviews for this book, we heard, over and over, "practice," "prepare," "perform." Many, probably most, performers have made gains in overcoming anxiety through simple hard work and repetition: practicing/performing incessantly until their performance-confidence increases. Yet other very accomplished performers—including famous ones who have been in the spotlight for decades—still suffer from stage fright, some to the point of vomiting before every performance.

Why? The difference lies in what they're telling themselves. Those who gain confidence are telling themselves positive messages, such as, "I know my material. I've done this a thousand times. I'll be fine," and "I should do fine, but even if I don't it's not the end of the world."

In contrast, established, accomplished performers who suffer stage fright are still giving themselves the negative, irrational messages they gave themselves at the beginnings of their careers: "What if I bomb? That'll be *awful*." "I *must* do well." "It'll be *awful* if the audience hates me. I'll be a total failure." Etc., etc., etc.

So, while practice, preparation, and performing all tend to decrease stage fright, they only do so if a performer's self-messages change from the negative ones to the positive ones. In most cases, this change is unconscious. But if a performer consciously changes his or her self-messages from the untrue, irrational ones to the rational/positive ones, progress in overcoming stage fright will likely be greatly accelerated.

• **Distraction**. The classic example of this is attempting to picture one's audience naked or in their underwear. The problems with the use of distraction are: 1) the performer is dividing his or her attention between the task at hand and the distraction; 2) the performer can become aware that he's simply playing mental games with himself and lose confidence in those games at any time; 3) it fails to undermine the core of the anxiety: the performer's irrational philosophy (expressed in self-defeating self-talk).

• **Deep, slow breathing**. The usual recommendation is taking in ten or twelve slow, deep breaths. Some also recommend the combination of deep breaths with a form of mini-meditation: closing one's eyes and blanking one's mind during the deep breathing. This can be temporarily calming, but it's a type of distraction and leaves the anxiety-creating thinking intact.

Beating Stage Fright—More Effective Strategies

Are there more effective ways to beat stage fright? Yes. As a fallible human being, you may never completely eliminate your performance jitters. But you can greatly minimize them, to the point where they become only a minor annoyance, surfacing only occasionally. How can you do this?

• **Abolish your musts**. Identify your self-demands, then rip them up. Replace *musts* with *preferences*: not "I *must* do well," but, "I *prefer* to do well." This goes hand in hand with developing anxiety tolerance. Not "I *can't stand* feeling anxious," but rather "I *don't like* feeling anxious, but I can stand what I don't like." The first statement is self-destructive and unrealistic; the second is helpful and realistic.

• **Uproot your awfulizing**. Not "I *must* do well and it'll be *awful* if I don't," but rather "I *prefer* to do well, but it's not the end of the world if I don't." Put things into a realistic perspective. If you don't speak or perform well, your family will probably continue to love you (or hate you) and the sun will most likely come up tomorrow. The way that David Brenner puts this is "No one's coming out of the alley with a baseball bat playing 'Let's get a Jew.' So what's the big deal? What am I nervous about?"

• **Abandon self-rating**. Self-valuing based on one's performance or on the approval of others is a recipe for hopelessness, depression, and giving up. Self-damning performers rarely live up to their unrealistic self-expectations, and even when they do, they often compare themselves with others who perform better than they do. Self-rating based on audience or other-performer acceptance is equally self-defeating. It has the added disadvantage of removing the locus of control from oneself to external entities. Self-rating can lead to grandiosity—"I'm the greatest thing since Charlie Chaplin!"—after an especially good performance or reception by an audience. More often, it will lead to self-downing and depression after an imperfect performance or audience rejection. Additionally, self-rating usually creates anxiety about the *next* performance or audience reaction.

Jason Alexander describes the benefits of getting away from self-absorption: "When I began to make the story the most important thing, I became much less the focus of my concerns." The lesson here is that the more you abandon self-absorption/self-rating, the more your nervousness will diminish.

• **Develop unconditional self-acceptance** rather than self-esteem. It's more reasonable and effective to focus on self-acceptance than on self-esteem. We're all fallible human beings who screw up fairly often. But we're alive, and life can be quite enjoyable, even thrilling in peak moments. Instead of rating yourself based on your performance or audience acceptance (which produces self-esteem, be it high or low), it's more realistic (and self-helpful) to accept yourself as a fallible human who screws up regularly and yet has an innate capacity for enjoying life. Further, even if rating yourself were rational—which it isn't—a rating based on performance cannot equal the rating of your being, your totality. To put this in other words, *your performance* is one thing. *You* are another. It can be helpful to rate how well you do, but it's not helpful to rate your*self.*

Moreover, you can strive to unconditionally accept your fellow performers as error-prone, fallible humans who are probably trying to do their best, rather than to rate them based on their performance or treatment of you. As mentioned above, intolerance of others triggers anger: "They *must not* perform badly or mistreat me! They're worse than useless if they do!" This over-critical attitude tends to worsen ensemble performances and to produce conflict with your fellow performers.

• **Develop unconditional life-acceptance**. As life is spelled h-a-s-s-l-e for just about everyone, it's essential to accept this harsh reality in all its adverse aspects. Make the best of it. Don't dogmatically rebel against it: "It *should no*t be this way, *I can't stand it*! It's not *fair*!" Acceptance doesn't mean liking it. Rather, it means acknowledging that it is what it is, while attempting to change what you can, and remembering that you *can* bear what you don't like. If you're on stage and the lighting, sound system, your fellow performers, etc., aren't up to snuff, that's tough! Accept it and do the best you can. Then try to improve whatever's wrong after the performance, without whining about it.

Specific Techniques

There are additional techniques for helping with stage fright beyond the traditional ones mentioned above:

• **Rational coping statements** are simple self-statements that tend to calm anxiety. Use them when you notice you're suffering stage fright and recognize your negative self-messages. Examples of rational coping statements include: "If I don't do well, it's not the end of the world"; "What's the worst that can happen if I don't do well? The audience won't like me? Tough!"; and "Even if they think I'm a total fool, their thoughts can't magically turn me into one."

• **ABCDEF** is a highly effective REBT tool for addressing negative emotions such as stage fright. Its components are:

A—**Activating event** you recently experienced about which you felt upset or disturbed,

B—**Irrational Belief** about or irrational evaluation of this activating event,

C—**Emotional and behavioral Consequence** of your irrational belief, resulting from A x B,

D—**Disputing** or questioning your irrational Belief,

E—**Effective new thinking** or answer resulting from Disputing your irrational Belief,

F—**New Feeling** or behavior resulting from Disputing your irrational Belief.

Now let's apply this to stage fright:

A—Activating event: I'm about to go on stage. Suppose I blow it?

B—Irrational Belief: I *must* perform well! Life won't be worth living if I do poorly!

C—Emotional and behavioral Consequence: Nervousness, sweating, shaking, vomiting. Divided attention between self and the task at hand. Poor performance.

D—Disputing: Why must I perform well? Where is the evidence life won't be worth living?

E—Effective new thinking: It's preferable I perform well, but not a dire necessity. I won't like it if I perform poorly, but I can stand what I don't like. It certainly may have disadvantages, but I'll still be alive and the world won't end. I've done poorly before and I've survived, and I'll survive this time. Having failed does not prove I'll always fail; rather it proves I did not succeed as I would have liked *this time.* Doing poorly only proves, at the very worst, that I'm an imperfect human. It's not the possibility of a bad performance that causes my symptoms, but rather it's my self-destructive thinking about blowing it that makes me nervous. With practice I can change my thinking and unconditionally accept myself with my imperfect performing —and if I practice, practice, practice, my performing will almost certainly improve. But I can still have a happy life if I blow it, although I would be happier if I do terrifically. The more I pressure myself to do well, the worse I'll tend to feel and perform. The more I accept myself with my mistake-making, the better I'll tend to do.

F—New Feeling or behavior: Diminished stage fright and lessened physical symptoms.

Write out this exercise a few times daily, the more frequently the better. (Use your own words—don't word-for-word copy the above example.) The further in advance of a performance you begin this discipline, the deeper the results will tend to be. Remember, reinforcement is the royal road to learning.

With practice, it's possible to write the ABCDEF in as little as three to five minutes. It's usually better to do the exercise in written form, although with experience you'll be able to supplement the writing by also using the process mentally. To combat spur-of-the-moment stage fright, in situations where it's not possible to write out one's ABCs, rational coping statements (see above) are a good alternative.

Considerations when doing the ABCDEF exercise

• Embracing the **E** is a significant step in changing your feelings. If you eventually don't deeply buy into **E**, your feelings rarely will improve.

• Some people conclude that the ABCDEF exercise doesn't work because it often doesn't yield immediate results. This may be because at **A** you failed to identify the most meaningful *must*; at **E** you weakly reinforced the new thinking; you were demanding that you not disturb yourself in the first place; or demanding that you must feel instantaneously better (creating secondary disturbance—disturbance over being disturbed).

There are ways to deal with these problems:

• To properly identify the *must*, it's often easiest to begin the ABC exercise with **C**—Emotional and behavioral Consequences. (Contrary to much pop psychology, people tend to be quite in touch with their feelings. They just don't know what to do about them.)

A

B

C—I feel anxious.

You can then fill in A—Activating event:

A— I've got a very important performance coming up.

B

C—I feel anxious.

This often makes it easier to find B (the irrational Belief), which you can then fill in. Remember, the irrational Belief is a *should*, a *must*, a *demand*.

Look for it. It's there. As we've found with ourselves over years of practicing REBT, when there's emotional disturbance (anxiety, depression, anger),
there is a demand.

Then identify **B**, your irrational Belief, your demand:

A—I've got a very important performance coming up.

B—I must perform well. If I don't, it will be horrible, utterly awful, the
worst thing in the world.

C—I feel anxious.

At **D**, question the idiotic thoughts at **B**. (Yes, irrational thoughts are idiotic.) Simply place the word "why" in front of **B**'s irrational thought and a
"?" after it.

A—I've got a very important performance coming up.

B—I must perform well. If I don't, it will be horrible, utterly terrible,
the worst thing in the world.

C—I feel anxious.

D—Why must I perform well? Why would it be horrible, utterly awful,
the worst thing in the world if I don't?

You are then free to answer the questions posed at **D**. (Remember, the
more thoroughly you tear apart your irrational, unrealistic, idiotic thinking,
the more viscerally you will drum out your well-practiced, decades-
entrenched, self-defeating irrationalities.)

A—I've got a very important performance coming up.

B—I *must* perform well. If I don't, it will be horrible, utterly awful, the
worst thing in the world.

C—I feel anxious.

D—Why must I perform well? Why would it be horrible, utterly awful, the worst thing in the world if I don't?

E—Nothing says I must perform well, except the ideas in my own nutty head. To hell with it! I can accept myself as a fallible human who foolishly makes himself upset. I also accept myself as a fallible human who might not always perform well. It'd be nice if I were superhuman, but I'm not and never will be. I can stop insisting that I perform well. I don't have to! I just don't! That's a dumb idea that gets in my way and I am determined to give it up.

Just you watch: it will *not* be horrible if I don't perform well. Performing badly is *not* the worst thing in the world. There are infinitely worse things—starvation, torture, terminal illness. Staking all of my happiness on my performance is senseless. I *can* stand it—I've stood bad performances in the past and am still here. It won't kill me. I will not explode. All of life will not be worthless. Even if I foolishly stake all of my existence on this performance, others really don't care that much. However upset I make myself, most people on the planet don't know me or care about me. And I don't need them to. As Ralph Terry told Jim Bouton, "Kid, just remember one thing: No matter what happens, win or lose, five hundred million Chinese Communists don't give a shit."

Once you've internalized these beliefs at **E**, your anxious feelings will change, which can be stated at **F**.

The entire ABC exercise, then, will resemble this:

A—I've got a very important performance coming up.

B—I must perform well. If I don't, it will be horrible, utterly awful, the worst thing in the world.

C—I feel anxious.

D—Why must I perform well? Why would it be horrible, utterly terrible, the worst thing in the world if I don't?

E—Nothing says I must perform well, except the ideas in my own nutty head. To hell with it! I can accept myself as a fallible human who foolishly makes himself upset. I also accept myself as a fallible human who might not always perform well. It'd be nice if I were superhuman, but I'm not and never will be. I can stop insisting that I perform well. I don't have to! I just don't! That's a dumb idea that gets in my way and I am determined to give it up.

Just you watch: it will not be horrible if I don't perform well. Performing badly is not the worst thing in the world. There are infinitely worse things—starvation, torture, terminal illness. Staking all of my happiness on my performance is senseless. I can stand it—I've stood bad performances in the past and am still here. It won't kill me. I will not explode. All of life will not be worthless. Even if I foolishly stake all of my existence on this performance, others really don't care that much. However upset I make myself, most people on the planet don't know me or care about me. And I don't need them to. As Ralph Terry told Jim Bouton: "Kid, just remember one thing: No matter what happens, win or lose, five hundred million Chinese Communists don't give a shit."

F—Less anxiety (or just possibly no anxiety).

Be honest with yourself at **F**. If there is no change of feeling, don't kid yourself about it. There are other exercises to fully hammer out your self-defeating thinking. Here's one:

Debating Until You Win

No matter how conscientiously you complete the ABC exercise, anxiety may still linger. Your long-held irrational beliefs may be quite stubborn. You may (irrationally) talk back to them: "I know intellectually nothing must be the way I want it." What you may really mean by this is that you don't deeply believe the *must* is false. Try zeroing in on your irrational beliefs by directly arguing against them using this rigorous format:

Begin by answering the questions posed at **D**.

D—Why must I perform well?

E—Nothing says I must perform well. That's just my own stupid idea.

If this does not hit home, or you don't know what to say next, argue with your irrational, self-defeating thought.

Irrational thought: If I don't perform well, I won't get this job, making my life quite hard. I *must not* have a hard life!

Rational thought: It's true I would profit from performing well. But nothing says my life can't be hard. I want to work as hard as I can to make things easy. But no matter how much I work, I cannot have a guarantee of success.

Irrational thought: I keep failing. This *proves* I can't succeed, as I must.

Rational thought: I am able to succeed. But being able to succeed and demanding I succeed are two different things. And previous failure does not ensure future failure. I'm not clairvoyant.

Irrational thought: But others have it so much easier! Life *should not* be so unfair to me!

Rational thought: It is unfair that some people have an easier life than me. It's also unfair that many other people have a harder life than me. If I would like my life to be better, good! I can still work as hard as I know how to make my life better, including performing well.

Irrational thought: Life is such a pain in the butt! It *should not* be this tough!

Rational thought: Since I don't run the universe, what's the evidence that life should not be tough for me?

(no longer) Irrational thought: I guess I really don't have any evidence.

Rational thought: Right! There's no reason life should not be a pain in the butt. But this doesn't mean it's *awful*, devoid of any possible pleasure. Even if I don't get what I want, it's not horrible. I can work as hard as I know how, as intelligently as I know how. I am committed to doing just that. If I do, eventually things are much more likely to go the way I would like them to. But there are no guarantees. What is virtually guaranteed is that if I hold onto my demands I am going to feel lousy. So, to hell with my demands! I am going to give them up, and if they return I will give them up again and again and again. I can continually work against my human tendency to make myself upset. The bottom line is: even though I want many things, I don't have to have them! And that's the way it is. I can accept that or whine about it. It's my choice, and I choose not to whine!

By continually challenging your irrational thoughts with rational ones, you'll eventually break down your demand that you must perform well. It's a matter of persistence in finding the *should*, the *demand*, the *must*, and repeatedly uprooting it until you begin to believe the truth: no matter how much you fail, it's not the end of the world; nothing says you must succeed; but if you prefer to succeed and work hard, you'll have a better chance of success than if you burden yourself with anxiety-inducing demands.

Internalizing such rational thoughts is your goal. This book provides the theory and techniques that will help you toward that goal. At the end of the day, though, it's the rational thoughts you profoundly believe, feel, and act on that will make you better.

Rational-Emotive Imagery (REI)

Step I: Vividly visualize your worst performing fear come to life. For example, if you're a comedian, visualize bombing like you've never bombed before—at an important gig in front of your most respected peers.

Step II: While picturing this scene, get in touch with your feelings of anxiety, dread, and panic, as strongly as you can. Really feel them.

Do Step II for just a few seconds.

Step III: Now, while still clearly imagining the scene from Step I, make yourself feel keenly concerned, deeply displeased, and profoundly disappointed, rather than anxious, dread-filled, and panicky.

Do this by making rational statements to yourself, such as: "I've survived this before and I'll survive it again. I really don't like bombing, but it's not the end of the universe. I will live through it, no matter how panicky I feel at the time. I *can* stand what I don't like." Also, "It's not bombing, or the possibility of bombing, that makes me anxious; rather, my self-defeating thinking about bombing causes my dread. With practice I can change my thinking and accept bombing—although I'll never like it. Looking at bombing this way will benefit me for the rest of my performing life."

Do Step III for three to five minutes, three times daily.

Bonnie Hayes describes her use of this technique very clearly (although she doesn't identify it as REI):

> Picture the worst thing that could possibly happen. And then imagine yourself living through that. And what is the worst thing that could happen? You're not gonna die. You're not gonna get hurt.

Ben Sidran notes: "Nothing is as bad as your fear of it. There's nothing in life, and probably even death, that is as bad as your fear of it."

This visualization technique is a powerful help in achieving that realization—and in defanging your fears.

Three-Minute Monologue (TMM)

Sometimes we aren't able to put pen to paper. Other times we talk ourselves out of working on something by telling ourselves that the task appears too tedious or daunting. However, it's quite hard to talk yourself out of working on something for three minutes. And, take it from us, if the three minutes of work are rigorous, worlds can change (with repeated use—it helps tremendously to do this exercise repeatedly). This exercise can even be done under your breath while standing in line at the post office or while you're involved in day-to-day activities such as washing the dishes, taking a shower, or getting dressed.

Here's how it works: Take the **E** section of the ABC and get right to the point: your rational, self-helping thoughts. Argue for your self-helping thoughts in a firm, sensible, and personally compelling manner. Here's a somewhat compressed example, citing our hopes for this book:

"Nothing says this book must succeed! It would be nice if it hit the big time. We would love to have great success and all it would bring, including riches and the opportunity to teach these self-help techniques to throngs of people. But nothing says it has to happen.

"If we want to help others, nothing says they have to be helped. If they aren't, it would be a shame. But that's the way it goes. The human race has suffered many tragedies, and not receiving the information in this book would hardly qualify as the worst. There's no guarantee things will go the way we'd like them to. Tough! That's reality and we can handle it!

"We never have to give up if we don't want to. This book is simply a tool for teaching people self-help techniques. But if this book doesn't do the trick, we can come up with another one. It would be great to have this book get the word out. But it does not have to happen. Nothing ever has to happen. What's the point in telling ourselves that this book must succeed? There are going to be people who don't think that what we've offered is valuable. There's no way that everybody who comes in contact with our book is going to buy into its ideas. We can accept this reality or whine about it. Great success, no matter how true our ideas, no matter how beneficial it would be to ourselves and others, does not have to happen.

"Nothing ever has to happen any particular way. It would be ridiculous to try to put ourselves above that reality. We are simply two humans who have something we believe can be helpful to almost everyone. And one of the most irrational ideas we can have is demanding success. So we refuse to demand that our book succeed. It doesn't have to. That's reality. Rebel against it and feel lousy. Or accept it, feel motivated, and be productive."

When practiced over and over, these exercises will take less and less time, helping you knock out your *shoulds* more easily. Occasionally a major *should* may surface, and it may take more work to get rid of it. But, by and large, the more you practice, the more effective these techniques become. Eventually, *shoulds* won't have nearly the power they once did. And you'll rid yourself to a great extent of the needless burden of self-demands.

MVP

While ridding yourself of your irrational, anxiety-inducing thinking, keep in mind three things: meaningfulness, vigor, and persistence (MVP).

• **Meaningfulness**. Make everything you write in your exercises your true thinking at the time. Avoid including anything simply because it seems like the "right" or the "rational" thing to say. For example, in the ABCs, at **B**, don't write "I absolutely *must have* the audience's approval" if this does not ring true. And at **E**, don't write "it's not the end of the world" if you really believe the end is near.

• **Vigor**. Question, confront, challenge, and contradict your unreasonable notions passionately, strongly, and enthusiastically.

• **Persistence**. Practice, practice, practice. Then practice some more. Refuse to give up.

Armed with the anti-anxiety techniques in this chapter, put yourself in performing situations as often as you can. By doing this, and through the repeated use of even the simplest technique in this chapter—rational coping statements: "I can stand it"; "It's not the end of the world if I do badly"; "I'm rehearsed; I know my material"; "The audience is here for a good time; they want to like me"—you'll find that your performance anxiety will decrease, probably quite rapidly.

A Final Word

There is another consideration in effectively employing all of these techniques. Having found them effective, many performers erroneously conclude that their problem is solved. This would be quite nice, and in some cases it may be true. But usually, as fallible human beings, we easily fall back into old, self-defeating thoughts. Fully conquering one's irrational beliefs often requires a lifelong commitment to identifying them and doing the work required to eradicate them.

With practice, practice, and more practice, your use of these self-help techniques will tend to become easier and more efficient. Depending on your level of dedication to eradicating your stage fright, you may eventually perform virtually anxiety free. (Remember, *demanding* that you eradicate your stage fright will only exacerbate the problem.) However, you will most likely not improve without making the effort.

Commit to getting rid of your stage fright with the same level of work you devote to other aspects of your performing career. Any top performer will say that it took them years to become a master of their craft. Using these techniques to eliminate anxiety is no different. However, when you practice these self-help techniques meaningfully, vigorously, and persistently, the relief and joy you'll achieve can be rapid and ultimately life changing.

So there ya go! Practice, practice, practice. Get rid of your demands, and you'll feel better, better, and better, while increasing your chances of achieving your goals, leading to a happier and more fulfilling life. And better performances.

Go get 'em!

P.S. To derive additional benefit from this book, while reading the interviews identify those statements by the stars tacitly reinforcing the above ideas and techniques, for example, avoiding demands, contradicting them, using rational coping statements, and refusing to be nervous about being nervous.

Carlos Alazraqui

Carlos Alazraqui is Officer James Garcia on Comedy Central's "Reno 911." He is also the voiceover artist for Mr. Crocker on Nickelodeon's "Fairly Odd Parents," Rocko on "Rocko's Modern Life," and Lube and Winslow in "Cat/Dog." Carlos also stars in two shows for the Cartoon Network—as Munroe, the Scottish Pug dog, on "Juniper Lee" and as Lazlo on their number one series, "Camp Lazlo." He also was the voice on one of the most recognizable commercials in TV history: "Yo Quiero Taco Bell."

Carlos starred in his own stand-up comedy special on Comedy Central, performs live at the Hollywood Improv, The Ice House, The M Bar on Vine, and The Knitting Factory in Hollywood, and has a steady corporate schedule. He has appeared in *Happy Feet* with Robin Williams, and the "Reno 911" movie. He currently appears on two series for children: "Handy Manny," as Felipe, Abuelito, and Mr. Ayala, and on "Wow Wow Wubbzy" as Walden, Earl, and all other male characters.

MB: How long have you been performing?

CA: I've been doing stand-up comedy since 1984. I had a college professor who noticed I was doing impressions at Sacramento State University, and he encouraged me to get up on stage at a place called Harry's Bar and Grill in Sacramento to do this stand-up comedy competition. I had the support of a lot of friends and students, so I did the contest and I took third place.

MB: What was the first time you were nervous on stage?

CA: It was that contest. It was my first time—pretty much, ever—on stage. I had to drink a beer and was sweating under my armpits. The fact that it was a contest just added to the pressure. Not only was I going to do stand-up, but I was also competing. I was going, "Wow!" It was a double whammy.

MB: Did you know beforehand that you'd react that way?

CA: No. But if I'd thought about it, I would've gone, "Why would I do that?" [Laughs] [But at the competition] I felt good. I felt nervous. I definitely felt that first shot of comedy heroin. People were laughing; they liked me. I came off, and the girls seemed to pay attention to me.

MB: As you continued performing, how did your stage fright change?

CA: It took a while. At first I had performance anxiety, and I just did not want to go up. Then my feelings suddenly changed. And what helped them change was that I got in a duo with this guy named Mark Fraser; we were called the Brew Ha Ha. That assuaged my nervousness, because I could share the stage with somebody else.

So gradually, after performing with Mark as a duo, I got used to the fact that the audience was liking us, so I was able to branch off on my own. Having a partner is almost like having training wheels. So I had the benefit of those training wheels for a year. And getting a year's stage time helped me get around the nervousness. It was almost like hiking on the back of a Sherpa guide and then going, "Okay. I can do this by myself now."

MB: You initially had some performance anxiety—how did that feel?

CA: It didn't feel good. I felt like a failure. I thought, "Oh God, I have this talent and I don't want to go up on stage. There must be something wrong with me. I'm a bomb. I'm letting my friends down; I'm letting myself down. How can I do this? I just want to go home."

MB: Can you elaborate on how it felt when you were nervous?

CA: I think there was just a general sense of pressure that I might get laughed at rather than laughed with. My pulse wasn't necessarily racing, but there was sort of a guilt feeling that I didn't prepare. So it was more a feeling of guilt rather than apprehension. Rather than thinking, "Oh my God, I can't believe this," it was more like, "Oh shit, I should've prepared."

MB: What were you telling yourself about that?

CA: Well, after I saw those other guys stopping and starting, I was telling myself not to worry about it. But before that, I was going, "You know what? You're good enough. You'll be fine. You've done this enough times and you're good at improving. If you forget something, it's just in your head—the audience doesn't know you did that."

MB: What were you telling yourself that was producing the guilt?

CA: I think it was, "I should have prepared." And that goes back to school and homework. [Using a big, ponderous voice of doom] *"You didn't prepare! You didn't do your homework!"*

MB: Can you think of the worst case of stage fright you've ever had?

CA: I think it would have to have been at a place called Café Croissant in Sacramento. It was probably the second or third time I'd been up on stage, not counting the comedy competition. And the place had a corner window where you could see people on stage inside. I remember pulling up [outside before my set], seeing a friend on stage, and going, "He's expecting me. I hope he didn't see me. I don't feel like coming in tonight." I just wanted to take my things and leave. And when I went in, my feeling was that people had such high expectations that I was responsible for their whole well-being that night. It was horrible. I felt the weight of the world.

MB: So when don't you get nervous now?

CA: Most of the time I don't get nervous, unless it's a private function and I'm in front of family and friends. Like when I hear, "My brother's really funny. Do that stuff." Then I feel put upon. If it's a family situation, or when I'm meeting people for the first time, that tends to get even more nerve wracking.

I recently met my girlfriend's family, and I was a little bit nervous that I would say the wrong thing in trying to be funny. But now, professionally, rarely. Almost never.

MB: What are you telling yourself that helps you not be nervous?

CA: Like I said, "I've got a career. I know I'm funny. I've done this for twenty years." It comes with the overall feeling, which is what stand-up comics have, that I'm secure with myself. I've gone to a lot of therapy and I'm growing older. And I'm secure with myself. So I tell myself, "I like myself and I don't really care if people think I'm fantastic. If they do, that's great. If they don't, I can't help that. I'm going to be myself."

MB: What role do your thoughts or attitudes about yourself play in performance anxiety?

CA: I think your thoughts about yourself play a huge role, because if you're not comfortable with who you are, you'll be nervous. If you're comfortable with yourself, confident in your abilities, and you're not worried about the outcome—whether or not people like you—that allows you to relax. It doesn't mean you're going to do great, but it allows you to relax.

MB: Is there any other advice you'd have on stage fright?

CA: Well, first, preparation really takes care of a lot of nervousness. It's going to help a lot. And then there's practice, which is right along the lines of preparation. Besides practicing your material, there's the mental preparation of liking yourself and telling yourself you're going to do the best you can. And if people like it, that's fine. That goes along with saying, "Just be yourself. Be true to yourself."

If you're doing comedy and have a point of view, write and deliver the things that you think are funny, and sell them. Don't write what you think anybody else is going to think is clever. And the same goes for public speaking. Talk about a subject that you're passionate about. That really takes care of preparation and practice, too. If you're passionate about what you're doing, and you have a point of view, you are going to practice. You are going to be prepared, and then you won't really care if people like you. You'll think, "I believe in this; I think this is funny."

Jason Alexander

Jason Alexander, as George Costanza on NBC's "Seinfeld," won six Emmy and four Golden Globe nominations, an American Television Award and two American Comedy Awards for "Best Supporting Actor in a Television Series." The Screen Actors Guild knighted him "Best Actor in a Comedy Series."

His Broadway debut was in "Merrily We Roll Along" (1981). Alexander wrote the narrative book for the revue "Jerome Robbins' Broadway" and played 14 different characters at every performance, winning the Drama Desk, Outer Critics Circle and Tony Award. Other theater roles include starring in the acclaimed L.A. production of "The Producers."

Film credits include *Hachiko: A Dog's Story*, *Pretty Woman*, *Mosquito Coast*, *Jacob's Ladder*, *Coneheads*, *North*, *Blankman*, *Dunston Checks In*, *Love, Valor, Compassion*, and *Shallow Hal*. He has directed the features *For Better or Worse* and *Just Looking*. He is currently directing and appearing in a number of television shows, and serving as the artistic director for Reprise Theatre Company.

MB: How long have you been performing?

JA: I started as a very ambitious six-year-old who performed magic shows. I was very serious about magic and thought it was going to be my life's work. But by the time I was a teenager, I realized that my passion was greater than my ability. Around the time I was thirteen, I made the quantum leap of looking at theater as a gigantic illusion, and one that I wanted to be a part of. So at age thirteen, I began studying voice and dance, and I performed in everything I possibly could. I was very lucky. About three years later, I stumbled into a modest but professional career. So I've been a professional for about thirty-two years.

MB: What were the circumstances when you started performing?

JA: As an amateur, I was part of the school shows and the teen theater troupe in my town. We would do musicals and contemporary comedies. Sometimes I was the lead, other times I was in a supporting role. I always felt very at home and very, very comfortable on stage. I craved it. It was where I felt most alive and most potent. It remained that way as I began to do commercials, which is primarily what I did professionally until I was twenty.

MB: Tell me about the first time you were anxious or nervous.

JA: When I was twenty years old, I made my Broadway debut. I had always dreamed of Broadway as the pinnacle of my career. I thought it was something I wouldn't see for many, many years. But suddenly I was there. And not only there, but working for absolute legends. My debut was in a Stephen Sondheim musical directed by Harold Prince—two gods of the theater. I had a terrific role and one that was very much in my wheelhouse. So I was stunned when we prepared for our first public performance. I'd always had butterflies before [performing], but not anything worse.

The show began with all of us on stage as the curtain rose. And as the curtain rose on that first night, I had a flash of intense vertigo, like I was going to pass out and couldn't find my center. It sent me into a cold-sweat panic. Luckily, I held on, managed to perform, and warmed into the performance. But the next night as I stood on the stage waiting for the curtain to rise, I was in a panic that the experience might repeat itself. I worked myself up so much that when the curtain rose, the vertigo was even worse than the first night. Every night became a nightmare at the opening of the show. Once I got past the first scene, I would settle down and be all right. But since this had never happened to me before, it was very unsettling.

The show didn't run [long] and the experience didn't last. The next professional show I was cast in performed in a small off-Broadway club, and I didn't experience anything other than the normal butterflies. But, throughout my career and up until about ten years ago, I would occasionally get panic and vertigo attacks *while performing*, and it took a lot of dealing with them to be able to continue.

MB: As you continued performing, how did your nervousness change?

JA: One of the worst periods for me was when I was on Broadway doing a Neil Simon play called "Broadway Bound." For a number of reasons, this show caused some of my very worst panic attacks. It may have been because it was the first time I was hired on Broadway as a non-musical actor, and that held significance for me.

The set was a two-storey construction, and a lot of my action was on the upper storey. I have a healthy fear of heights, so that added to my anxiety. But the worst thing of all was that my character had a moment in the play where he went to sleep on stage for about fifteen minutes. Lying on that bed, on that second story, on that Broadway stage—that combination literally scared me to death.

Night after night, I would get panic attacks. I just wanted to run. I wanted to do anything I could to get off the stage. But I was afraid to move because I didn't want to pull the audience's attention away from the action.

If I had been able to actually fall asleep, it might have been okay. But I was responsible for hearing the end cue and starting the next scene, so I had to stay acutely aware. It was a nightmare.

That went on for months. I would anticipate the horror every day. I saw therapists. If I had any inclination toward drugs, I'm sure I would have used them, but that just wasn't an option for me. Anyway, I never truly overcame those attacks on that show. I tried many, many things over the course of the run. I would try to do math problems or mental puzzles in my head. I would just count and see how long I had to count before my cue came up. I would sing in my head. I tried relaxation exercises to try to let go of the anxiety in my body. I tried self-reason—I told myself that I had gotten through this so many times that it was certain I would get through it again. And I eventually tried getting mad at myself. I would yell at myself in my head, daring myself to give in to the panic and vertigo. Telling myself to faint or run and just ruin the show and my career. It all worked for awhile, and then I would have to try something new. As the show ran, the severity of the attacks lessened, but they never truly went away until long after.

MB: Do you ever get nervous now?

JA: Of course, but it's a very different experience. Nervousness isn't a bad thing if you care about something that you have to present to others. If you've worked on it and want it to succeed, then nervousness is natural. Especially when you're only beginning to present it. As the presentation gets more and more into your bones, it becomes easier. Really, nervousness is just an indication that you care. And you should care. But there's a world of difference between nervous butterflies and real anxiety and panic. I'm happy to say that I haven't experienced that for many, many years.

MB: What advice would you have for performers who experience stage fright or nervousness?

JA: Well, what eventually was the answer for me? I had a wonderful acting teacher who I confided in about this experience. He told me that he believed that that kind of debilitating fear was a result of misplaced ego. He used to say, "Jason, these people are not here to see you; they don't really care about you. They are here to see the story. Just tell them the story."

Just tell them the story. Big idea. When I began to make the story the most important thing, I became much less the focus of my concerns. I realized that I was one small element on the stage, working with my colleagues to tell our audience a story. The information is what people want, the experience is what they want. They're not there for me. They would be just as happy having someone else tell them the story. The material—the work—is everything.

Realizing this was very, very freeing to me.

Now eventually, as I became a celebrity, people were in fact coming specifically to see me. But the idea still held. Seeing me was a momentary thing. Seeing what I could show them, tell them, sing to them, etc.—that was what they were paying for. So, my material had to be wonderful. My preparation had to be wonderful. My commitment had to be wonderful. If all that was wonderful, I just had to be able to stand in front of other people and deliver what they were there for.

It may not sound like much, but this idea has been enormously helpful to me in confronting my fears. And here's another good tip—it's my personal mantra that I repeat and breathe with before I go out for a live performance of anything, whether it's a play or a concert or a lecture or a master class. I tell myself that what I do is extraordinary. It isn't something that just anyone can do. I tell myself that it's a privilege to be able to do it. Not everyone has the opportunity to show what they can do. And I repeat the following words:

"STRENGTH: Know that you're healthy and sound and vital and that you are enough. You don't have to pretend to be more than you are. You are enough for the task.

"COURAGE: Be brave. Others fight greater battles and risk far more than you do. This is your battle and battlefield. Have the guts to go out onto it with dignity and pride. Know that you're prepared, and be prepared. And take comfort from your own courage. Yes, it can be scary. If everyone could do what you do, you wouldn't be special. So be brave.

"CONVICTION: Believe in what you're doing. Do it with everything you have. Do it fully. Commit. We can't control the result, but we can demand that we commit to the process or the project.

"And most importantly, JOY: This is a gift we've been given. To be able to uplift or inform or amuse—or just make a difference—that is a blessing. It gives our lives purpose and value. Not everyone gets this opportunity. So greet it with joy and gratitude. Be grateful for something that challenges you. Challenges make life worth living. They make life sweet. So take joy in your ability to challenge yourself and succeed."

This mantra has gotten me through all the worst nerves I've ever had to face.

Mose Allison

A musician's musician, Mose Allison has never, in over 60 years of performing, missed a single gig. Crossing musical boundaries, Mose has recorded and/or performed with jazz greats Stan Getz, Zoot Simms, Al Cohn, Jerry Mulligan, rock star Van Morrison, and Country legend Willie Nelson. His music has been covered by The Who, Robert Palmer, Hot Tuna, Van Morrison, Bonnie Raitt, Eric Clapton, Vassar Clements, Bill Wyman, Diana Krall, John Hammond, the Yardbirds, John Mayall and the Kingston Trio.

Years ago, someone took a photo of Mose with BB King on one side and Lou Donaldson on his other side. That picture was how Mose saw himself at that time, between Bebop and the Blues.

A reporter once asked Mose, "You were a poet before Bob Dylan, you were satirical before Randy Newman and you were hip before Mick Jagger, how come you are not a big star?" Mose answered, "Just lucky, I guess."

MB: How long have you been performing?

MA: I'm in my fifty-fourth year.

MB: What were the circumstances when you started performing?

MA: I started performing in Lake Charles, Louisiana in a little nightclub on the outskirts of town. I had a couple of friends I had a little trio with, and we played there six nights a week for about six weeks.

MB: Can you describe the first time you were nervous performing?

MA: As a child when I had to perform in public, I got nervous, I got stage fright. But after I started doing it professionally, I don't remember getting that kind of nervousness. I get anxious to go on sometimes—I don't like to be delayed.

MB: What were the circumstances the first time you started feeling anxious?

MA: I can't remember exactly, but it was when I first started going on the road, started playing concerts and clubs on the road. Sometimes I'd be playing a concert somewhere at a college and the contract would say eight o'clock and I'd get there and they'd say, "Well, there's an opening act; you're not going on until nine." And since I get myself prepared to go on at a certain time, I don't like it if I have to sit around.

MB: So how do you feel if you have to sit around?

MA: I start getting anxious and nervous, because what I do before I go on is have a cup of black coffee. And if I have to sit around, the coffee is beginning to work and I'm sitting there.

MB: Is there anything you're telling yourself during times like those?

MA: Oh, I don't have to do that. I don't do any visualization things. I'm just anxious to get out and start the first tune, because I don't exactly know how it's going to go until I start that first tune, and then I can almost tell from the first tune how the whole set's going to go.

MB: How do you feel if the set isn't going to go well?

MA: Well, I work. Playing becomes work.

MB: Since you don't get nervous very often, can you remember some of the times in earlier performances when you were nervous? You mentioned Lake Charles as the first regular professional gig.

MA: Yeah. I wasn't nervous there, either. I was anxious to play. I've always been anxious to play. I can walk in anywhere, anytime, and play.

MB: So if it's really easy for you to play, do you know what's going on in your mind that's making it so enjoyable for you?

MA: Well, there are a lot of things going on in your mind. Sometimes you're playing sort of automatically, not really making any effort. You can sort of get into a state of self-hypnosis or something. When that happens, you might be thinking about something completely unrelated to playing. It's hard to explain, but every musician knows about it—every jazz musician knows about it. Those times, you go on and you feel like unrelated. You're not even playing the songs yourself; the playing is just happening. You just appreciate it when that happens.

But when you have to really work hard, when it's not going right and you have to really work . . . well you have to concentrate all the time; it's just a matter of concentrating on the music and trying to put your mind on the keyboard and what you're doing. Trying to manipulate the instrument—execution, that's the whole thing. If you're executing smoothly and without any problems, that's the time when it's easy. But If the things you try to do don't come out exactly right and there's a little lapse, ninety-eight percent of the audience will probably never know it. Maybe one hundred percent of the audience will never know it. But you'll know it.

MB: So as you continued performing, would you say your attitude about performing changed at all?

MA: Not much, man. I still look forward to the gigs like I did when I first started out. Getting there is a drag. The travel thing is getting worse all the time. It's getting worse on it's own, but it's also getting to me more because I'm getting older, you know? So my attitude about that has changed. But once I get to the piano and the microphone, I'm usually fine.

MB: Is there anything you do in addition to drinking the coffee to get prepared?

MA: I use these Hall's citrus vitamin C drops. I have one of those right before I go on because it gets my throat to cool out. But that's it. A cup of coffee and the Hall's drops. Then, during the performance, I have water—just plain water with no ice.

MB: What's the worst case of nervousness you've ever experienced?

MA: There've been times when the sound system was bad or the players weren't that good. I experienced a lot of that in the early days when I would go out on the road and play with whoever was there. Sometimes it didn't go too well.

I played some gigs, man, where the piano was really bad. I remember one piano in San Francisco at the Matrix. That was a big club at the time, but they had the worst piano I ever played. So we had a joke going, the musicians and myself: Any time we ran across a bad piano, I'd say, "Man, this is a Matrix piano."

MB: Isn't there anything about your attitude that makes it easy for you not to get nervous? Do you worry at all about making mistakes?

MA: Nope. If you make a mistake playing jazz, sometimes it throws you into something you haven't done before, which is good.

MB: When people hear you perform, they're generally blown away by you and think, "Man, the guy's flawless." But I imagine you wouldn't classify yourself as flawless.

MA: I have my flawless sets, sometimes, I think. But who knows? You can't even tell. You don't know yourself how flawless it is. Because, as I found out from recording live, sometimes when you felt it was really going good while you were playing, when you listen back to it you don't like it. And sometimes when you were working like mad and couldn't get anything going, you play it back and it's better. So you don't even know yourself; you can't really judge what you're doing. You just do it and hope for the best. When people ask me, "How'd the show go?" I say, "Well, man, you tell me."

My performance is for a certain temperament. People of that temperament are more likely to dig what I'm doing. And I always say, "Man, there's more and more of us all the time," because the situation and the environment is getting so weird.

Maya Angelou

Dr. Maya Angelou is one of the great voices of contemporary literature and a remarkable Renaissance woman. Poet, educator, historian, best-selling author, actress, playwright, civil rights activist, producer and director, Dr. Angelou travels the world making appearances, spreading her legendary wisdom.

She has authored twelve best-selling books, including *I Know Why the Caged Bird Sings*, *A Song Flung Up to Heaven* and *Even the Stars Look Lonesome*, and holds a lifetime position as the first Reynolds Professor of American Studies at Wake Forest University. In January 1993, she became the second poet in U.S. history to write and recite original work at the presidential inauguration.

She has been nominated for two Grammy Awards for Best Spoken Word or Non-Musical Album for "On The Pulse Of Morning" (1993) and "Phenomenal Woman" (1995). In 2004, she received a Grammy Award nomination for Best Spoken Word Album for "Hallelujah! The Welcome Table." She holds over 50 honorary degrees from colleges and universities worldwide.

MB: How long have you been appearing before audiences?

MA: In one way or another, for about fifty years.

MB: Most people know you as a writer and a poet. But you've done a considerable amount of acting and singing.

MA: And dancing.

MB: What were the circumstances when you began performing?

MA: I was a mute from the time I was seven until I was thirteen, or there-abouts. But I memorized poetry. I loved it.

A lady in my town had told me (encouraging me to read and memorize) that I didn't really like poetry. But I wrote her back and said, "I do, yes ma'am!" She wouldn't even look at it. She said, "You will never love it until you speak it. Till you speak and feel it come across your tongue, over your lips, you will never love poetry."

In my privacy, I decided to try. And I realized that I had left my voice, my voice had not left me. So I accepted that I could recite poetry aloud. And then in San Francisco, at about fourteen, I received a scholarship to a college at night. And I studied drama and dance. And I was almost six feet tall. [Laughs]

MB: you probably still are, too.

MA: I shrunk a little bit. I shrunk a half an inch.

MB: What were the circumstances when you first performed on stage? Was it in drama?

MA: Yes. The first time I can remember, I was around fifteen, and I recited "The Raven" for Mr. Paul Robeson. I flung myself over the stage like a wounded huge bird.

MB: How did you feel while you did that?

MA: I was so nervous. But I had memorized the poem. And I had it—I didn't blow my lines. There were only about four people there, but I knew he [Mr. Robeson] was in the front row and was watching. And my knees . . . I could have just lost everything then.

But I did something that still stands me in good stead, and that is: I went into the poem. When I'm very, very nervous—like, when I recited the inaugural poem [at President Clinton's inauguration]—I have to believe that the poem is important. And I have to get into the poem, and give it its due. To respect it enough to let it be heard.

MB: So, the importance of the material overrode the feeling of being nervous?

MA: In a way. I mean, I was still nervous. But I didn't think about it because I was thinking of the material.

MB: So you were thinking about the material, rather than thinking about being nervous?

MA: Except for every other second. [Both laugh.]

MB: Is there a way that you think you could have viewed things differently the first time, so that you wouldn't have been as anxious?

MA: I don't think so. I don't know any way but to use the nerves, use the discomfort, the edginess. I spoke last night at the Kennedy Center in Washington, along with Miss Odetta, and Miss Della Reese. We've known each other for forty years, or thereabouts. And each one of us was nervous before we went out onto the stage. But by talking to each other, we shoved the nervousness back. Still, it can't be forgotten that there are thousands of people sitting there listening and evaluating, whether you like it or not.

MB: So you still get nervous at times.

MA: Absolutely.

MB: I'm particularly curious about when you spoke recited your poem "On the Pulse of Morning" at President Clinton's inauguration. There can't be a bigger audience than there was for that, or a more important appearance. I know you said you get into the material. Is there anything else that you did at that particular event to deal with the pressure?

MA: Not really. From the moment the announcement was broadcast that I was writing a poem, I would get onto an airplane and people would say, "Hello there, Ms. Angelou. Finish your poem yet?" [Both laugh.] So I just wrote and rewrote and wrote and rewrote that poem until I could say it as closely to what I meant as possible.

MB: What changes when you're nervous?

MA: The physiognomy is changed. My voice is not the same voice I would have if I wasn't nervous. So physically, my presentation is enhanced by the nerves. I think it's better.

MB: More concentrated?

MA: More concentrated. And there's an urgency. As it comes out of my mouth and my throat and larynx, it reaches other people with an urgency. The content is strengthened by the voice itself.

MB: Are there any particular thoughts that you're telling yourself when you're performing to intensify your awareness and emotions?

MA: No. There's nothing. I don't tell myself anything. Unless it's "Remember the poem. Remember what you're saying."

MB: Are there performing circumstances in which you don't get nervous?

MA: I don't think there are any. There may be. No, I don't think so.

MB: Can you tell me about the worst case of nervousness that you've experienced?

MA: Yes. Some years ago, I was on the board of the American Film Institute, and I went to the Century Plaza Hotel in Los Angeles. It was a big affair, and I was to make a presentation, just to introduce some new members of the Academy. There were maybe five hundred or a thousand people in the ballroom, and as I looked around, I saw people like Loretta Young and Gregory Peck. And all of a sudden Charlton Heston introduced me. I went to the microphone, and I had the people's names, but I just froze.

I looked at those faces, some of which I had seen when I was a child in Arkansas in a theater when, in order for me to go to the movie house, I had to walk up the outside stairs. We would buy the tickets, and the woman who took the tickets wouldn't take my dime in her hand. She'd take a ruler and rake it into a cigar box. And then I would go up the sides of the outside stairs—rickety stairs—and go into what was called "the buzzard's roost." And there'd be trash on the floor and peanut shells. And the stench . . .

At my presentation, as I looked at some of those faces I had first seen at that movie house—only because my brother insisted; I didn't want to go to that movie house—I was so, so traumatized that I couldn't think of a thing. And Charlton Heston came and started to take me away. And I said, "No. I will speak. I will speak. And I'll speak here." I said something about the industry, and something about the people I was to introduce. And I said, "Someone else will introduce you." Then (to another individual) "But I will have a name in this business."

And then I walked out through the kitchen. Not through the front door. Not through the lobby. I left my mink stole—that would be my first. And the waiters and the men who worked back in the kitchen were all Mexican or Spanish. And they asked me what I wanted, and I started speaking to them in Spanish. So they helped me get out of that hotel.

MB: Wow.

MA: You asked me for one.

MB: Yeah. I really appreciate that. It's really wonderful to share that. Because so many people feel like, "Oh, Dr. Maya Angelou! She would be oblivious to being nervous."

MA: Oh, no!

MB: What advice would you have for anybody who appears in front of a crowd and experiences stage fright or nervousness?

MA: I would say, "Accept it; don't fight it." My mother used to tell me, "If you're afraid, tell yourself you're afraid." She said, "When a snake approaches a bird, the bird—if it knew it was afraid—could fly above the snake in a second. But the bird doesn't say to itself, 'I'm afraid.' It just allows itself to be paralyzed."

I think this is true for a performer. What he or she should do is say, "I'm nervous as the dickens. I'm as nervous as I can be. And I'm going to say this piece." That's better than trying to ignore it.

Lawrence P. Beron

Actor, humorist, and raconteur Lawrence P Beron is a native New Orleanian and still resides in New Orleans. In high school, a family move to The Netherlands led him to graduate from The American School of The Hague, where he appeared in a number of plays directed by Richard Freedberg. After moving back to New Orleans, he began performing stand-up comedy and acting in local productions.

In 2008, he was cast in his first supporting role as Detective Anthony Merchant in the upcoming *Beyond a Reasonable Doubt*, starring Michael Douglas and Amber Tamblyn and directed by Peter Hyams. Professionally, he has studied with Alan Dysert and David Keith at The Actor's School in Nashville, TN; and with John "Spud" McConnell and with Lance E. Nichols in New Orleans. He is a member of the Screen Actors Guild.

MB: How long have you been performing?

LPB: My first performance was in kindergarten. It was some kind of school play. I don't remember anything about it except I was cast in the role of a big, golden carrot. I had a couple of lines and I got some big laughs. But I felt embarrassed because at that time I had a really bad speech impediment. A lisp. And the lines were really funny because I said them with a lisp: "I'm a big golden carrot/ You can eat me cooked or raw/ Some people like me in their soup/ Other people like me in their slaw." You can see how a kid with a lisp is going to think he sounds funny.

MB: Do you ever get nervous now when you perform?

LPB: I do get nervous, but my method of dealing with that is to look at it not as nervousness as much as anxiety, and look on that anxiety as positive and exciting, as opposed to nervousness. I recognize and anticipate it. And I'm a preparation freak. I know I've done it before and I'm ready to go. There's some nervous tension in the air, and that's a good thing because I'm getting ready to do something fun.

MB: So how do you view it differently now that makes it easier?

LPB: Preparation and experience are the keys. I think all performers come to realize that they just need to keep going. As far as the audience is concerned, nobody's sitting there with a script, noting that you dropped a phrase. And from experience you anticipate that some things are going to work and other things aren't. And that's not in your control, and it's not supposed to be.

If you're just working by yourself, some audience member is going to cough at the wrong time, or are you going to forget something? Is there a way to reinsert it at the end of the monologue or just go on without it? These things are going to come up. Part of the preparation is foreseeing the possibility of problems and not being thrown when they occur. Because they are going to occur. I don't even call it "going wrong." It's what's going to happen.

MB: Can you tell me about the worst case of stage fright you've ever had?

LPB: Probably the worst was a Showtime contest. It was almost an open mike, and if you made it in the top ten you came back the next week. And I got in. With nothing. I didn't even plan on going on stage. I had jokes; but I didn't have a stream of one thing leading to another.

[But] I felt pretty good, because the DJs stole the one that was my joke and told it on the air the next day. So that was gratifying. But the problem with that contest was that when they said, "Okay, come back in a week and be just as funny, if not more funny," I now had the pressure of "Man—I have a whole week. Should I stick with the same stuff or try to come up with new stuff?" And then there was "Now we're in the top ten. Before it was a lark. Now people are coming for the finals." So that was unnerving. I didn't have a routine that got me into the top ten, let alone have one for the finals.

MB: Do you think there's any way you could have viewed it differently that would have made it easier?

LPB: Oh yeah. If I knew then what I know now, I would have done exactly the same stuff. Chances are that it's not going to be the same people seeing you, so nobody's going to demand that you come up with a new routine within a week. It was funny the first time, it's going to be funny to again.

MB: What do you think you were telling yourself that created more pressure?

LPB: That it was an accident that I was funny, and that they were certainly going to see that if I did the same stuff, so I'd better come up with new stuff. And that was a killer mistake. I had tested material and threw it overboard for untested.

MB: Is there anything else you'd like to mention about dealing with stage fright?

LPB: I used to think the best way to get ready was to have a couple of beers. But I make sure not to do that now. It's going to help you suppress stage fright, but it's not helping make you a better performer. As Tommy Staub [a New Orleans casting director] told me: "If you gotta get drunk, where's the enjoyment?"

MB: Any other advice?

LPB: You're not going to eliminate anxiety from a performance. You have to make it positive energy. You have to address it, accept it, meet it halfway, and channel it into the performance.

Mark Bittner

Born in 1951 in Vancouver, Washington, Mark graduated from high school and spent four months in Europe hitchhiking and taking trains, then moved to Seattle and spent three years learning music. He moved to Berkeley, California, worked as a street singer and ended up in North Beach in San Francisco, spending fifteen years on the streets studying Eastern religions, history, Italian, guitar, and clarinet.

In 1988, he took a job as the caretaker of a house. Two years later he spotted four parrots nearby. Eventually the flock grew to 26, and he was in love. Making friends and learning their ways, in 1996 he began a book, *The Wild Parrots of Telegraph Hill* (Harmony Books, 2004). Mark starred in a documentary of the same title, released in 2005, written and directed by filmmaker Judy Irving. Mark and Judy are now married and living in the gardens of Telegraph Hill. Mark is currently working on a book about his years on the street.

Mick B: What was the first time you were were nervous in front of a crowd?

Mark B: Well, that would be all the way back in eighth grade. I was in this little four-piece band, and, uh . . . terrified! I used to have a real problem with stage fright, but not much anymore.

Mick B: If you don't have a problem anymore, can you attribute that to anything?

Mark B: Well, for one thing, I think I've matured. But when I was doing music, I always felt that I was doing something that I shouldn't be doing. I worked hard at it, and I got to be okay. But I always had to force myself to pick up my guitar—and I always figured a "real" musician had to force himself to stop. So when you feel like you're not really doing what you should be doing, you get nervous about it.

Another part of it was wanting to be a star. When you want to be a star, you're into it for sort of an ego reason, and that will make you nervous, too. You really worry about how you're going over.

Mick B: You said, you were terrified when you first started performing in eighth grade. What were your thoughts about being terrified?

Mark B: I think being nervous on stage comes from two things. For one, you're worried about your ego—how you're coming across, and whether people are liking you.

The other thing has to do with being on stage and having all of that energy directed at you. If you're not selfish with it, if you're feeding it back to the audience, and it's continually going back and forth, you shouldn't be nervous.

I always use the moment that I'm on stage to try to focus. And if people are giving you a lot of energy, it makes it easier to focus. And when you're focused, and you've gotten rid of all the crap that's in your mind, then you can give people back something that's more real.

Mick B: And the crap in your mind would be?

Mark B: Oh, just all kinds of neurotic thoughts. You might start thinking that person over there doesn't like you, if you spot someone particular in the audience. And it's purely paranoia. Most people want to like the performer on stage, and I think most performers even know that. But once you're in the midst of performing, it's hard to deal with that thought if you've got it going already.

Mick B: What do you think you would be telling yourself about that? If a person doesn't like you, what could be the results of that?

Mark B: Well, now I don't care. Back then, I would have cared a lot.

Mick B: So if they don't like you, that's okay?

Mark B: You can't please everybody. If you're doing your best, I don't think it should matter so much to you.

You're putting out the best you can. If you're doing that and you know what you're talking about—and you know that you stand on solid ground—that gets rid of a lot of that nervousness.

Mick B: And "standing on solid ground" is?

Mark B: Well, in my case [now, when I'm doing bookstore appearances and slide shows], I know my subject; I know what the parrots are about. And I've done [these presentations] so many times that I haven't encountered a question in a long time that I've never dealt with.

Mick B: Is there anything else you'd mention about stage fright?

Mark B: Yeah, one thing is that now I have a different idea of what performing is about. To me, it's not so much getting up on stage and showing off. I try to create a kind of communion. I respect the audience's energy. I understand that it's real stuff and that people want to be moved. So rather than do something selfish, I just try to create a flow whereby people are moved by what is happening. If you've got people going that way, then performing isn't for a selfish end; it's to try to create a sort of community between you and the audience.

Mick B: You're not nervous because you're not doing it for yourself?

Mark B: Right. You're just doing it. It's like with music. If you're really into the music, you don't think about what people are thinking about you. You're just trying to keep the music going.

Mick B: How does what you're telling yourself help prevent your being nervous?

Mark B: I don't know what I really tell myself anymore. I used to have this little mantra I told myself when I performed, which was, "Just tell the truth about the birds." But now I don't really think about it; I just get up and start talking. And I know at the beginning there's going to be some distance between myself and the audience. But if I keep going—I've seen it over and over again—if I keep going—then I stop being so stiff, things loosen up, and I can get that flow going.

I've done it so many times that I don't think about it. I just start talking about what I know, and once I'm relaxed I'm just there with it. I just talk about what I know, and I'm constantly trying to find a place where the audience can feel inspired by that. Because that's the thing about a public performance. When people go to a public presentation, they want some kind of inspiration. They want to come away moved.

Mick B: What's the worst case of stage fright you've seen in somebody else?

Mark B: [Laughs] There was a woman who was presenting an author at a bookstore. It was difficult watching her, she was so nervous. I'd seen her offstage and she was usually very poised. But when she was up on stage, she was very nervous.

I think part of her nervousness was caused by a little gesture she wanted to make at the end of her talk when she'd finished introducing the author. She wanted to shout a revolutionary slogan, and I think she was nervous about that; I think she had it in her mind during her entire presentation. Any time you set something up like that, the whole thing is harder to pull off.

Mick B: Do you have any other advice for performers who experience stage fright?

Mark B: Well, you have to know your stuff. Whatever you're doing, you have to be in command of your stuff. And I think it always works better if you're not trying to be an egotist. I think most people get into show business for egotistical reasons. I mean, I did. I wanted to be a star. And that's always going to be difficult. You get self-conscious when you want to be a star.

Walter Block

Walter Block is a Harold E. Wirth Endowed Chair and Professor of Economics, College of Business, Loyola University New Orleans. He earned his PhD in economics at Columbia University in 1972. He has taught at Rutgers, SUNY Stony Brook, Baruch CUNY and the University of Central Arkansas. He is the author of 300 articles in professional journals, two dozen books, including the classic *Defending the Undefendable*, and thousands of op eds. He lectures widely on college campuses and appears regularly on television and radio shows.

MB: How long have you been performing?

WB: I first started giving public speeches in 1966. I began my teaching career in about 1968. I ran for political office in the early 1970s, for the New York State Assembly.

MB: What were the circumstances when you started speaking publicly?

WB: I had become a libertarian in 1962. I wanted to promote liberty. There were two ways of doing this: writing and publishing, and public speaking.

MB: Tell me about the first time you were anxious or nervous. What were the circumstances?

WB: Both writing and speaking were occasions for nervousness and anxiety. In the former case, I had bouts of "writer's block." In the latter case, when I had a public speech scheduled a few weeks in advance, and I contemplated going through with it, I would get a dry throat, upset stomach, and general discomfort.

MB: How did you feel?

WB: I felt horrible. How could I have a career in promoting liberty through writing and speaking if writing and speaking were accompanied by anxiety? Yet, so strong was my desire to pursue such a career that I persevered. I did the writing and speaking—I forced myself to do so. But I was not a happy camper.

MB: What were you telling yourself? What were your thoughts?

WB: Regarding public speaking, I told myself that I would be a failure. I would be a disgrace. I would be unable to attract anyone to the cause of free enterprise because I would be so tongue tied. After my talk, I would be asked hostile questions that I would be unable to answer, further humiliating myself. I would be an embarrassment to the cause of free markets.

As for writing, I would sit there and sit there in front of my typewriter looking at the blank page. I would tell myself that if I couldn't write, why was I just sitting there? Wouldn't I be better off if I stopped fooling myself into thinking I could become a professional writer? Maybe I should get a job where I didn't have to write.

MB: How could you have viewed it differently so that you wouldn't have been anxious?

WB: With the benefits of hindsight, I can now say that had I been aware of the benefits of Rational Emotive Behavior Therapy (REBT)—the psychological philosophy of Albert Ellis—ninety-nine percent of my nervousness and anxiety would have disappeared. This, indeed, is what did happen to me when I understood the philosophy.

Here's the story. I went to several shrinks for this problem of stage fright and writer's block. The shrinks were singularly unhelpful. I don't think that my early recollections of my mother, or my dreams, or free associating, had anything to do with my abject failures in overcoming this problem. (Well, I should clarify; I wasn't an abject failure in my early days of writing and public speaking—I wasn't polished, but who is, when they first begin? My failure, rather, was that I was driving myself crazy with my anxiety, and I was unable to write as much or as well as I wanted, if I weren't continually giving myself a pain in the butt.)

One day, or rather, Friday evening, I bumbled into a workshop run by Albert Ellis in midtown Manhattan. His style was very appealing to me; he made it clear that people had problems of all sorts because of the crap they kept telling themselves. His solution was to argue his patients out of the crazy statements they were plaguing themselves with. This was very appealing to me, because I flattered myself that I tended toward rationality.

Soon after attending this Friday night workshop, I entered into one of Ellis's group therapy sessions. I attended for several months. I read over a dozen of his books. I did the homework assignments Al and the other group members assigned me. Pretty soon, I had thrown off my irrational thoughts on these matters and my anxiety and nervousness pretty much disappeared. What a relief! Now, I could pursue my career freed of the impediments I was placing in my own path. Whoop-dee-do.

MB: As you continued speaking publicly and writing, how did the state of your nervousness change?

WB: It changed remarkably for the better. I would actually look forward to upcoming speeches. Getting in front of an audience no longer terrified me. I would enjoy and anticipate the pleasure of getting words down on paper (nowadays, filling up the screen).

MB: How did you effect that change?

WB: I kept challenging my irrational thoughts about these matters. I asked myself: If I gave an imperfect speech, would this be awful or intolerable? Hah! Neither I nor anyone else has ever given a perfect speech. Yes, giving a poor speech had a definite downside. I wouldn't be listened to, invitations to lecture would decrease, and I wouldn't be promoting liberty as well as I could, had I been able to give a better account of myself. But this was not awful. It was not intolerable. The proof that it was tolerable was that I was tolerating it.

The prospect of a less-than-perfect performance no longer held any awe for me. Why not? Because, after Al argued me out of my old thinking patterns—many, many times—I could no longer accept the view that there was something over and above disadvantageous about failing, or doing relatively poorly. Mere disadvantages I could tolerate. I learned that there was nothing over and above that.

My thoughts changed from, "Well, if I give a poor speech, it will be horrible" to "If I give a poor speech, it will be unfortunate." "Unfortunate" I could live with.

A similar pattern emerged with writing. In my early days, I used to post little signs on my walls. For example: "The next article I write will be perfect; this one, I'll just finish." I didn't mean this, of course. I never thought that any future writing of mine would be perfect. I don't even know what a perfect publication would be. Another one was, "The perfect is the enemy of the good." Here are some more: "As it says in the men's rooms of the nation, 'The job's not done until the paper work is completed.'" Don't ask— these things helped me; they inspired me. Heck, these sayings are no more weird than the way my critics view my substantive output.

Here's another one: "If it is worth doing, it is worth doing imperfectly." This one helped me quite a bit, too: "A good book is a book that I actually finish [writing]." In the bad old days, I would think that the "eyes of history" were looking over my shoulders—who's grandiose here?—and be saying things like, "You must be kidding" or "Give us a break." So I came up with this aphorism: "The eyes of history are looking over my shoulders at what I'm writing and poo-pooing my efforts? I'll tell them to avert their eyes."

Michael Edelstein once mentioned a technique he used for writing, which I also adopted for myself: When nothing was "coming," he'd just hit the keys on the keyboard in a random manner. He'd type undecipherable nonsense, just to get his fingers moving. Works for me, too.

MB: What else did you tell yourself to overcome your fears?

WB: Other thoughts I fed myself—taking the place of "If I don't do a perfect job, I'm a shit"— included the following: "If people don't like my talk or my publications, that's just their opinion. If they're correct, then I do indeed need to improve. But, just because I may be rejected by some people, that doesn't necessarily mean that what I did was improper."

I remember once some student asked me a question that I couldn't answer. In the bad old days, that would have been truly devastating. After all, I'm supposed to be the expert. But, armed with my REBT training, I simply congratulated the student on coming up with a question I couldn't answer. I said I'd have to think about it, and I'd get back to him on it. I even had the temerity to explain to the audience that what they were now witnessing was not a disgrace. We're all just human beings. None of us have all the answers always at our finger tips. The earth doesn't open up, and you don't fall into the pits of Hades, if you can't answer a question. Okay, if this would occur too often, I might even at this late date want to take up a different profession. But failures of this sort on my part now hold no horror for me.

As for my publications, every once in a (happily) rare while, someone points out an error in an article or book of mine. I have not yet committed suicide over any of this. I simply write in a later publication that I no longer hold the views that I earlier articulated, and I explain why. No big deal. No horror.

MB: Do you ever get nervous now?

WB: Very, very rarely. And, when it occurs, it is of much of a shorter duration and is less debilitating.

MB: What are the circumstances when you get nervous now?

WB: Sometimes, right before a speech, just as I'm about to go on, someone will ask me if I'm nervous. Before that point, I wasn't at all nervous. But, before I can think my way out of it, I get a little tinge of nervousness.

MB: When don't you get nervous now?

WB: Nowadays, I'm pretty good at public speaking, if I say so myself. I actually enjoy public speaking—the adulation of the crowd and all that. People seem to appreciate what I say. (At least when I'm not talking to actively hostile audiences, which I do a bit of—heck, sometimes I like that even better, pervert that I am.)

Jim Bouton

Jim was a bench warmer in high school with the nickname "Warm-Up Bouton." His guidance counselor recommended a career as a forest ranger. People are still having trouble predicting what Jim Bouton might do next. This Yankee twenty-game winner, author of *Ball Four*, TV sportscaster, actor, inventor, and businessman, is also a major league speaker. His presentation is a highly entertaining combination of anecdotes, insights and inspiration, tailored to his audience. And he's very very funny.

Bouton believes in focusing on the process to achieve goals. He encourages his audience to think like athletes, get into the fun of the enterprise, the challenge of long odds, the satisfaction in details, the thrill of extraordinary effort, the joy of work. His love of a challenge led to his unprecedented comeback to the major leagues at the age of 39, after an eight-year retirement. "The irony," says Bouton, "is that by focusing on the process you reach the goals more often."

MB: When did you start playing baseball?

JB: When I was about six years old.

MB: Can you remember the first time you were nervous while playing?

JB: I never called it nervousness. I always thought of it as excitement and fun.

MB: How did you feel?

JB: Energized. And focused.

MB: Can you tell me what your thoughts were?

JB: Well, it really depends on what stage of my life you're talking about. I think at some point along the way I realized that the butterflies in my stomach were an asset, not a liability. The way to be successful in performance situations is to see nervousness as a source of electricity that you can plug into. There have been some situations where I didn't feel nervous, I didn't feel butterflies, and I had to manufacture butterflies to get a better performance. While pitching with the Yankees, for example, games became routine after a while. So I would create an imaginary dire circumstance. I'd put the welfare of mankind at stake. Tonight's win will end starvation in India.

MB: I remember in *Ball Four* you talked about how you would get butterflies when you had friends or family in the stands. You wrote about imagining that your family actually was in the stands, even though you knew they weren't going to be there.

JB: I did that to create the feeling I was looking for. I've always thought of nervousness as an asset. And that's what I tell kids today, when I speak to Little League groups. I say, "Don't push that away. Embrace that feeling. It's your body telling you that you're ready. That's going to help you."

MB: As you continued to play baseball, did your nervousness change? Or did it stay about the same?

JB: No. I was just as nervous—or excited—about pitching in a high school tournament as I was in the World Series. I once cried after a high school game. I never cried after a World Series. [Both laugh]

MB: How were you feeling when you cried after the high school game?

JB: It was too long ago. I never thought baseball was the most important thing I could be doing with my life. What helped me a lot was keeping sports in the proper perspective. None of it matters much when you think about it. Whether you're good on the stage or not good on the stage, whether you win the game or lose the game. Nobody is going to die—or even get sick.

MB: Could you elaborate on "putting it in the proper perspective"?

JB: Yeah. I remember before I went out to pitch my first World Series game, Ralph Terry, a veteran pitcher, was sitting next to me on the bench and said, "When you're out there on the mound today, kid, just remember one thing: No matter what happens, win or lose, five hundred million Chinese Communists don't give a shit." [Both laugh] So when you realize that half the world doesn't care, then the game becomes just that: a game.

MB: Do you see people who don't have that attitude?

JB: All the time. I had a lady call me last year. She played the piano and, whenever she had to give a recital, she would get so nervous she would make mistakes. She said she never made mistakes when she was playing by herself or just for the fun of it.

I said, "What are you afraid of?" and she said, "I'm afraid of making a mistake." I said, "Well, you should be making a few mistakes." She said, "What do you mean?" I said, "If you never make a mistake, that means you're not playing all out. You're not playing as open and free as you can. You're playing too tight, too controlled—that's not the way to play. You'd be better off having a full-out recital with half a dozen mistakes, than having a mistake-free boring recital. Because the one in which you've allowed yourself to make mistakes is going to be more dynamic, more powerful, and more musical." So she was able to see that error-free playing is not a good goal. [Both laugh]

MB: You're doing a lot of public speaking now. Are there times when you're speaking when you're not nervous at all?

JB: Yeah, but those are the times when I am nervous. [Laughs] Because I want to feel those butterflies. I look forward to them.

MB: Do you do anything now to manufacture the butterflies? Do you ever have to?

JB: I spend some time alone, and talk to myself about the importance of what's coming up.

MB: So even though there are five hundred million Chinese who don't give a shit, there's still importance to what you're doing.

JB: You have to strike the right balance. If it's a World Series, you have to tone it down. That's when "five hundred million Chinese Communists don't give a shit" works. At the other end of the spectrum, with nothing at stake, you have to tell yourself: "Five hundred million Chinese Communists do give a shit." [Laughs] That their lives are depending on this game. You have to reframe the situation, up or down, depending on what's needed.

MB: What effect does thinking have on your performance?

JB: I try not to think. I try to get more in touch with feelings. I want to perform as instinctively as possible, so I try to get rid of conscious thoughts. I want to find the right feeling for the situation.

For example, I never liked committing myself in those pre-game meetings where we would go over the opposing hitters, and they would want to know how I'm going to pitch to each batter. I would always say, "I can't tell right now. I have to wait until I'm on the mound. My body will tell me what pitch feels right." Two men on, one out, eighth inning; I'm going to have a feeling. I'm going to trust that feeling more than I'm going to trust a decision I made two hours earlier inside a clubhouse. As someone once said, "Don't think. You're hurting the club."

MB: I don't need names, but can you tell me the worst case of stage fright you've seen in someone else?

JB: When kids are out on the field and their coaches and parents are screaming at them. I try to help the kids deal with these kinds of parents and coaches.

MB: What do you do to help them with that?

JB: Whenever I'm asked to speak to little leaguers I say "Okay, but I want the parents and coaches to be there too." I start by asking the kids "What do you think a major league batter is thinking in this situation: bases loaded, the score is tied, two outs, it's the ninth inning. Is he thinking, 'I've got to get a hit'? Or is he thinking nothing? How many think it's 'I've got to get a hit'?" Everybody's hand goes up. How many think he's thinking nothing? No hands go up.

"Wrong," I say. "He's thinking nothing. He's not thinking, he's feeling.

He's trying to feel loose and confident, because he knows from past experience that's the feeling that gives him the best chance to succeed."

Then I ask, "What do you think a pitcher is thinking who has just walked the bases loaded?" Is he thinking, 'I've got to throw a strike'? Or is he thinking nothing?" By now they know the answer.

That's why the worst thing a coach or a parent can holler in that situation is, "Just throw strikes!" As if you weren't trying to throw strikes the rest of the game! [Laughs] Instead of thinking about the bases loaded and throwing strikes, you want to go for the feeling that you've just struck out three guys in a row.

Of course, my message to the kids is really intended for the parents. Left to themselves, kids would choose up their own sides, attaching their own importance to the event or not, and play for the pure fun of it.

Parents and coaches are frequently trying to achieve something through their kids that they weren't able to achieve in their own lives.

MB: Is there any other advice you'd have about stage fright?

JB: No. Just put things in perspective: Nobody's going to die. Don't be afraid to make mistakes. And above all, have fun.

David Brenner

David Brenner debuted on national TV on "The Tonight Show," and has made the most appearances of any guest on that show—158. He is the most frequent talk show guest of any entertainer, which is confirmed in *The Book of Lists #2*.

Today, he is recognized as a political pundit, appearing on MSNBC, CNN and The Fox Network. He's had four HBO Specials. His last, "David Brenner: Back With A Vengeance," was one of HBO's highest rated specials. *The Hollywood Reporter* proclaimed, "He's edgier and more insightful in his skewering of popular culture than ever before . . ."

Before doing stand-up, he was a successful writer/producer/director of 115 television documentaries, and headed the documentary departments of both Westinghouse Broadcasting and Metromedia Broadcasting. In that role he earned nearly thirty awards and citations, including an Emmy Award. He is the author of five books, including the best seller *Soft Pretzels with Mustard,* and *I Think There's a Terrorist in My Soup.*

MB: How long have you been performing?

DB: Thirty-nine years.

MB: What were the circumstances when you started?

DB: Well, I never wanted to be a comedian; you have to understand that. I was a writer, producer, and director of documentaries for the networks. I headed up documentary production for Westinghouse and Metro Media. And I just got burnt out. I'd been working since I was eight-and-a-half years old. I said, "Well, that's enough of this." So I took a year off, saved enough money to just squeak by for a year in New York.

I just wanted to have something to do, because I'd had this work ethic since I was a child. You know, I'd always been funny, and people had always been telling me, "Oh, you oughta be a comedian." But, I had no interest or desire to do it. But then I thought, "You know, why not? It'll give me something to do for a year."

So I started hanging around comedy clubs. And, to tell you the truth, when I sat there, seeing most of those comedians, I'd think, "Well, I'm as good as that guy." Or, "I'm better than that guy. If I'd want to do this. I don't think he's that funny."

So I started doing it. I wanted to do a television show, so that some day, when I told people, "I once played around with stand-up comedy," and they didn't believe me, I could whip out a video, and show it. So, I gave myself a year. And in a little over a year I got on "The Tonight Show." The response was so great. . . . I had ten thousand dollars worth of job offers the next day, including a gig in Vegas, and I realized that I'd hit the mother lode. And this lark of mine has lasted thirty-nine years.

MB: So, were you nervous when you first started out?

DB: Yeah, because I had never really been on stage. When I was in—I think it was fourth grade—I played a cloud in a school play. I had to puff out my cheeks, and they glued cotton balls on me, or some stupid thing. And then, in the orchestra, I started out playing the triangle. But I was screwing around so much they made me bang the sticks. In another play I was a whip. I had to take off my belt and use it as a whip. It was a stupid thing.

So I had never truly been on stage. But as a producer for television, I had worked with a lot of actors, comedians and all that. I knew the production end of it. So I was a bit nervous, to the point where I would take an over-the-counter pill before I performed. I think it was called "Miltown." It was a tranquilizer, and it would calm me down. So I had no trepidation about performing.

Then I went with Steve Landesberg to a club down in the village. He's a very good friend of mine, played Sergeant Dietrich in the Barney Miller series. He's a terrific stand-up comedian, a very funny guy. So he and I went down to the Gaslight Club. A lot of the great folk singers and comedians had been there in the early days. They had this Hootenanny night, or open mike, whatever you want to call it. This was back in '69, so this was a time when most performers were folk singers, and they had missions, you know, to correct the world. They were all peace and love, and making V's with their fingers, and blowing kisses to the audience. It was the time of Aquarius and all that crap.

So the night I was there with Steve Landesberg, the place was packed with folk singers, their managers, their relatives, and their friends. And in those days, comedians weren't on the top billing. We were pretty low down on the ladder. We were like the bastard child of the show business family.

Anyway, I was going on. And then about five comedians later, Steve would go on. So I thought about how fascinating it was to me how the folk singers perform, and I got up on the stage and said, "You know, I've been watching all you folks singers, and truly, it's so fascinating to me how you spend five minutes or so telling us how you wrote the song, why you wrote the song, what it means to you, what it's supposed to mean to us, what it's going to mean to the world, how it's going to change everything. And I thought, 'Wow, wouldn't it be great if comedians could do that?'" And I made believe I was holding a guitar, and dealing with the frets, and all that. And I said (as a comedian now), "I was living in Haight-Ashbury"—and I was tuning this air guitar— "with this woman Esther." (Of course none of this is true.) "And we had an argument." (Again, a little tuning.) "And I broke off with her. I decided to leave." (A little more tuning.) "And Esther got upset and tried to stop me. But she slipped in the tub, and she broke the big toe on her right foot. And it was at that moment that I created this joke which I call 'the broken big toe on Esther's right foot,' and I'd like to say it for you now. If you've heard it, please say the punch line with me." [Both laugh.]

See, you're enjoying it. [DB laughs] I enjoyed it. They fucking hated it. [Both laugh] Not only was I bombing, but there were glares, and you could hear, like, snakes hissing. It was a horror. And Steve Landesberg . . . In the back of the club, there was a big pillar, a structural pillar. Steve leaned out past it and waved goodbye to me. And left.

So, I managed to get through the crowd and to get outside without getting harmed. I walked out onto the street, Mulberry Street. [Both laugh] And Steve and I were walking, and I said to him, "God, can you imagine a worse bomb? I mean, it was perfect. Not only did I not get laughs, but everyone in the room hated me."

MB: How did you feel after that happened?

DB: Well, what I said is, "Well look at me, Steve. My legs are working. My arms are working. My brain's working. My mouth's working."

And then I came up with a line which I used from then on. I said . . . and you know the way I grew up . . . I said, "No one's coming out of the alley with a baseball bat playing 'Let's get a Jew.' So what's the big deal? What am I nervous about? That experience was nothing compared to what I've been through."

And I took those tranquilizers, those little pills that I took, and I tossed them into a litter basket on a corner somewhere around Fourth and Mulberry. And I was never nervous again till this very moment.

MB: Wow!

DB: And I was never nervous on the first "Tonight Show." First of all, I was going to do it, and then I'd decided I was quitting the business. That's number one. So there was no pressure. Number two: having been a television producer, I was very familiar with television stages, so when I walked out on "The Tonight Show," I knew what everyone was doing. I knew that the guy pulling those weird-looking cables was actually dressing the stage so that the camera could dolly. And I knew about the boom mike. I mean, I knew all this. And I knew all that. So I was on familiar ground. When I was in a nightclub, I didn't know what the hell to do on stage. But on a television stage, I knew.

When Johnny [Carson] introduced me, he said that I was weird. And he said, "You have to be weird to be a comedian. You have to be weird. And here's David Brenner." And I took it as an insult. I thought "Weird? What the hell do you mean I'm weird? I'll show you how weird I am." And I went out and I blew the roof off the place.

As a matter of fact, that's around the time when I got a nickname among the young comedians. They used to call me "Ice Blood," because—and I do it to this day—I stand around backstage and I talk about something that's in the paper, some national issue, or something in my life, until I hear my name, and then I just walk out on stage. So . . . I'm the antithesis of what you're focusing on [stage fright], because I have no absolutely no trepidation, no fear, no worry, no anxiety. I don't break out.

Look, I've had friends who were sitting on the toilet in the dressing room when they were supposed to be introduced. I know all about that. I can remember walking off the stage once when I was co-headlining with a singer down in Florida. I went up to him and said, "Hey, how ya doin'? It's a great audience." Then I said, "They gave me three cabanas. I understand you're down here with your wife and kids. They gave me three cabanas. I don't need that. It's just me and my manager. If you want, I'll meet you there tomorrow. You can have the cabanas." And he was staring straight at me, but didn't answer me. Then they introduced him and he walked out. I turned to my manager and I said, "What's wrong with him?" He said, "David, not everyone's like you. The guy is in shock. He's going on stage. He's scared." [MB laughs]

MB: So, you never get nervous now?

DB: No, never.

MB: Would you say it's due to that experience at the Gaslight and saying to yourself, "Look what I've been through in my life. This is nothing compared to that"?

DB: Yeah. It's no big deal. And the thing is, in a hundred years, they're not going to remember what any of us said or did anyway. What the hell's the difference?

One time I did a television show . . . This is a little bit of a deviation, but anyway . . . I went on a TV show, and some camera broke—the color wouldn't show—and the audience was getting restless. And I know that's not good for any performer. So I went up to the producer, and I said, "Listen, if you want, put a stool out there, and I'll go and take questions from the audience, and goof around with them and keep them happy." He went, "Oh, great, David. Sure. That'd be great."

So they did. And I walked out. As I was walking out, someone spotted me and yelled, "David Brenner!" and they start applauding. Then a guy yells, "David, you're going to live forever!" And I said, "Look, I really appreciate you telling me I'm going to go on forever, but the truth of the matter is whatever we say or do, in a hundred years no one's going to remember what anyone said or did." "No, you'll be remembered forever," he said. And they were all applauding. So I said, "Well, let me ask you a question"—and this was in 1985. I said, "Let me ask you a question: Who can name the number one actor, the number one singer and the number one comedian in 1885? Raise your hands." [Both laugh] And no one did. I said,

"Ya see, in a hundred years, none of this is going to count. But let's have some fun while we're here." And I went on and I took their questions and entertained them. So, that combined with the idea that no one's coming out [alive] . . .

You know, I grew up in a slum in Philadelphia, with fights, and poverty and all that crap. This [performing] is a piece of cake. I don't get [stage fright] at all. But the guys who get the most nervous, and panic and throw up and all that, when they get out and hit that microphone, they can be way better than somebody who's an "ice blood" like me. It doesn't make you a better performer or a worse performer because you're not nervous or you're nervous.

MB: You've made it clear that what you tell yourself makes it so you don't get stage fright. Can you speculate on what goes on in the minds of people that make themselves nervous?

DB: They're being judged. It all boils down to the fact that they take it personally and they're being judged. When you bomb and you personalize it, it would be—if you're a man—it would be like walking out in front of fifty thousand women, dropping your pants, and they start booing, and they give you the thumbs down. That's the feeling if you're personalizing. And if you don't personalize, it's: "So what? In a hundred years who the hell's going to care?" Even tomorrow morning. You're as good as your next show, not your last show. So the next night you recover.

Look, I believe that every comedian is assigned "X" number of bombs in comedy heaven. You know, like this guy's got two hundred sixteen. You gotta get it out of your system. And some of us are very lucky: we don't bomb very much. We hit that stride. We're just lucky that way. But others, God, they bomb for years. But they come out of it, and they go on.

Larry "Bubbles" Brown

Larry "Bubbles" Brown is a San Francisco-based comedian. In first grade, while watching clouds at recess, he realized we were all going to die. He then lay in under the swings until the teachers brought him back to class and sent him home with a note.

His stand up career began at the Holy City Zoo in San Francisco in 1981, and he rode the comedy boom of the 1980s. He explains it crashed because "anything in life you like will be taken away from you." Brown stayed at it because "you can't beat working half an hour a night."

He has appeared on over 25 TV shows (twice on David Letterman), in the movie *Kiterunner*, in numerous clubs in California and Las Vegas, and he frequently opens for Dana Carvey and Dave Attell.

He hopes to start a vegetarian minimalist pessimist movement. Though he once was a certified glider pilot, flying terrifies him. His philosophy of life: "Expect the worst and you will never be disappointed."

MB: How long have you been performing?

LBB: Since March 3rd, 1981. It was a Tuesday. Absolutely true.

MB: What were the circumstances?

LBB: I always wanted to do stand-up, but I never thought I could. Then I heard about open mikes. So I started to hang out at The Punchline and the Holy City Zoo. I think I watched the open mikes for about a year. Then I finally put a few minutes of material together and I went up on March 3rd. The rest is history. A toboggan of failure.

MB: Tell me about the first time you were anxious or nervous on stage.

LBB: I just remember the first few months I did stand-up—I had a day job then—and I remember being so nervous about going on that night that I didn't eat for the whole day. Then I came home after I did my set and ate like five pounds of food at midnight.

MB: So how did you feel? Can you elaborate on that?

LBB: I just remember feeling anxious until I did the set, then after I did it, it was a real relief.

MB: How anxious?

LBB: Not being able to eat. And I'd be thinking, "I'm going to be doing this for five minutes in twelve hours." That's all I could think about the whole day. In fact, I used to walk up to the Holy City Zoo on days I wasn't performing, and I'd be nervous just being in the area.

MB: So what were you telling yourself? What were your thoughts?

LBB: Just "Please don't bomb." That was the big thing.

MB: So what was so bad about bombing? What were you telling yourself about that?

LBB: It's like it is today. Although the first few times I went on stage I did pretty well. I don't think I bombed until I got six weeks into it, and I remember how traumatic that was.

MB: What were your thoughts then?

LBB: Well, when you're standing up in front of a bunch of people who are staring at you in silence, you look like a complete dork. And my humor tends to be somewhat personal, so I take that as a real personal rejection.

MB: How did your nervousness change as you continued to perform?

LBB: It just lessened. The more you do it, the more you get confidence.

MB: What were the circumstances when it lessened?

LBB: I don't remember. I just remember before the end of the year [1981] I was actually able to have a meal before I went on stage. And keep it down.

MB: So how did you feel then?

LBB: It got to be kind of a good nervous. That was when the comedy boom was starting, so it was an exciting place to be around.

MB: So what were you telling yourself? What were your thoughts then?

LBB: After I started doing well, I thought, "Wow. It's so cool to get paid to do a gig." And after three years, I got to where I could quit the day job, and I actually made a living doing comedy.

MB: So were there any thoughts you were telling yourself that made you feel more excited than nauseous?

LBB: No, I think it was just doing it for a few months and getting over that initial horror of going on stage.

MB: Did you feel different?

LBB: When you do well, you feel pretty good. But when you bomb, you hate the world.

MB: So you hated the world. Did you ever get to where you weren't hating the world?

LBB: No. I still hate the world to this day.

MB: [Laughs] Now come on.

LBB: These days, whether I bomb or kill, I still hate the world.

MB: Do you get nervous when you perform now?

LBB: No, it's like bombing is just really uncomfortable. You can't wait to get off stage. But it doesn't have the same effect it did twenty years ago. Same with killing, too.

MB: So rather than being horrible . . .

LBB: It doesn't mean anything. All you can hope for is to meet a hot chick after the show.

MB: So before it felt horrible?

LBB: Before, it was like a life or death matter. Like, "I gotta kill or die." Now, it's just, "I do what I do. If they don't like me, screw 'em; if they like me, great."

MB: What's different about your attitude now?

LBB: I guess I have the attitude "I don't care," which is supposed to be good. If I bomb, I think, "It wasn't my night." I forget about it in five minutes. Whereas in the old days, if I bombed I'd think about it for a week.

MB: What's the worst case of stage fright you've ever had?

LBB: When I did Letterman, I was so wired up I couldn't sleep the night before. I was so nervous, and I had dark rings under my eyes, because I hadn't slept in thirty-eight hours. And they changed my set around. Fortunately, I got bumped. That may have been the worst. They brought me back a month later. Of course I took a Valium the night before and slept like a log.

MB: So under those circumstances where you didn't get any sleep, and they rearranged your set, how did you feel then?

LBB: It was awful. I was dead tired, but I was so wired I couldn't sleep. And I thought about bombing on national TV. It would've been horrific.

MB: So what were your thoughts about that?

LBB: Sheer panic.

MB: What were your thoughts connected to the sheer panic?

LBB: [Laughs] That maybe I could fake my way through it.

MB: But if you bombed on national television, what would that have meant to you?

LBB: I would have quit the business at that point; it would've been so humiliating. Back then, a lot of comics did bomb on Letterman. They didn't have the audience miked, and I saw a lot of guys go down hard. I literally would have quit comedy.

MB: When don't you get nervous now?

LBB: I rarely get nervous now. If there's an audition for something that's big, I get a little antsy.

MB: But aside from that you don't get nervous?

LBB: No. I feel numb. I just go in and do it. I'm like a factory worker. Plop those jokes in and get out.

MB: What are your thoughts around that?

LBB: I just hope I can keep doing this. It's a tough way to make a living, but I don't want to do anything else.

MB: In considering your own nervousness, what role do your thoughts, beliefs or attitudes about yourself play in it?

LBB: Hmmm. I don't know. The only thing that I think about nervousness now—and I've thought this ever since I first went on stage—is that I've never been able to remember all of my material. And that must come from nerves. I cannot go up and do everything I intend to do. I always go up and leave stuff out. And it's always been very frustrating.

MB: So what role do you think your thoughts play in that?

LBB: A self-sabotaging role. They say a lot of performers have it [stage fright]. They don't want success or something. I don't remember all of my stuff, and I don't always do the best editing. I'm going down like the Hindenburg.

MB: What advice on stage fright would you have for other performers?

LBB: Take lots of drugs.

MB: [Laughs] And aside from that?

LBB: Just keep doing it. It'll get better with time. You'll get used to it. It's like hitting a baseball—just keep doing it and it won't be as hard. You just get tougher. The more you do it, the tougher you get. You get rid of the stage nerves. It's like anything. Like jumping out of a plane. I'm sure it's terrifying the first time, but after ten times you might get to where you like it.

MB: As people become more seasoned, what do you think they're thinking that helps them not be as nervous?

LBB: They might realize, "This is a great way to make a living; it's fun. So why be nervous?" Although I think you need a little nervousness to give you a certain amount of energy.

MB: Is there any last thing you can mention that's been really helpful to you in dealing with nervousness on stage?

LBB: I remember what Mike Pritchard told me when I was really upset one night. He said, "You're in a small room. Maybe thirty people in there. Outside of that room, no one knows who you are or what you did. It doesn't matter." That made a lot of sense.

MB: What were you thinking to yourself before he told you that?

LBB: I was just thinking, "God, I suck. The world hates me." And hell, the world hadn't even seen me.

David Burns

Dr. Burns graduated magna cum laude from Amherst College, received his M.D. from Stanford University School of Medicine, and completed his psychiatry residency at the University of Pennsylvania School of Medicine. He has served as Acting Chief of Psychiatry at the Presbyterian/ University of Pennsylvania Medical Center (1988) and Visiting Scholar at the Harvard Medical School (1998) and is certified by the National Board of Psychiatry and Neurology.

Currently Adjunct Clinical Professor Emeritus of Psychiatry and Behavioral Sciences at the Stanford University School of Medicine, his awards include the Outstanding Contributions Award from the National Association of Cognitive-Behavioral Therapists, and Teacher of the Year three times from the class of graduating residents at Stanford University School of Medicine.

American mental health professionals rate his *Feeling Good: The New Mood Therapy* (over 4 million copies sold) as the #1 book on depression, out of 1,000 self-help books.

He conducts workshops for mental health professionals throughout the United States and Canada.

MB: How long have you been making public appearances?

DB: Since I was a research fellow. That's when I did my first academic talk, at any rate. That would have been in the mid-1970s. After *Feeling Good* became well known, I had the chance to do quite a bit of talking both for the general public and for mental health professionals.

MB: Can you tell me about the first time that you were anxious or nervous appearing in front of a crowd?

DB: Well, I was giving a talk at Oxford University, when I was a fellow at the University of Pennsylvania Medical School. I had the chance to present some of my research at a very prestigious meeting to scientists who were involved in brain research. I was doing research on brain serotonin metabolism at the time.

MB: How did you feel?

DB: Well, I was very anxious because my research was challenging some findings that were coming out of one of the high profile laboratories at the National Institute of Mental Health [NIMH] on brain serotonin metabolism. I was convinced that the scientists at NIMH had been using incorrect methods. So I repeated one of their studies but analyzed the data quite differently, and came up with the opposite conclusion. This was exciting and potentially important, but there was one problem. I had heard that the fellow whose work I was challenging could sometimes be a little bit on the feisty side. He had a reputation for screaming at people at academic conferences. So I was very anxious.

To make it worse, I was one of the few junior investigators at the conference; there were only eighty scientists who were invited to attend—it was sponsored by the NATO Advanced Study Institute on Metabolic Compartmentalization in the Brain. Nearly all the people were senior, world famous researches, the top people in their fields. So I was very anxious because my presentation was scheduled toward the end. I kept fantasizing that I'd get up and mumble, and I was terrified that the man whose work I was challenging would be in the audience. In my fantasies, I imagined that he would scream at me at the end of my talk, and I'd be humiliated. I was in a state of high anxiety for four days, waiting for my turn to present. It was like waiting to be executed. The night before my presentation I couldn't sleep at all. I just wandered around the Oxford campus. Even owls seemed to be scorning me and hooting at me. It was a nightmare.

So the next day my turn to speak finally came; I was the last speaker of the day. I walked up to the podium with my notes, and lo and behold, here was the fellow I had feared sitting in the front row right in front of me, staring at me in this icy way, just as I had fantasized. I was so nervous that I decided to kind of read and mumble my talk, rather than giving it in a spontaneous and dynamic way. At the end, there was silence for a few seconds, and no one said a thing. Then the scientist I feared jumped up out of his chair and started screaming at me. He said, in essence, that I didn't know what I was talking about. Then he sat back down, and there was another prolonged silence in the room. Finally, the chairperson said, "Does anyone else have any questions for Dr. Burns?" And not a single hand went up.

Then the chairperson said, "Now we're going to walk to dinner to a restaurant about two blocks from here." And I remember when we were all walking no one would walk next to me. I felt so humiliated—it was my worst nightmare come true. I just felt like such a loser.

Then I got on the plane back to the United States, and I began to think about what the critical scientist said from a scientific point of view, and it dawned on me that his criticisms didn't seem to be valid. So I went back and shared my concerns with my research colleagues, and we did a few more analyses using sophisticated computer simulation techniques. We proved very clearly that what he was claiming was the opposite of the truth. So I submitted my research to a journal called *Biological Psychiatry*. It was my first scientific article.

Four weeks later I got a call from the editor, and I thought, "Oh boy. Now I'm going to be criticized some more." Usually, they just send you letters with the reviewers' comments. Often, articles are rejected flat out. Occasionally, they ask you to revise the article and submit it again for another round of reviews. But they never call the authors, so this was unusual.

However, the editor said, "This article you sent is amazing. Your article has been accepted for publication and we're going to publish it without any changes. In fact, the reviewers were so impressed with your work that we were wondering if we could submit it for the A. E. Bennett competition this year in the category of basic research?" That was quite a surprise. The A. E. Bennett Award was considered the world's top award in the area of brain research for an investigator under 35 years of age. People all over the world compete, including the people from the lab at NIMH whose work I was challenging. I said, "Sure. Go ahead and submit it."

Several weeks later, he called me again and said, "You're the unanimous winner of this year's A. E. Bennett Award for Basic Research. There was tremendous competition this year, but you received all the first place votes. Can you present your findings to the annual meeting of the Society for Biological Psychiatry in New York in a month?" I said that I'd love to.

But this time, I fantasized it very differently. I imagined that I would speak without my notes, and with great enthusiasm, and just talk to the people like they were my friends. I used a visual imaging technique to try to fantasize this as vividly as possible every night before I went to sleep. And even though it didn't seem particularly believable, I figured that it couldn't hurt. In my fantasy, I imagined that people would rush up to the podium at the end of my talk and congratulate me, and ask questions, and tell me they were thrilled with my presentation.

I bought a new suit, went to New York, got up, and delivered my presentation spontaneously, without any notes, and with a lot of enthusiasm. There were hundreds of scientists and psychiatrists in the audience, and at the end they all started clapping and cheering. Lots of people rushed up to the podium to congratulate me, just as I'd imagined. So that really kind of made a huge impact on my career. Although, as you know, I eventually went in a different direction with cognitive therapy. But that was the first real recognition I'd ever received as a psychiatrist.

Since then, I've done a lot of presentations. I now do approximately 25 two-day workshops to mental health professionals around the country every year. Of course, my public speaking techniques have evolved a lot. I've received standing ovations this fall in a great many of the workshops I've given recently. And I've really discovered what people are looking for, what's the difference between a great presentation and a presentation that's only so-so, and the attitudes and the mind sets that go along with that.

Recently I've been doing an anxiety workshop called "Scared Stiff"—it's a two-day workshop. At the end of day one, I often treat someone with public-speaking anxiety live in front of the audience. It's meant to illustrate all the negative thoughts that trigger public speaking anxiety and how to turn them around. It has been very dramatic, because someone gets right up on stage with me and their voice is trembling, and they have all these negative thoughts. I use cognitive therapy techniques, and nearly always see a profound shift in the person who volunteers for the demonstration. They usually defeat the problem right there on the spot. It only takes about thirty minutes to complete this live mini-"treatment" on stage. And that makes the audience believers, because you've actually shown your work rather than making claims about it.

MB: How could you have viewed that situation at Oxford differently so that you wouldn't have been as anxious?

DB: From the cognitive therapy perspective, the thoughts and perceptions that cause anxiety and depression are distorted and unrealistic. But you don't realize this when you're feeling upset—you may be telling yourself, that "Everyone will see how nervous I am. My voice will tremble and my legs will shake. My mind will go blank. And I'm really going to blow it. The people in the audience will all look down on me." But the funny thing is, these distorted thoughts can act as self-fulfilling prophecies. So you don't know that you're creating your own universe. You feel like a victim, a powerless victim, but you're actually hypnotizing everybody to treat you in just the way you imagined.

Now, when I give a workshop, I view the situation quite differently; I view the audience almost like children—they're burned out, they want some inspiration, they want to laugh, they want to cry, they want to have fun, and they want some magic to occur. They want someone to care about them. I expect them to be incredibly warm and responsive. So I get all excited now, and it nearly always turns out the way I expect.

If you perceive the people in the audience as enemies who are highly judgmental and critical, they will suddenly appear to be like that. And if you perceive them as warm, loving and responsive, and you react to them like that, they will usually be just like that. If you treat them with warmth and respect, they'll give you their hearts and minds. It's a magical thing; it's more than just learning how to give a dynamic presentation. There's a spiritual component to it.

MB: Do you ever get nervous now when you're making a presentation?

DB: Well, not very. But occasionally, I'll get anxious or annoyed because the audio isn't working right, or whatever. But I always remind myself that the negative predictions that we make can be way, way off base, and that's very reassuring to me.

MB: My next question, though I believe you've already answered it, is "What role does your thinking, what you're telling yourself, play in your nervousness?"

DB: That's the whole ball of wax.

MB: What's the worst case of stage fright you've seen in someone else?

DB: None of my patients have done as badly as I did, because they usually avoid the speaking situations they dread. Whereas I went ahead and did it and blew it.

MB: Is there one particularly effective technique you'd recommend to someone with public speaking anxiety or with any other type of performance anxiety?

DB: No. Looking for one panacea or magical technique that will work for everyone is the biggest error in psychiatry and life in general. We're all so different. In my latest book, *When Panic Attacks*, I describe how to overcome every conceivable type of anxiety, and how to select the techniques that are the most likely to work for you. But trial and error will always be necessary. One person might respond to a Paradoxical Cost-Benefit Analysis, and another might respond to Cognitive Hypnosis.

That's the a technique I used last week during a workshop in Canada: Cognitive Hypnosis with Time Travel. The woman who volunteered had severe public speaking anxiety. So we went back in time, and she suddenly remembered a horrible experience when she was little. She had moved to Canada from Eastern Europe and didn't speak English. However, she was thrown into an American classroom. During her demonstration with me on stage during the workshop, she suddenly remembered that she could understand the teacher, but she couldn't yet speak English; she didn't know how to speak the words yet. So when the teacher asked her to do some simple arithmetic, she understood the question and knew the answer, but didn't know the names of the numbers. So the teacher started pressuring her, and humiliating her, and made her stand up. Probably, the teacher didn't realize that she couldn't speak English yet. She didn't know how to say "three" or "seven" or "fourteen" or whatever the answer was. So the teacher told her to write it on the board. But she didn't know how to write the American numbers, either. She tried to draw a picture of the answer—to put the number of dots, or something. And everyone started laughing at her and she's been feeling inadequate and humiliated ever since.

We did Cognitive Hypnosis and went back in time, and I had her talk to that little girl and to tell the little girl that she loved her. It was very emotional and touching. It seemed to pull the cork out of this particular person's champagne bottle. She might also have wanted to talk to the teacher in the hypnotic state, and to tell the teacher how much she'd hurt her. However, talking to the little girl seemed to be sufficient, and she suddenly began to feel much better.

Another volunteer during one of my workshop demonstrations had the thought, "Everyone will think I'm a fool," or "They'll think I'm a loser," or something like that. This was her worst fear. I said, "Well, why don't you confront this? Why don't you just walk down the middle aisle and ask everyone to stand up and shout, 'You're a loser! You're a fool!'" And she did. So everyone in the audience jumped up and said, "You're a fool!" It was so cathartic that she started laughing uncontrollably at how ludicrous the whole thing was. That experience absolutely crushed her public speaking anxiety. This technique is called Cognitive Flooding, but you could also call it a Shame Attacking Exercise.

The week before, a woman had this negative thought during the demonstration: "Everyone in this audience will look down on me because I'm not enough of an expert. I don't know all the answers. I'm nervous. If I give a talk, I won't be smart enough." She was afraid to look at the audience, so she took off her glasses and would only look at me, because she was certain they were all out there scorning her and looking down on her. I asked, "Would you like to confront the monster you're afraid of and look at them?"

She replied, "No, I'm afraid to. I could look without my glasses because I have blurred vision."

I said, "Put your glasses on and look out there," and everyone started waving and smiling and cheering for her. She was so moved that she started sobbing. She couldn't believe it.

So for each person it's going to be a different path out of the forest. . .

Stage fright is quite a problem. Because, you know, I've suffered from it myself, and that makes it a lot of fun when someone has this problem. I think, "Oh boy! We're going to have fun showing you how to defeat it."

MB: We're having a great time writing this book. And one of the reasons we wanted to do it is that it's so common.

DB: It's common and curable. In most cases, with people I've worked with, it just takes the one shot. But it's got to be up in front of a live audience, because they get the exposure. And the self-disclosure is a part of it. If you just do it in the office, then you've got to complement that with actual exposure, so you face your fears outside the office.

MB: Lastly, I just want to personally thank you for writing *Feeling Good*. The thing that attracted me to it was—I forget the words you used, but—I think it was learning how to stop being a love addict. Before that, I always assumed that my feelings created my thoughts. It took a lot of work, and I still have to stay on top of my tendency to needlessly upset myself.

DB: We all drift in and out of enlightenment, and no one can be happy all of the time. So you do have to keep working at it. I think that what we can hope for is having tools that will work for us, so that whenever you fall back into that black pit of self-doubt or despair, then you can climb right out again, because you've discovered the method that works for you.

MB: One of the most insidious dysfunctional thoughts I had—and my co-author pointed this out to me—was demanding that Cognitive-Behavioral Therapy, in the form of Rational Emotive Behavior Therapy, work one hundred percent of the time. Because if you do that, you're going to drive yourself nuts.

DB: That's a relapse prevention concept as well—and it's a Buddhist concept. The Buddha says, "We drift in and out of enlightenment." In other words, "We all relapse five or ten times a week." The key is knowing how to get out of that trap when it hits you.

Tony Castle

Tony Castle has been making a fool of himself in front of people since he was five years old. He emceed his first show while in the Cub Scouts. He was in his first play in 1961. And he spent the next 30 or so years in live theatre. He began doing stand-up comedy in 1987, and in 1992 was asked to perform at a retirement community. Since that day in 1992, Tony has developed his One-Man Vaudeville show that he performs 300 or more times a year. His favorite audiences are WWII Veterans and Rosie the Riveters.

MB: How long have you been performing?

TC: Since I was five years old, tap dancing at my aunt and uncle's wedding.

MB: You're serious?

TC: I'm dead serious. Then, when I was about eight, I got up in front of my grandparents' fiftieth wedding anniversary celebration and sang "Oh Come All Ye Faithful" in front of a combo. That's the first time I ever saw an audience that was truly stunned. They didn't quite know how to take that. It didn't help that it was May!

MB: Tell me about the first time you were nervous about performing. What were the circumstances?

TC: Oh man, that's a good question. The first time I had a lead role in a play was the first time that I really, really had butterflies. It was about a two-hour play, and I was on stage for all but twenty minutes of that time.

MB: Could you just elaborate a little bit on what you meant by "having butterflies"?

TC: Well, the best way to put it is that it was probably one of the few times when I felt insecure. I thought, "Am I going to be able to do this without the whole thing collapsing in on me?"—the actor's nightmare. Of course you've heard of the actor's nightmare.

MB: Right. But describe "the actor's nightmare," because I want to make sure everyone knows what it is.

TC: The actor's nightmare—and every actor has had it, and I've heard some stand-up comics have had it, too—is that you're standing back stage, you haven't been to a single rehearsal, and all you know is that you're going to have to walk out on stage in a second and they're going to say, "You're on!"And you don't even know what the play is. And you wake up in this cold sweat. You rarely make it onto the stage. It's sort of like those death dreams where you dream you're falling but you wake up before you hit the ground.

MB: What were your thoughts that contributed to being nervous when you had that first lead role?

TC: I had never been a lead before, where the whole thrust and focus of the play was on me. Before, I was always in a supporting role, so I could throw lines off, do my thing, and let the weight of the whole play rest on someone else. Suddenly, the whole weight of the play was on my shoulders, so that's what contributed to my being nervous. I was not just the lead. The play opened with me, it closed with me. I had never been in that situation before. Even when I was in a large role, I was always in a cast with a lot of people throwing lines back and forth. All of a sudden it was like doing stand-up with no stand-up training.

MB: And what were you thinking that made it feel perilous?

TC: The weight on my back was the thought: "Christ, this whole play is on me. This play will either rise or fall from my performance. No one else can save it."

MB: Suppose it had been a flop because of you. How would you have felt?

TC: I never allowed that thought to enter. It's like doing stand-up. You get up in front of a crowd and you've seen other comics just die in front of this crowd, just get buried—there's a hole in that stage like the Grand Canyon. You'll get up there, you throw something at the audience, and you get your first big laugh. Then you go, "Oh Jesus, it's going to be okay." Then all the preliminary thoughts go away after you get that first laugh. When I hit the stage in this play and the first night was a rousing success, I didn't have to think about all that other stuff. Once I was over the first night, I was no longer nervous about it.

MB: How did you feel when you weren't nervous, then?

TC: It really comes down to ego—it really does. Because if you ask a hundred people, "What is your greatest fear?" They don't say, "Getting mugged." They say, "Speaking in public." It's the greatest fear. Millions of people, you could put a gun to their head and they wouldn't speak in public. Then you start looking at smaller and smaller groups within that set [who will speak or perform in public]. There are musicians. There are singers. There are actors. And then there's this tiny, tiny, tiny little set of people who are stand-up comics who get up in front of other people and not only try to make them laugh, which isn't that easy, but try to make people laugh with stuff that they wrote. In order to do that you have to have an ego. You have to go up there and say, "I'm a member of an extremely elite group. Because all of these people who are sitting out there, they may not like me, but none of them would get up and do what I'm doing." It really does come down to ego. People will try to sugarcoat it, and put chocolate frosting over it, but I'm telling you, it's ego.

MB: As you continued to perform, did your nervousness change?

TC: It's not nerves so much as there's an edge that you never want to lose. You never want to say, "I've got this stuff down pat," because as soon as you say that you'll crash and burn on your next show.

MB: So what changed as you became less nervous?

TC: If you're talking about a play, it's getting out of the rehearsal process and getting out in front of an audience for the first time and having the play work. You know, you hear the laughter—or if it's a drama you hear the applause—and you hear that connection with the live audience. That's why you and I aren't in movies. We want that connection with the live audience. I think most people say that applause is better than sex. Applause is our drug. I've always said that performing is like breathing. Once you start, you can't stop. It's like a virus: once it gets in your blood, there's no cure. Performing is literally the most important thing in your life. Period.

MB: Now that you're less nervous and are feeling good about performing, what are your thoughts about doing it?

TC: I've had maybe twenty-five to thirty jobs in my life. I've never had a career. The only thread in the tapestry of my life, since the time I was a child, is performing. So I finally made that leap, quit the day job, and said, "No matter what, I'm going to find a way of making my living as a performer, 'cause my grandfather used to tell me, 'Work at something that's play to you and you'll always be happy.'"

MB: Do you ever get nervous now?

TC: I really don't. But then I've never been backstage at the Paramount Theater [in Oakland] with three thousand people out there. Maybe I'd be nervous then. Until recently, the biggest crowd I ever performed for was three hundred. But I have performed in front of a crowd of over five thousand people, just once, and I was not nervous because, on a big band stage when the crowd is in a pit pretty far away from you, the scene is less intimate and you don't feel as exposed. But it was fun when I did the bit about my Dad. When I said "How far did your Dad walk to school?" It was pretty cool to hear five thousand or so people shout, "TEN MILES! . . . IN THE SNOW! . . . UPHILL . . . BOTH WAYS . . . BAREFOOT!!!!" That was fun.

MB: And every once in a while—I don't care who the comedian is—every once in a while you still bomb.

TC: Oh, absolutely. Anyone who says he doesn't is a liar.

MB: So how do you feel when you bomb?

TC: Well, while it's happening, it's like when people describe being in combat, and they're asked, "Well, weren't you scared"? They'll say, "I was too busy. I got scared later. I was just trying to stay alive."

MB: What advice would you have for performers who are dealing with stage fright?

TC: I tell this to young comics all the time: The very fact that you can even get up there, that you're willing to get out there bare-assed naked by yourself with your own material, means that you're a member of an extremely elite group. And the very fact that you're willing to attempt it means that you've done something the other six billion people on the planet would not even attempt to do. That alone should help get you through your next show.

Peter Coyote

Peter Coyote has performed as an actor for some of the world's most distinguished filmmakers, including Barry Levinson, Roman Polanski, Pedro Almodovar, Steven Spielberg, Steven Soderberg, and Sidney Pollack.

Voice-over credits include an Emmy as the "Host" for a nine-hour series called "The Pacific Century," announcer of the 2000 Academy Awards Ceremony, and most recently a 12-hour series on the National Parks for Ken Burns. Recent movies in which Mr. Coyote had principle acting roles include *Femme Fatale*, directed by Brian DePalma, *A Walk to Remember*, starring Mandy Moore, and *Bon Voyage* by Jean Paul Rappeneau. Recent major television roles include playing the Vice-President to Geena Davis's President on "Commander in Chief," Rod Lurie's "Resurrecting the Champ," with Samuel. L. Jackson and Josh Hartnett, and "Brothers and Sisters," with Sally Fields.

Mr. Coyote has also written a memoir of the 1960's counter-culture called *Sleeping Where I Fall,* a chapter of which, "Carla's Story," won the 1993/94 Pushcart Prize for Excellence in nonfiction. It will be reprinted this May by Counterpoint Press. He is currently working on two new books.

MB: With all the experiences you've had, it seems hard to believe that you could ever be nervous about performing.

PC: Well, I'm not too nervous anymore. It's different on stage because there's no safety net. Once the curtain goes up, you're off and running. My experience has been that if you're really thinking about what you're doing, and concentrating on what you have to do, there's no space left to be nervous.

If you think about it, stage fright is imagining somebody else, out in the audience, thinking about you in a disparaging way. That means that your attention has gone out into the audience and you're not concentrating on stage. To me, stage fright's a dead give away that your concentration is off.

MB: When did you first start performing?

PC: I started performing in college, and I went as a writer—I was part of the black turtle neck sweater crowd. One day, the drama coach dropped into our little soiree in the coffee house and said, "Have you ever considered that drama is an argument of great import played out before the public?" I said, "No." He invited me to audition. I went, and I had the opportunity to do play after play after play for four years. That really got me interested in theater.

MB: Can you remember the times that you were nervous then?

PC: Yeah, I can. You get nervous about all the things that can possibly go wrong.

MB: What were you telling yourself to induce nervousness, and also to overcome it?

PC: Well, I don't think I was telling myself anything in particular. I think that what I was doing, before I felt comfortable, was acknowledging that there was a huge amount to remember, and I didn't have quite enough rehearsals to have it locked into my body.

"Am I going to forget my lines?" I think that's a big one. And, "Is somebody else going to forget their lines?" And, "Am I going to be put into a situation where I'm going to have to cover for them?" Those are the kind of things I think most people worry about.

MB: How nervous did you feel at times?

PC: Sometimes I would be nervous to the point that my legs would be shaking—really out of breath and anxious and nervous. But once you start [performing] it sort of goes away. And there's actually a degree to which stage fright gives you energy.

MB: So your method of dealing with it was knowing that once you began things would be cool?

PC: Yeah. You just have to get over the anxiety enough to get out from back behind the curtain.

MB: You mentioned that one aspect of stage fright is worrying about what somebody in the audience is thinking of you. Do you think there was anything you were telling yourself that was making that worry a little more pronounced?

PC: Oh, yeah. When I was in college, I figured the people that I was competitive with would be looking for the worst about me.

I had a really good friend who's now a really famous poet. And he was completely hampered by stage fright. I mean, he was just paralyzed by stage fright and just couldn't deal with it. I cured him in about fifteen minutes. What I told him was to "Imagine you're on stage. Imagine that now you're frightened, you're not feeling confident. Look out on the audience in front of you, and see who's out there from your past whose critical reactions you're afraid of." He identified somebody, and I said, "Okay, just for the hell of it, look at them carefully and ask yourself how old you were when they were that age."

He went, "Oh my God!" He realized that when he was afraid of that person he was about six. And I said, "Okay. Now bring that person up to the age that he or she would be today, and fast forward to where you're at your age today. Do you still feel that way?" And he said, "No, I don't."

Then I said, "Okay. Now turn the picture into black and white. And move yourself and that person way up in the far balcony in the back end of the theater. Just change their scale and their vividness." He did that, and he never had stage fright again.

He went off and had a long career. He now performs with a piano player, and he reads poems.

MB: Can you speculate about what he was afraid of?

PC: Whatever it was, it was taking his attention away from what he was doing and bringing it [his fear] into the audience.

MB: You mentioned that your legs would sometimes shake when you were performing in college. How did your nervousness change as you continued performing?

PC: I don't know. I just developed an ability to not care if I was afraid. It used to be that being afraid would make me worry that I was going to mess up. But at a certain point, I had enough experience working despite my fear that I stopped being concerned that it would stop me.

MB: What are the circumstances when you get nervous now?

PC: You know, I just don't seem to get too nervous anymore. I don't exactly know why, but I just don't.

MB: Do you think it's due to your being focused on the material rather than worrying about the reaction of people in the audience?

PC: Yeah, I do. I no longer care what people think. No matter what I do, there are going to be people who like it and people who don't. And there's not much I can do about it.

MB: So you accept that if there are people who don't like it, that's just the way it is?

PC: Yeah. But you know, it's interesting because the number one phobia of people from Western European cultures is speaking before a group.

You can't imagine a rattlesnake bite, but you can and you have experienced shame and confusion. And that's something that people really shy away from.

MB: What role would you say your thinking has in creating shame?

PC: Well, I think shame is induced in early childhood in parental situations. And I think that it's so powerful as to almost obliterate the ego and self-image. I think it's so powerful that people will do almost anything rather than feel it. Shame is at the root of most addictions. People will do anything rather than feel great humiliation and shame. I don't know why it comes, exactly, but I do know that it has a very, very powerful effect on people.

MB: So it goes back to people forming an opinion of you?

PC: I think that's at the root of a lot of stuff. Part of it is your own opinion about yourself. You want to do your best work. You want to feel that you've acquitted yourself well.

MB: Can you think of a bad case of stage fright you've seen in someone else? I don't need any names, but an example would be useful.

PC: Well, I can put it another way. You know when audiences go to the theater, they want to see you succeed. And the last thing an audience wants to see is someone really frightened up on stage, really humiliated. Because it embarrasses them. They want to have enough trust in the performer they're watching to believe that that person can manifest an accurate representation of fear or anxiety. But they don't want [real fear or anxiety] to leak out.

Of course I've seen that. I've seen nervous people trying to be casual or trying to present themselves as relaxed to cover what they're feeling. It's not so bad when people are nervous and they admit it. You know, they say, "Oh my God, I'm scared to death." There's something kind of charming about it—you can identify with it. But to see somebody who's really trembling and not doing well, that's upsetting.

MB: Okay. In one of these instances you've seen of someone not doing well, do you think the person was telling themselves something that made it worse?

PC: Yeah. I think they were telling themselves that it was bad to feel anxiety, that they shouldn't be feeling that way.

People who are leaking and inadvertently showing you their fears are people who are not accepting how they're feeling. It's okay to feel frightened.

MB: Is there anything else that you haven't mentioned yet that might help people with stage fright ?

PC: I do think physical stretching and relaxation exercises help. I think paying attention to your breathing is a huge piece of [dealing with nervousness]. You can actually define anxiety in a certain way as holding your breath. People do that when they're anxious. So if you're breathing slowly and regularly, and taking deep breaths, it's going to really moderate your anxiety.

Phyllis Diller

Phyllis Diller is recognized as one of the world's leading female stand-up comics. With five decades of performing, she has starred on television, in movies, and on stage, including the "Jack Paar Show," Carnegie Hall, Caesar's Palace in Las Vegas, the Waldorf Astoria in Manhattan, Soldier's Field in Chicago, and Madison Square Garden in New York City. She appeared on Broadway in "Hello Dolly," in Elia Kazan's film *Splendor in the Grass*, co-starred in three other films, and appeared in 29 specials with Bob Hope. From 1972 to 1982, she performed as piano soloist with over 100 symphony orchestras in the U.S. and Canada. Author of four best-selling books, she has also received a plethora of awards, including Celebrity Business Woman of the Year (National Association of Women Business Owners), Lifetime Achievement Award (Annual Comedy Awards), and the 1993 Lifetime Humor Award (National Humor Institute). She also has her own star on Hollywood Boulevard.

MB: Hello, Madam. I've been told to call you Madam.

PD: Well, I like that.

MB: Thank you so much for doing this. My first question is—if this isn't too scary—how long have you been performing? I understand you're no longer doing it, but how long was your run?

PD: Fifty years.

MB: Wow! Were you nervous the first time you performed?

PD: That doesn't even come close to describing it. [Laughs] Words like "terrified" would be better. [Laughs] Or words like "shaking so bad that I was a blur." [Laughs] Words like "blank brain." [Both laugh]

MB: Was there anything that you were telling yourself that was causing you to be so frightened?

PD: Well, it's only natural. If you're a beginner, you have no experience. You do not know that making a mistake isn't fatal. [Both laugh] You're sweating. The sweat is running down your back onto your buttocks and tickling. That doesn't help either. The sweat is running into your boots—to the point that it's so strong and poisonous and toxic that it actually eats the leather lining of the boots. Have I made it clear?

MB: Yes. Do you think there's any way you could have viewed it differently to lessen the stage fright?

PD: Not at the time, because I was already into mind control and fearlessness. Look, I was so into wanting peace and quiet that my nickname was Mother India. But I couldn't manage it. The fear overpowered what I was trying to learn.

MB: As you continued to perform, did the nervousness become less severe?

PD: Oh my, yes. In fact . . . let's go this far . . . Out of all the twenty-four hours of any day, I was most comfortable in the hour that I was standing in the spotlight. That was my most comfortable hour. That's what it became. That perfect joy.

MB: What do you attribute that to?

PD: Experience. But also great material. When you first start, you don't have any of that. You don't have material. You don't have expertise. You haven't found all those wonderful magic things. You write every day for many years to get great material.

And when you first start out, you don't even know who you are. You don't know whether you're a singer or a comic. You don't know what you should do. So you learn all that from the many audiences [that will see you].

MB: Were there any differences in the way you approached things?

PD: In the beginning, at my first job. there was no way I could have walked out on that little teeny—it wasn't even a stage. It was on the same level as the audience, and it was the size of a postage stamp. So I had to have one martini. That was my approach to getting a little bit calm.

However, I did have a technique that I invented very early, which I used all fifty years. I had to be absolutely quiet and talk to nobody for five minutes [before going on]. Simply meditate and get my head screwed on right.

MB: Can you be a little more specific?

PD: Silence. And then I thought about the audience.

MB: So what were your thoughts about the audience?

PD: That I loved them, and I wanted to make them happy.

MB: They no longer were your adversary?

PD: Well, they never were. I don't know what I was afraid of. I was afraid of myself. Because I've always loved the audience. My God, I'm crazy about 'em. I love people. I love to be with people. And I have a good approach to all kinds of people. That's something you're born with, in your DNA, where you can talk to a king or a bum and everybody in between. And I have that ability.

MB: Would you say that your thinking played a big role in lessening your nervousness?

PD: Oh my, yes. When you perform, you're constantly trying to reach a point of having no nervousness. Now I know of entertainers, in long, long careers, who never got over it, to the point of throwing up before every performance. [Both laugh]

MB: So experience, for them, did not do the trick.

PD: And neither did grasp of the material. You see, as my material got better—it's like having a better life raft. That first raft is full of leaks [Both laugh]

MB: So what was the worst case of stage fright you ever experienced —your first performance?

PD: That would have been a pretty good one.

MB: Yeah, I don't see how it could get much worse.

PD: No, it couldn't. I did shake. You know how you hate to see people shake—the real shakes? I had that. And I'm always embarrassed when I meet somebody and they have the shakes. I try to grab them so nobody sees them, because I know how embarrassing it is. But over the years, I became a real pro: I didn't need a martini; I was together. I would never have a drop of booze. I wouldn't even drink at lunch. I wouldn't have any alchohol till after the show.

MB: Regarding cases of stage fright you've seen in other people—I don't want you to disclose anybody's identity—could you tell me about some of the worst things you've seen in other performers?

PD: [Laughs] Well, I think throwing up is the worst. I've heard of both men and women who had that problem. And they were big, big stars. It just shows it can happen. That would be a subconscious reaction—they don't want to throw up.

MB: You wouldn't think so.

PD: No. But you see, I think it shows extreme sensitivity, which is what an artist must have.

MB: With the people that threw up, can you speculate as to what was going on in their minds?

PD: Well, it was subconscious. They never got a handle on it. Every person, from kindergarten to the biggest stage in the world, when the performance is over, they're elated! The word is relieved. They have a high. There's no high like after a show. One of the most important things about getting over stage fright is being prepared. It depends on your material, and really believing in your preparation, believing in what you're going to do.

MB: I understand you've performed as a concert pianist.

PD. That was the worst! [Both laugh] Because now we're into a whole other field. A *serious* field. [Both laugh] When I talked, it was comedy. But when I played, I had to be serious. And remember, I was with seventy concert musicians. And therefore the terror started all over.

MB: Was performing as a pianist different from performing stand-up?

PD: Of course! Because it *was* serious. And it was a different audience. Sure, they were there to see me, but they weren't really sure what they were going to see. They were really astonished that I could play at all. But it was wonderful. That amounted to about ten years of me being at the peak of what I can do.

MB: So, last, let me just ask if there's any other advice you can give to people with performance anxiety?

PD: Well, they should all have that period of silence before they go on, and be alone with their thoughts. Calming thoughts. Meditation thoughts.

MB: This has been immensely helpful. Thank you again.

PD: You are really fun to talk to. [Both laugh] Because, you know, when you hear a gag, you laugh. And I love you for that.

MB: Well, I've got to say it's a thrill to hear your voice live. I remember being ten and watching you on television—and loving you with my sisters and my parents. It's just wonderful when you can do comedy that reaches across the generations.

PD: You know, that was my original plan. I had that in mind. I wanted to appeal to everyone from three to a hundred and three.

Olympia Dukakis

Olympia Dukakis is a renowned stage, film and television actress, director, producer, teacher, activist and author (best-selling memoir, *Ask Me Again Tomorrow*). She has appeared in hundreds of movies and television shows, receiving an Academy Award in the Best Supporting Actress category, the New York Film Critics Award, the Los Angeles Film Critics Award, and the Golden Globe Award for her work in the Norman Jewison film *Moonstruck*. Other movie credits include *Away From Her*, *Steel Magnolias*, *Tales of the City*, *Dad*, and *Picture Perfect*. She has also performed in well over one hundred stage roles, received Obie, Drama Desk, Lost Angeles Drama Critics Circle, and Outer Circle awards, and has taught acting at New York University and Yale. Of her most recent works, she is the executive producer and co-star, with Haley Joel Osment, in *Montana Amazon*, scheduled for release in 2009.

MB: How long have you been performing?

OD: Since about 1958.

MB: What was the first time you were nervous?

OD: The first time I was nervous, I didn't even realize I was nervous. It was the first part that I ever did in any play. I was Mrs. Cliveden-Banks in "Outward Bound." I went on stage, couldn't remember a single thing, and never moved from my chair for the whole first act. The other actors were ready to kill me, I had no idea what was happening; I was unaware of being frightened or anxious.

MB: Can you tell me what was going on in your mind then?

OD: At the time, I think it all felt very unreal.

MB: Was there anything you might have been telling yourself that contributed to the nervousness?

OD: No. I just think that it was because it was my first time in front of people. I had gone to graduate school for two years, and I had never been in a play before. I started off wanting to direct, but then ended up acting, and this was my first part. It was stunning. I still can't believe what happened.

MB: So, obviously you outgrew that phase. How soon did you start to overcome that?

OD: Well, the next night I went on stage and said my lines, and did my blocking, and left the stage when I was supposed to.

MB: And how did it feel that time compared to the first?

OD: Well, a little realer. I still didn't feel the fright that must have been in me.

MB: Have you felt stage fright?

OD: Oh, yes. I then proceeded as the summer went on—in summer stock —to realize that I was going to the bathroom a lot before I went on stage. My first clue that I was scared. And that still happens to me.

MB: Is there anything you can see in your own approach to performing —that is, what you're thinking or telling yourself—that makes things easier in terms of overcoming pressure?

OD: Well, the first thing I realized was that I had to keep my mind focused on what I was doing. So I would go backstage a good half-hour before I went on, and try to focus myself on the play and what I was going to do, because if your mind isn't focused, then all kinds of other concerns come in. That was probably the first thing I learned: to stay focused.

When I went back to school, I talked with my acting teacher and he pointed out that if you leave your head a vacuum, and don't really learn to concentrate, to discipline yourself, then you are prey to a lot of emotional conditions.

MB: Could you elaborate on that—on falling prey to negative thoughts?

OD: Well, I think the important thing is not to think of anything as negative. [But the thoughts would have been:] "Am I believable in this? Am I doing a good job? Will people say I'm a good actress?"—all those things that plague us, especially when we're younger.

MB: So how do you avoid thinking those thoughts?

OD: Actors do many things to get themselves concentrated. Some do physical exercises in the wings.

MB: How has your management of performance pressures changed over the years?

OD: Well, I don't fight it [the nervousness] anymore. I let it happen. If that's who I am, that's who I am.

A lot of stage fright has to do with excitement. It also has to do with the fear of being seen and known. Pretty soon you get to the point where you realize that you can live with people knowing a lot of things about you that you thought you couldn't reveal.

MB: What would the fear be that you thought you couldn't live with?

OD: Being known. Aspects of myself being known that, I think, would have negative connotations.

I've recognized that embracing all aspects of who I am is part of what being a human is about. And if I'm going to be so judgmental about all of this, then of course I'm not going to want to be revealed, and I'm not going to be more fully available for my work.

MB: So eliminating the self-judgment was a big factor?

OD: Yes, not eliminating the judging, but actually taking it on.

MB: And acceptance of the particular traits that you were portraying?

OD: Not just acceptance. That's a little passive. But really taking them on, almost to the point of having an appetite for it. Going towards it. Which is, of course, the thing that actors do that most people don't do. Actors go towards what is painful, ugly, vulnerable, they go towards what is angry, what is frightening. Most people try to avoid those things in their lives. [Facing these things] makes them uncomfortable; it makes them insecure.

An actor's work is about that. Being believable—whatever system of acting you use—to be believable in the world of the play. So you have to go through all these negotiations with yourself. It's either that, or you just play the same kind of part over and over again. (Which a lot of people do.)

MB: You said that now you don't try to fight stage fright. Do you sometimes still get nervous?

OD: Oh, yes. Sure. Now I try to make a distinction between "fear-excitement" and "fear-danger." I'm really not in danger when I go on stage. But when you're younger, you think you are.

MB: So the distinction is "Well, I'm not actually in danger now"?

OD: Right. The audience didn't come here to judge me, to criticize me. They came to have a good time.

MB: Is there any advice you'd have for people with stage fright?

OD: I think you've got to be really honest about what's going on—what you're thinking and what you're concerned about. Because [if people feel they're] out of control, it makes them feel very frightened for themselves—depressed. The trick is to try to be as honest as possible.

MB: By "honest," do you mean admitting that you're experiencing stage fright?

OD: Well, beyond that, [you should ask yourself:] "How do you view yourself? How do you judge yourself? And what do you think other people are thinking?"

For me, the most frightening time I had was when I did a play called "Rose" at the National [Theatre] in London. It was a one-woman show, with me sitting on a bench for two damn hours, talking to an audience. It ended up being sixty-seven pages of lines, from top to bottom, margin to margin. And not only were the lines an issue, but it was hard just holding the whole play emotionally, holding the audience.

It was okay the first night. But the second night, all of a sudden, I had hardly even begun, when I felt myself actually pitch into a black hole. My body just jerked forward as if I was falling into a pit. It was awful. I just looked at the audience—and I've never ever done anything like this—and I said, "I'm up." And I walked off the stage.

I said to the stage manager, "What are the lines?" The stage manager had been too far away, so I said, "You have to be closer, 'cause if I go up, I'm going to call for lines." So the stage manager went, "Okay," and I said to the stage manger, "What should I do?" because I'd never done anything like that before. Should I apologize, explain?

"No, no," she said. "Don't say anything. Just go out and sit down." And the moment I walked out and sat down, the audience burst into applause. It so moved me . . . It was just so kind. I thought, "What am I so worried about out here? Look at these people. Look how much they're on my side."

I realized that I had to prepare myself during the day to walk on and need an audience, which is a lot different from informing them, pleasing them, impressing them, making them cry, making them laugh.

MB: When did that all take place?

OD: That was in 2000.

MB: I'm impressed that you can admit to this so easily. It's quite impressive that you don't mind people knowing about it.

OD: Oh, no. It's just all part of the work. It's part of how I have evolved (and continue to evolve, I hope!) as an actress and as a performer. We're confronted constantly with new experiences, new experiences that shake us up: If you deny that, it's going to catch up with you.

Will Durst

As the sacred cows smear bullseyes on their foreheads begging to have their pomposity punctured, America yearns for a man with the aim, strength and style to hit them where it hurts the funniest. Will Durst is that man. Comedy for people who read or know someone who does.

According to the *New York Times*, Will Durst is "quite possibly the best political satirist working in the country today." He reads five papers daily, is a regular commentator for audible.com, Air America, CNN and NPR, writes a nationally syndicated op-ed column, daily website jokes, and performs hundreds of comedy shows every year—at clubs, corporate events, theaters and benefits, with the occasional acting and voice-over role. He has made more than 400 television appearances in fourteen different countries.

C-SPAN's favorite comic (eight appearances,) Durst is a five-time Emmy nominee and recipient of seven consecutive nominations for the American Comedy Awards Stand Up of the Year. He was the first comic invited to perform at Harvard's Kennedy School of Government and the first American to be nominated for the prestigious Perrier Award at the Edinburgh Fringe Festival, for the show "Myth America." His heroes are Thomas Jefferson and Bugs Bunny, while his performances are made possible by the First Amendment.

MB: How long have you been performing?

WD: Oh, geez. I started way, way, way, way, way early—as a kid.

I did stand-up in high school. It was me and my buddy Bob Bielefield; we were juniors. We entered one of those talent contests that every school has. We did this old vaudeville routine, and we added our own jokes to it: "I hear you buried your wife last week." "Had to . . . dead, you know." It was very funny. We also sang some songs.

Then, when I went to college, I had my first class in theater. It was weird. It was when theater was tickling the edges and trying to find new ways to stay current. So it was kind of like a performance art class. And in one class, I created a comedy club. I brought in ashtrays, and beer, which was great, 'cause the kids all loved it, and I did a comedy routine that worked for the kids.

Then I auditioned for a part in a stage review, with singers and Broadway show tunes; and it had a hokey part for a comic who wore a tuxedo. There were eight people sitting around in a semi-circle on chairs drinking scotch out of coffee cups [at the audition]. It was the height of Milwaukee sophistication. It was incredibly intimidating. I died a horrible death. I was so nervous about that audition that I didn't actually perform the stand-up set. I did it on tape, and I played the tape. That's the reason I died. That's how nervous I was. [Laughs]

MB: How did you begin performing if you were that nervous?

WD: There was a showcase, a Monday night open mike. And I went down there with the act I had practiced and taped. They were used to stand-up comedy, and I was used to performing, because I'd been in theater, so I did okay. The first time I went on stage in Milwaukee, I did the fourth or fifth best out of fifteen [comics].

MB: Were you nervous then when you went on?

WD: Very nervous. I know two people—two of them—who did stand-up only twice. The first time, they had so much nervous energy, and had worked and worked on their acts, that they killed. The second time, they used the same material, but they didn't have the same preparation or the same energy, and they died. And they could not reconcile that in their brains. It was like a computer error. The same material, and it didn't work—"does not compute." They never went back up [on stage to do comedy, again.]

MB: Why do you think that they couldn't reconcile it?

WD: I don't know. Maybe the early success skewed their expectations too high. You need a cast-iron stomach to handle all the rejection.

MB: I'm assuming from what you've said that you didn't have a cast-iron stomach when you started. How did you develop one?

WD: By failing. And the ratio of desire to fear of rejection has to be 51-49 at least. If it's 50-50, people can see it when you're on stage. If it's 51-49, you can build it up to 95-5, which is probably where I'm at now.

MB: Is there anything that went on in your mind, anything that you told yourself, to build it up to 95-5?

WD: Probably that I'd have a better chance of getting laid if I made it. There's the big carrot, which is fame and fortune. And then there's the little carrot, which is every night. It's not just getting laid. It's also the free drinks and getting the respect of your peers. There're so many things.

I'm in a play right now, a musical comedy about stand-up. And one of the songs is about doing corporate gigs. There's this comic on stage, slogging through his material, and then you hear his inner voice: "Forty more minutes." [Both laugh]

MB: How did you develop your confidence?

WD: You learn tricks every time you're on stage. Have a routine. Know your material.

It's like when I try to give counsel to a guy doing a competition. I tell him, "There are so many things to worry about on stage. Don't worry about your material. If you know your material, you'll be comfortable."

You know, when you're killing, it's all a blur. You can't remember anything you did. And when you die, everything is highlighted and outlined in parentheses, in italics, in bold. You remember everything when you die. Time just slows down, 'cause you don't have that adrenaline.

So one of the tricks is to know your material—know what you're doing so you're comfortable with it. And [remember that] every time you go in a space, you're more comfortable in that space. New places always freak you out—at least me.

MB: What do you do to get over "dying"?

WD: If I die, I allow myself four hours of self-pity. But that's it. I can wallow in it for four hours.

MB: And then that's the end of it?

WD: Correct. Nobody likes a whiner. There's a comic in town who whines more than me, and I just realized how annoying that is, so it made me stop.

MB: So you still get nervous sometimes?

WD: Every time. I have a little routine. I drink a lot of coffee—my drug of choice—before I go on stage. And I pace. And I actually try to write my set line-up every time because it's a reinforcer of what I'm doing. I don't care how many times I've done it, if I write it down before the show, I don't even have to look at it. Writing it down makes me familiar with my material.

MB: Do you think that your thoughts or attitudes about yourself have a role in your being less nervous now than when you started?

WD: If you do anything long enough, you get to the point where you're either halfway decent or people will tell you to stop doing it.

MB: Quite a few people have told me they get nervous when there are celebrities in the audience. Do you?

WD: Family is worse.

MB: Do you have any advice for people with stage fright?

WD: No, I don't have any advice. The only people still working are the ones who never quit. Just do it.

Albert Ellis

Dr. Albert Ellis (1913–2007) was the founder of Rational Emotive Behavioral Therapy, the first of the cognitive therapies. He received his PhD from Columbia University in 1947 and began to practice classical psychoanalysis. Disappointed with the lack of positive results, citing psychoanalysis as "unscientific and even antiscientific" and too long winded and inefficient, he began to formulate his own approach, which he introduced in 1955 as Rational Therapy. It focused on helping people change their dysfunctional behavior and disturbed emotions by teaching them to identify their irrational beliefs and to replace them with rational ones. Author of close to 80 books on a variety of psychotherapy issues, he is held in the highest esteem in his field. In 2001 *Psychology Today* stated, "It's safe to say that no individual—not even Freud himself—has had a greater impact on modern psychotherapy." Dr. Ellis died some months after our interview with him.

MB: Tell me about the worst case of stage fright you've ever experienced. When was it? What were the circumstances? How did you deal with it?

AE: The worst time was when I was a child in the first grade, and I knew the answers to all kinds of questions; but I never raised my hand because I was so afraid of speaking badly. When I was a student at college I was president of a political group, but scared shitless of making speeches. I forced myself to make them, telling myself that I would do my best, however uncomfortable, to do what I wanted to be more comfortable at—if I died, I died! Not only did I survive, but I discovered that I had a talent for talking in public, and once I was over my fear of it, I enjoyed doing so.

MB: Did you have any difficulty as an adult?

AE: Practically none, because I've made myself do all kinds of exercises over the years, including my shame-attacking exercise, where you deliberately do something foolish, ridiculous, or silly in public, and work at not feeling ashamed. Since I've done those exercises, I'm practically never nervous except once in a very great while.

MB: You mentioned the shame-attacking exercises. Could you tell us about them?

AE: Well, you might get onto the subway and yell out the stops—"42nd Street!"—and then stay on the train. Or you could go to a hotel lobby and say to a stranger, "I just got out of the loony bin. What month is this?" Or you could wear peculiar clothing.

All the while you work on not feeling ashamed. By doing these exercises many times you get over that crap.

MB: Did you ever have clients that had a great deal of problems getting over stage fright, and how did you work with them?

AE: I've had some clients who were practically numb and dumb. They just didn't speak at all, they were so afraid of speaking. Most of them were just afraid of important audiences, and things like that. But I show them that they are just about always telling themselves that, "If I speak badly, I will be no good. And if people don't like what I say, they'll put me down. And they'll be right. I deserve to be put down."

So I show them that they're always taking a preference to do well—which is fine in itself—and making it into an absolute must; and they put their own worth on the line, which they never have to do. Then I always give them homework assignments to get out and speak and speak and speak.

MB: So they should repeatedly put themselves in the uncomfortable situations?

AE: Yes, preferably. Take risks.

MB: Have you ever worked with anybody who wasn't able to get over stage fright or being nervous?

AE: Several, because they just don't come to sessions after awhile and never keep doing the hard work to get over it. So I never see them again, and presumably they never did get over it.

MB: So they give up, then?

AE: Yes, they give up.

MB: Do they usually give up after a few sessions, or have you seen somebody for half a year and then they still give up?

AE: Rarely, because after half a year I have most of them pretty well cured.

MB: Is there anything you can do that will encourage people not to give up?

AE: I show them that discomfort won't kill them. They can get by with it, and not take it too seriously. So they become less uncomfortable.

MB: Would you say that stage fright is, in almost all cases, about the person rating themselves over the possibility of doing poorly?

AE: Yes. First they rate their performance, which may be accurate. "I don't speak well. Other people don't like my talk." That may be okay. But then they say, "Therefore, I'm an incompetent speaker or person or no-goodnik." So, like most of the rest of the human race, when they can't do something that they consider very important, they almost always put themselves—not merely their performance—down.

We teach them "USA"—Unconditional Self-Acceptance. Always accept yourself unconditionally, because no matter how badly you do, you are not your performance. And therefore you can rate your performance, your act. But you can't rate yourself, because if you were a no-goodnik, you would always and always fail.

MB: Have you ever seen somebody who had no confidence or no hope that they would ever be able to get over their fear of speaking? Have you seen somebody that was in that bad of a shape?

AE: Yes, I've seen people with severe personality disorders who spend their whole lives putting themselves down.

MB: And by seeing you, they're able to eliminate that? Get rid of it?

AE: A few people are not. They have severe personality disorders—they're semi-psychotic. There are a few who never get over it.

MB: Would you say that your method will not work for them?

AE: No. They will not work for it.

MB: Okay. So if somebody was using your shame-attacking exercise and they didn't find it effective, are there one or two reasons why they aren't finding it effective?

AE: We get them to keep doing it and doing it and doing it until it is effective for them.

MB: So it's repetition and hard work?

AE: Right. Of those who really keep working at it—I'd say that probably ninety-five percent get over it.

MB: Have you seen other negative attitudes about stage fright that get in the way, besides self-rating?

AE: They always compare themselves to other people and put themselves down if they think their speaking isn't good enough. They can always find some people who speak adequately or very well and then they say, "I'm not as good as he or she is, therefore I'm no good."

MB: Are there any other exercises besides the shame-attacking ones that you could recommend?

AE: All kinds. Take risks. The risk of getting thrown out of school, of not getting a good job—any kinds of risks that you consider important, even if they're not shameful it's important that you win.

MB: Right. So shame is the main reason people have stage fright?

AE: Right.

MB: Is there anything else that you'd like to add about stage fright?

AE: Well, mainly that people had better see that they are responsible for their stage fright, that they make themselves disturbed. They don't "get" disturbed. The situation doesn't disturb them. They make themselves disturbed about it.

MB: Right. But some people might not believe they are doing it. How do you convince them that they are making themselves upset?

AE: I show them that, obviously, if a hundred people fail at almost anything—at sports, at work, or anything else—that not all of them will get upset. So most people do upset themselves about failure, at speaking or writing or anything else, because it's the human condition to do it. But I show them that unless they admit it, then they're never going to get over it.

MB: How do you get them to admit it?

AE: I get them to face the fact that, "Yes, I definitely fail at speaking. I'm a very lousy speaker. That's too damn bad, but it's not the end of the world. And, again, my worth as a human is not included in my worth as a speaker."

MB: How would you say that your worth as a human is included?

AE: It's not included in anything unless you asininely include it.

MB: So human worth is an asinine concept?

AE: Yes, and I always quote [Alfred] Korzybski [founder of the Institute of General Semantics]. He says that you cannot be what you do. Because you do thousands of things, good bad and indifferent. And therefore you cannot be any one of those things, no matter how bad it is. You generalize: "I failed, and I don't like failing." And then you over-generalize: "I failed and so I am a failure." So I show people over and over that whilst they may fail at some things, they are never, never, never failures.

MB: Would you say that fear of speaking or stage fright is a very common experience among human beings?

AE: Yes, very common.

MB: And people that experience it, if they work at it, can get over it?

AE: They can practically all get over it if they keep working, working, working, failing, failing, failing, and not taking themselves too damn seriously.

Melissa Etheridge

Beginning with her debut album "Melissa Etheridge" (1988), she has written and performed innumerable hits, including "Ain't It Heavy," (Grammy®, 1992), "I'm the Only One" and "Come to My Window" (Grammy® Award for Best Female Rock Performance, 1995). She then issued her highest charting album, *Your Little Secret*, leading her to receive the Songwriter of the Year honor at the ASCAP Pop Awards in 1996.

Ensuing albums include *Skin* (2001), *Lucky* (2004), and the DVDs *Live And Alone* (2002) and *Lucky Live* (2004). *Her Greatest Hits: The Road Less Traveled* (2005), recently re-released, included Melissa's Oscar® winning song, "I Need To Wake Up." In 2007, she released her ninth studio album, *The Awakening,* (One of *Rolling Stone* magazine's Top 50 Albums of 2007).

In April 2007, Melissa Etheridge received the distinguished ASCAP Founders Award honoring the anthemic power, compassion, and generosity of spirit of her music, and her enduring status as one of the greatest all-time female rock icons.

MB: How long have you been performing?

ME: Well, I first got up in front of a group of strangers when I was eleven years old. And I was hooked after that.

MB: What made you hooked?

ME: The thrill! I was sick to my stomach, but when I was done they all applauded, and I went, "Wow! All right! Let me do that again!"

MB: So you started out sick to your stomach and you ended up thrilled. Could you say what caused that transformation?

ME: First you actually have to have the dream; first you have to have the desire to actually want to sacrifice yourself on stage. That desire is a crazy one, but it gets inside you. For me, that feeling first came when I was three years old and listening to The Beatles' "I Want to Hold Your Hand" on a transistor radio. I was just transported.

I listened to all kinds of music [when I was young]. My father brought a guitar home for my sister when I was eight years old, and I begged to play it, begged to play it. I wanted to learn because I had been pretending to play on badminton rackets, jumping around the house. But the guitar teacher said, "No, you're too young." And I said, "Please let me try." He went, "Well, all right." And I was out of my mind; I wanted to play the guitar so badly. My fingers were bleeding, but I was playing it. And so he taught me. Then I let guitar playing go when I was nine years old, but when I was ten, got back into it. I learned chords. And once I learned chords, I said, "You know, I can write a song." (This was the early seventies. There was a lot of folk music.) And I would visit my friends and sing; I would write these songs and we would all sing them.

One day, my friend called and said, "Hey, there's a talent show. Do you want to go sing your song?" And I thought, "Why not?" So I went. There were two other girls singing one of my songs with me. And I felt this nervousness, and also excitement. That's what I tell people: that feeling that you attribute to nervousness is also excitement.

I try in my mind to go, "I'm excited. That's what's making my stomach feel this way." And my desire to be on stage and transform this energy, to get this music out, and to give it to the people is greater than any fear I have.

MB: Did your nervousness or excitement change as you continued to perform? Or is it the same now as it was when you were eleven?

ME: No, no. Gosh, no. The guy who headed that talent show, the emcee, put together a variety show that he would take around to the old folks' homes, to the prisons and schools and stuff. So I started performing on that level. I was part of this whole big thing, and I would go out and do one or two songs, and I would be nervous. But by the fourth of fifth time I did it . . . I would make mistakes, but I would forgive myself for them and go through with it. And the next time I got up to do it, it was a little easier.

Then the stakes were raised. There was a musical group that knew one of the singers in the variety show, and they asked if I would come play with them. They had real gigs, playing for Parents Without Partners and Knights of Columbus—real, paying gigs. That brought a whole new kind of nervousness.

After I did that for a while, I became a member of the band. Then I'd play every Friday and Saturday night. So now I'm twelve or thirteen years old, and I'm getting in front of people every week and doing this, on top of doing things in school. And there would always be a certain amount of nervousness. But I'd also recognize that it was excitement and that I really loved doing this. And at each step along the way, there would be more comfort.

When people ask me, "Don't you ever get stage fright?" I say, "Look, everything that could possibly happen to you on stage has happened to me: My clothes have fallen off; I've fallen off the stage; every single piece of equipment has stopped working. Everything that could happen to you has happened to me."

The bottom line is that the audience is really on your side. I've always thought that way about an audience. They want to have a good experience, so if you just keep that in mind, you can handle whatever comes along.

MB: Is there anything else that's been helpful to you in thinking about stage fright?

ME: Well, just that entertainment is an exchange of energy. And that's bigger, so much bigger than any one entertainer, any one person. I'm fortunate that I've been able to craft this idea into my work. This is my work. This is my life's work. I'm just very fortunate that I show up someplace and people pay money to come see me. That blows my mind—that's awesome! And knowing that these people paid really good money to see me, I have a responsibility. These people are expecting a good time now. So on that level, I don't have stage fright at all. It's a joy to be there.

I remember when I would open for acts. I was opening for the Eagles one time and thinking, "Who am I?" During those sorts of times you just have to believe in the music—in the music that you're making, in the exchange of energy—and you have to have faith in yourself as a conduit, as the thing that the energy comes through. You have to have a great belief in that, and a great love of it. And if you don't love doing it, if you don't love going out on stage and doing whatever you're going to do for the people, that also comes through. And that manifests itself in a lot of ways. So you have to really love yourself and love what you're doing.

MB: Has it ever been a challenge to get to that feeling?

ME: Yeah, probably in the early days when I would play and there would be nobody in the bar. You see people get really drunk and you're going, "Oh my gosh. What am I even doing here?"

I've had a few of those times. If my audience was off, I would look to the people who worked there, the bartenders. And I would perform for them. There's always someone who's willing to listen. I would try to focus my energy there.

MB: Do you ever get nervous now?

ME: I get nervous if I'm doing something out of the ordinary, like the Oscars. It's "Here's your three minutes." There's a billion bazillion people. At times like that, I get nervous. But when I say nervous, I also mean I feel a great amount of excitement. It's an incredible opportunity. I get nervous if I sing the national anthem at a World Series game. Because it's not about me. And you don't want to mess that up.

MB: I've actually done that nine times for the San Francisco Giants, though it was on the hammered dulcimer. Everybody knows the song.

ME: Yeah, if you mess that up, you're "back to go." With those kinds of things, I still get a little excited. And when I'm first starting a tour, doing something completely different or doing brand new material, the newness will get me. But I also like that; it gives me an edge.

ME: Has there been an occasion where things went wrong, or when you were really nervous?

ME: Well, I've fallen down on stage. And that's terribly embarrassing. Yet, the audience is totally with you, and it doesn't take long to recover from that. Usually I'll come back with some great performance to cover up the mistake. It drives me to do things better. I've never done anything where it was really hard to recover. I can't even think of one time.

MB: Have you seen stage fright, or extreme nervousness in another performer (and I don't need any names here)? Can you tell me about that?

ME: Well, I saw a performer once who was literally shocked by her microphone. (Sometimes the ground between your guitar and microphone can be bad and you'll get shocked.) And she ended up storming offstage and not finishing the show. And if you let those kinds of things overcome you, then those things win. But I don't mean to judge her experience, because it's an awful experience to get shocked. I just see people's choices. I would make them differently.

MB: Could you elaborate on things not "overcoming you"?

ME: Well, for one thing, there's a lot of embarrassment involved. You like to make the audience think that you're in control. If something happens that's out of your control, it can really throw you. And getting shocked is a big thing. If you have things that aren't dealt with, they'll bubble up and they'll become out of control.

I always believe that to have people's attention is priceless. There's a reason they call it "paying" attention. They are giving you this attention. There you are. And your presence, and what you have to give them, is worth more than any equipment or any effect. I've always believed that even if all the equipment breaks down, then you know what you do? You do a set; you get your guitar out and sit on the edge of the stage and you play.

MB: Is there anything else that you'd like to mention about dealing with nervousness?

ME: You know, it's funny. I get a lot of requests for stuff like this. Now that I'm on this spiritual journey, I understand positive thinking and intentional creation. I know that if you let fear drive you, then the things you fear are going to happen. You cannot ever underestimate the power of positive intention. And you can't get on stage and say, "I don't want this to happen! I don't want this to happen! Oh my gosh, I hope this doesn't happen!" Because then it will.

You need to get on stage and go, "I am here. I am blessed." You have to feel such gratitude that people have come to see you, and that you have the opportunity to be in front of them. If you come at the experience with gratitude and love, your experience is going to be a great experience. And after thirty-six years of performing, I know that is true.

Tony Freeman

Tony Freeman has appeared in over 250 plays and movies, including Broadway and national tours of "The Lion King" as Zazu (the wacky, British bird) for over 1,500 performances, and Tony Kushner's musical "Caroline, or Change." Mr. Freeman's television credits include guest roles on "Law and Order" (twice) and "Law and Order, SVU." He recently worked on a new musical "All About Us" with showbiz legend Eartha Kitt. Mr. Freeman's other credits include a Barrymore Award in the Arden Theatre's production of Stephen Sondheim's "Merrily We Roll Along," and nominations for three others. He has been a Guest Professional Actor in Residence and Acting Teacher at Cornell University and Teaching Artist for the Roundabout Theatre Company in NYC. In 2008, he appeared in "Applause" at the popular Encores series in NYC, directed by two-time Tony Award winner Kathleen Marshall.

MB: Have you ever experienced stage fright?

TF: I don't usually have stage fright when I'm in a show. I get stage fright when I stand up to speak as myself. If I stand up and say, "Hi, I'm Tony Freeman," I get nervous.

MB: Have you ever had stage fright when you've been in a play? If so, how did you deal with it?

TF: Oh, yeah. Years ago I would get nervous when I was in shows. What I did to get over the nerves was to concentrate on the other person on stage instead of on myself—to put my focus more on them than on the audience, so that it became just about me and another actor rather than me in front of an audience.

MB: Was there anything that you'd tell yourself to calm yourself down?

TF: I would just say, "Concentrate on the first line you're supposed to say." Just think about your first line or your first action. That gives you the impetus to come onto the stage with a purpose, as opposed to thinking, "Oh my God, once I walk through this door, there's going to be an audience."

MB: Why do you think you don't get stage fright now?

TF: I guess because I've been in over two hundred shows. Once you've done something so many times . . . But I have heard of people who have been in a lot of shows who still get really nervous before every performance. Some even throw up before every show.

MB: Do you ever get stage fright in higher pressure situations, such as an opening night, rather than six months into a run?

TF: Certainly you get more nervous on opening night, because your performance is an unknown at that point. You don't know if the audience is going to respond the way you hope they respond.

MB: So you can still get nervous on opening night?

TF: Yeah, I feel like there's a difference between nervous excitement and stage fright. With nervous excitement, the feeling is tinged with the hope for positive reinforcement, as opposed to stage fright, which seems to me to only be thinking, "I may fuck up."

MB: So you've never found it paralyzing to be nervous under those circumstances?

TF: Never. There are those moments, though, where you have the split second thought, "Oh fuck, I don't know the next word that's going to come out of my mouth." But then either the word has always come to me or I've been able to work through it. So I've had moments of panic, but never more than that.

MB: How do you keep them to only "moments" of panic?

STAGE FRIGHT • 121

TF: By being well rehearsed. If you feel confident in your rehearsal, you'll know that even if you can't think of the exact words, you still know what the scene's about. If you know why you're doing the scene, and you know what you want in the scene, and you know you can talk, you're going to be able to say something that makes sense, even though it may not be the exact lines you're supposed to say. You're not going to be standing there dumb-struck as long as you know why you're there.

MB: When you've seen people that have had really bad stage fright, could you see anything that they were doing that was creating it?

TF: You can see the exact moment when somebody panics on stage, because their eyes go from looking out to looking inward at that exact moment they're thinking, "Oh shit!" Or you can see their concentration go from being focused on the other characters on stage to being focused on the audience. You can see it on their face. But what causes it? I guess just that overwhelming realization of the audience's existence; their focus on the audience becomes more powerful than their focus on the material.

MB: Do you have any realizations about performing now that you didn't have twenty years ago that help you avoid stage fright?

TF: I think the more you see mistakes happen on stage, the more you realize that the audience doesn't know about them, and that it's okay. I've seen people totally screw up on stage and it was okay. The world didn't end. Also, the audience loves to see people screw up on stage. The actors hate it, but the audience loves it. [Both laugh] When the audience sees something go wrong, it's fun for them—it's not like it's a tragedy for them. It's one of those moments where they go, "Oh my God, I've just seen something no one else has ever seen."

MB: Could you name one of those moments?

TF: In our show ["The Lion King" on Broadway], things have gone wrong. There's a scene in our show where Pumbaa is supposed to fart on the hyenas. And then at the end of the show, Simba climbs to the top of Pride Rock and you hear the voice of his father say, "Remember!"(implying "Remember your pride, remember you're my son," and all that).

But this one time, Pumbaa is running across the stage, he lifts up his butt [to fart], and his ass goes, "Remember." [Both laugh] And the actor's going, "How am I supposed to cover for *that*?" You can't ad lib your way out of your butt saying, "Remember." [Both laugh] Because that was not supposed to happen.

The other thing that happened—it didn't happen to me, but to this other actor on stage—was after he had a soap opera audition during the day. And he got the lines mixed up in his head that night. So when he got to the confrontation with Scar, he was supposed to say, "You give me one good reason why I shouldn't tear you apart." Instead, he said, "You give me one good reason why I shouldn't tear your clothes off!" [Both laugh] And Scar was looking at him like, "*What!!??*" With things like that, you can only think, "Move on. The audience will think they've heard it wrong."

MB: Do you have any advice for other performers on getting over stage fright?

TF: I would say two things. Make sure you feel well rehearsed. And make sure you know what you want in the scene. I tell this to my students sometimes when we're doing improv. We'll do an improv, they'll talk for fifteen minutes, and I'll say: "You guys didn't know any lines, and yet you were able to talk for fifteen minutes without me giving you a single line only because I told you what you wanted. So just remember that as long as you know what you want, you'll think of something to say."

MB: What advice would you give to someone who performs or does public speaking, but isn't an actor?

TF: That's hard. But make it like it's a play. Think of it as a performance, not as a talk. Think of yourself as a character—show this confident version of yourself.

Dave Goelz

Dave Goelz is a principal puppeteer with The Jim Henson Company. His Muppet characters include The Great Gonzo, Bunsen Honeydew, Zoot and Beauregard from "The Muppet Show"; Boober Fraggle, Traveling Matt and Philo the Rodentia from "Fraggle Rock"; Digit from "The Jim Henson Hour"; Rugby and Ditz from "Jim Henson's Secret Life of Toys"; Stinky from "Jim Henson's Animal Show with Stinky and Jake"; and Randy the Stupid Pig and Gary Cahuenga the Vent Dummy from "Muppets Tonight!" His feature film credits include *The Muppet Movie*; *The Great Muppet Caper*; *The Dark Crystal*, as the Skeksis General and Kira's pet animal, Fizzgig; *The Muppets Take Manhattan*; *Labyrinth*, as the character Didymus as well as several strange objects, including a hat and a door knocker; *The Muppet Christmas Carol*, where Gonzo starred as Charles Dickens; *Muppet Treasure Island*; and *Muppets From Space*, where Gonzo learns his origins.

MB: Do you ever get nervous? And if so, when?

DG: What unnerves me is working live on television. And that has always fascinated me because ninety-eight percent of my work is done in a recording environment. The state I'm in when I go in there is alert—alert, and I know where the doors are. So if it really goes bad, I can get out and they'll never see me again. [Laughs] I'll be out the side door, get a taxi, and I'll never run into those people again.

It's a weird state to be in. First of all, I'm tired, because a lot of our publicity is done on the East Coast, so I have to fly back there. It's not fear so much—but it used to be fear. I used to be very afraid of these settings.

MB: When?

DG: Oh, fifteen or twenty years ago. I've been doing TV for thirty-five years. In 1979, the whole Muppet crew guest-hosted "The Tonight Show." I remember at the time thinking, "Jim [Henson] is mad; he's lost his marbles. Maybe he's comfortable doing this, but I shouldn't even be in Burbank. I should be somewhere else." In that particular instance, luckily, I had a small part. All I did was wiggle Gonzo's eyes at Bernadette Peters. If I put a lot of pressure on myself to do it right, if I care too much, it doesn't go well.

On another occasion we were doing "The Tony Danza Show." And they were very casual. We'd gone in and rehearsed, not with Tony, but just with the crew, and we were about twenty minutes into the show. And they came and got us after a commercial break started. So we were thinking they must be planning to do a segment. No. It turned out that was the commercial break we were going in after. And the set wasn't there; we were behind a little board. So we were just standing on the stage, waiting. There was a studio audience, and we were going on live. So finally the set came in and they put it down. I had the script pages; it was seven pages of material. And it was all ready to tape up into the set, which would take a minute or two. We were just about to squat down and get into position, and the floor manager said, "Thirty seconds!" Steve [Whitmire, performer of Kermit since Jim died] and I looked at each other and thought, "Oh, this is a problem. We have about a minute and a half of stuff to do before we're ready."

Then they said, "twenty seconds!" And we realized they really meant twenty seconds. There was no way to delay this, because it was being broadcast live. But because Steve and I have worked together for thirty years, we really didn't get ruffled. And we did absolutely fine. Steve went up with Statler who explained that Waldorf's alarm hadn't gone off. Meanwhile, I taped the script pages to the set. Then I brought Waldorf up and made excuses. Neither of us was nervous; we didn't miss any of our jokes.

But it was interesting because it absolutely didn't throw us. We just thought, "Well, we have to muddle through it; we'll figure out something."

MB: So by this time in your career you were so experienced that you didn't even come close to getting nervous.

DG: No. We didn't worry about that one. It was happening in real time anyway, and there was nothing we could do. It was too late to get scared. If somebody had told us, "You're going to have twenty seconds," I would have said, "Taxi! I'm outta here!"

MB: Were you ever in a situation where your job was on the line?

DG: Oh, no, no. Our company was never structured that way . . . Oh, I know one situation—one I was horrified by. We were on the first episode of "Saturday Night Live." We were on the whole first season, actually. But for the first episode, Jim had asked me to be one of these five characters that he had created for "Saturday Night Live." It was basically a royal family with a king and a queen, a voluptuous daughter, and a pothead son. And then there was a mighty god who would grant wishes. I was supposed to do the pothead son.

And I was horrified at the thought of working on live television. I was at the beginning of my career. We hadn't even done "The Muppet Show" yet. I had only been in one special.

Jim said he wanted me to do this character, and I thought, "Well, he knows what he's doing." But my socks are going up and down like window shades. As it got closer and closer, Lorne Michaels would come over with his writers, and I was terrified by them, terrified by Lorne Michaels. Luckily, a week before the show, Jim said, "I think I'll have Richard [Hunt] do that character." And I said, "Oh, thank you." I was so relieved. And he said, "Don't worry. In the future we'll have lots for you to do." And I said, "This is a good thing. I'm very happy you said that."

MB: What do you think you were telling yourself that was contributing to your fear?

DG: Well, what we do is very complex, even simple things. It's multi-tasking. I can tell you eight things that we do at the same time. . . .

You're literally thinking on eight levels at once. And it's very hard to do. It's similar to drumming in the sense that once you get that [limb] independence . . . well, even when you have independence, when you try to learn a knew rhythm, you have to do it methodically until you get the muscle memory going.

MB: It's muscle memory with the Muppets?

DG: It absolutely is. It took me about eight years before I started to think, "Maybe I can do this."

MB: Really?

DG: Yeah. It took a long time. And I was already doing major characters by then. It's still hard. I still can't believe how hard it is.

MB: What scares you now?

DG: The only thing that scares me is that sometimes I'll be asked a really dull question and I can't think of an answer for it. One of the worst is an internal reality question, like "What was it like working with Miss Piggy when she was the Wicked Witch of the West?" The question was to Gonzo in this case.

First of all, it's not like asking me what I think of the guy who does Miss Piggy. It's asking this character, Gonzo, how he feels about that character, Miss Piggy. But then it's not just about that character, but about that character playing a role. So you gotta get inside, and then inside again. And within those constraints, you still have to then think of something funny. It's tricky. That kind of question, especially when it comes out of left field, is hard.

I just saw Kermit on a late-night show. Kermit did a huge, long segment. I remember watching it. And every now and then during the show I'd get uneasy because I realized the host was throwing off-the-wall questions at Kermit. I was sitting there watching, thinking, "How would I answer this question?" And then all of a sudden I would just get this big jolt as the host asked a tough question.

MB: Did you ever see Steve [as Kermit] when he wasn't at ease?

DG: What I saw was the difficulty in making the transition to doing Kermit right after Jim died. We did a tribute special six months after Jim's death, where the characters didn't quite know who Jim Henson was, but they were supposed to be paying tribute to him. And then as the show went on, they began to remember, "Oh yeah. I remember. He was some guy who was down below." And so forth.

For that show, Kermit made an appearance at the end of the show. And that was so emotional for all of us. Steve had been given the puppet, like, a month or two before. He lives in Atlanta, so he was rehearsing on camera at home. He was on video camera getting ready. And when we went to do the read through for that show we all broke up. The idea of somebody else doing Kermit was just so unthinkable and so sad.

But in terms of what you're getting at: I'm realizing that we don't see a whole lot of stage fright, and I don't know why that is, because God knows we should have some. We should have a lot more than we do, given some of the things we've done.

MB: Has there ever been a time when fear got the most of you, to the point where you backed out of doing something?

DG: After the London premier of the London movie. Afterward, there was a party. And this little man, this little short guy, walks up to me and says, "They tell me you're the guy who does Zoot." And I said, "Yeah, I do." "Well, I'm Sammy Cahn. Hi. I've known so many sax players just like Zoot. He is an incredible character." Well, thank you, I thought. Gee. Ironically, I have no character. That's what works. [Laughs] The man said, "I want you to come and see me and Tita sometime. I'm on Canyon Drive in Beverly Hills. Here's my address. You call us up and come over and see us. Hang out with us." And I never did, because I was too afraid. But Sammy Cahn— Sammy Cahn! It turned out that years later he was doing an appearance at the Clift Hotel in San Franciso. I went over and had breakfast with him one day, when I'd gotten over some of the fear.

It would have probably been good to go hang out with Sammy and Tita. But at the time I thought, "What will I do? I'll get there and he'll have this lexicon of all the people he's worked with." He sent me a set of five LPs, full of sixty songs that were just classic standards. Frank Sinatra is singing, you know, Lena Horne is on there. And I thought, "This twenty-six-year-old kid is going to go sit on his couch? What am I going to have to say? 'Well, I went to Taco Bell today?' This guy is going to have this world of experience that I just don't have." I was too scared to go.

MB: Is there any last piece of advice you'd give to somebody about overcoming stage fright?

DG: I think what I would say is it's good to be as prepared as you can be, and then forget it. Forget your preparation.

The reason I say that is, it is nice if you can memorize a lot of stuff. But you don't want to be mechanical about it. Even if you have a photographic memory, you don't want to just read lines as if you were reciting by rote. You want to be in the moment. An example of that is what we do with choreography.

During intense choreography, we'll have characters moving around within the set. There's a whole traffic flow that goes on. And while they're moving, they're doing specific choreography moves. It's all tightly rehearsed with music and so forth. I notice that when I rehearse that it's good if I can learn the music the night before. I'll sometimes chart it on my script, and if I'm Zoot playing sax I'll make musical notations so I know where all the bits are. And so that would go right on the script. I'll be studying it, and correlating it to the script, trying to remember it, trying to get it into my head so I can just do it by rote.

Then I show up on the set and start doing takes. And it may take five or eight takes, or ten takes, before it'll all start to congeal. And at that point I'll realize, "Ah, I'm finally getting all the beats. I'm hitting all the choreography points. I'm doing the lip-sync right, I'm getting the emphasis on certain lines of the song, etc. (We use prerecorded vocals. Thank goodness we don't have to worry about singing, too.) But I'll realize at that point that what I'm doing is mechanical. It's all just me hitting these things. So I'll ask for one more take and I'll try to forget everything and just feel it. And then it's sort of like inner tennis. It's this other level you can go to, to just trust your knowledge at that point and just feel it.

Bonnie Hayes

Bonnie Hayes is a songwriter, musician, singer, producer and educator. Her songs include "Have A Heart" and "Love Letter," which anchored Bonnie Raitt's multi-platinum, multi-Grammy CD "Nick of Time." Writing for artists as diverse as Bette Midler, Robert Cray, Adam Ant, David Crosby, Booker T & the MG's, and Cher, Hayes crafts songs described by one critic as "sparkling clockwork mechanisms with a tendency to do the unexpected."

She has released five CD's, including "Good Clean Fun," which yielded her first hit song "Shelley's Boyfriend," and two songs for the sound track for the iconic 1980s movie, *Valley Girl*.

Bonnie has performed as a keyboard/vocalist with Billy Idol, Belinda Carlisle, Bruce Springsteen, Bonnie Raitt, Tommy Castro, Elvin Bishop, and Robben Ford, as well as many wonderful, unfamous, unsung musicians.

Ms. Hayes currently produces independent records at her San Rafael studio, teaches songwriting in the Bay Area, and continues to rip with her live band, the Superbonbons.

MB: Tell me, what was the worst case of stage fright you've ever experienced?

BH: I've been playing music for a long time, since I was very young, and I've never been nervous about playing. But when I started singing in my band, I couldn't find a lead singer that worked with us, so I ended up becoming the lead singer by default, really before I could sing at all.

And I had my first gig. We were playing a show with a couple of other bands in San Francisco. It was no big deal, but for some reason I was literally paralyzed with fear. And then I proceeded to get so drunk I couldn't walk, but at least I was able to get on the stage. [Laughs]

I didn't perform as a singer without drinking for several years. But I quickly figured out that if I got too drunk I couldn't sing. So I would get just drunk enough. It kind of took the edge off, and then I would proceed. It was a lot easier for me. Drinking sort of became a way out. I don't recommend it, but it was what I did in my terrible fear.

MB: It's okay to print all this?

BH: Yeah. A lot of people drink to ease [the fear of performing]. Drinking is known to lower inhibitions and to relieve nervousness. Right? Like I said, it's not recommended. It's really bad for your voice, and it makes you stupid. [Laughs] But it worked for me, until I figured out how to do it without drinking.

MB: How did you do it without drinking?

BH: Well, there are ways of training yourself to look past your fear. I mean there are a bunch of tricks. And when I did finally decide to learn how to perform without drinking, I started to use some of those tricks. The main one is trying to picture the worst thing that could possibly happen. And then imagine yourself living through that. And what is the worst thing that could happen? You're not gonna die. You're not gonna get hurt. I think the fear just comes from your pride, and as soon as you realize that it's just sort of an egocentric fear in the first place, its meaning is diminished—at least it was for me. The fear of being laughed at is real, but it's not something that I take very seriously any more when I'm deciding what I'm going to do or not going to do. And there are also ways of physically calming anxiety—taking deep breaths and meditating—and I found them very helpful.

MB: Where did you learn about imagining the worst thing that could happen?

BH: I can't remember where I heard that. I'm sure that there are therapists who prescribe that to people. But I remember doing it in other contexts. I think I mentioned it to someone else as I was trying to calm their fear about something, and then I realized, "Wow, that's really a great way to get through anything"—unless the worst thing that could happen is that you are going to get killed, and then you maybe should listen to your fear.

MB: So you don't get nervous very often now?

BH: No, I don't. Most of my fear now centers around boring myself, and then by default boring the audience.

How many times have I been on stage? It might be seven or eight thousand times. So you do—or at least I did—get over that terrible, crippling sort of fear, because you've walked on stage so many times, with so little preparation, that you're no longer afraid. I rarely feel afraid. I mostly now just worry about being good, and how to really be there. And how to be in the moment on stage. I'm usually worrying about the next step up, which is how to be great.

MB: Well, it seems to me you've already achieved that.

BH: Oh, thank you, that's so nice. I don't know if that's true. I mean, it's not a general greatness, but it comes from "being there"—being truly present on stage, not going away. And that's almost like another kind of fear. You can perform without really being there. I think a lot of people do that; they just put on a show and they're not really present. And so that's the thing I'm interested in now: trying to really be "in the now" as I'm there, channeling the thing that's coming through me that's worth listening to. Concentrating on that has made me see how stage fright is almost a way of avoiding what's really going on, what's really important about performing. And it's like you're a key or a talisman for other people. You're doing something they can't do, and that's an important thing.

MB: So you think that's one of the most important things about performing?

BH: Yes. I don't do it for others, I do it for myself, obviously. But it's not just an ego thing. I started to realize that it is important to the people who are watching that you're able to be true. It's important that there be authenticity. So being interested in that has taken away all that front stuff about stage fright. That stuff's kind of fallen into the background for me.

MB: Do you get nervous about wanting to be great, then?

BH: Well, maybe not great, but I get nervous about being as good [as I can be]. I want to be worth watching. Okay?

MB: How do you deal with nervousness about that?

BH: I basically challenge myself to be worth watching. And sometimes I handle it, and sometimes I don't. Sometimes there's this weird flow thing with performing. And flow is kind of hard to calculate. And that's the whole point. It's not supposed to be something that you can turn off or on. It's like when athletes are catching every single thing that gets thrown at them. Reading every offensive or defensive move. And there's a zone that you can get into as a performer, too.

MB: So when you achieve that, stage fright doesn't even come into play?

BH: I think that's right. Yeah. I think you're almost in kind of a different place in your head. I mean, it's not a real ego place.

And I'm not saying that people who have stage fright are egomaniacs, because I know they're not. I know so many great performers who experience stage fright before they go on and then get in the zone. But I think that's sort of the same thing. Stage fright happens before you go on, and then once you're on, you're not really feeling it anymore. But so for me, it's knowing I've gone through that many times and then I got on stage and just clicked in. I don't really feel stage fright anymore. It's like I know that nothing bad is going to happen.

MB: Do you have any tips on getting in the zone?

BH: [Laughs] I don't. I just try. The drinking thing is a really interesting issue, because I still use it as an "unlocker." And I really have gotten into this thing of not drinking until I've already hit a place, because I think that drinking actually inhibits you getting into the zone. And so do drugs. And even coffee. For me, all of that stuff kind of falsifies [the performance]. And then I have to really try to find a way to calm my mind from chatter. For me, that's about making sure that I have some time during the day to meditate or to take a walk or something. Some time when there are no words, nothing to distract me or pull me into a chattery place.

But everybody has their own way of doing that. A lot of people get into the zone by getting high. I'm just saying that's what works for me, after twenty-five years or thirty years of doing it.

MB: What I find I generally do is I just get emotionally committed to what I'm doing.

BH: Yeah, that's so right on. And that's kind of what I was saying about being intent on that: "This is what my goal is for this performance. I'm not gonna give up." Huey Lewis used to tell me, "A show is like playing a round of golf." Golfers really talk about this zone thing a lot, 'cause with lots of people, if they screw up their drive, they throw it away. Right? They quit, they get too distracted by having screwed up their drive. And so with their approach shot, they don't commit to making a great shot.

But you have to make each shot, and in the set that's like each song —and actually each moment in each song's a turning point. Which means that I'm constantly bringing this fresh mind to performing. Not, "Oh, I just screwed that up. The whole set's ruined. I might as well go home and go to bed." But, "Whoops, okay. Moving on."

MB: Are there any other thoughts, beliefs or attitudes that have helped you get over stage fright? Anything you haven't mentioned yet?

BH: Well, the other thing is preparation, which helped me a lot. I do a lot of lecturing, which has also contributed to my being comfortable on stage. So not only have I been on stage seven thousand times, but I've been lecturing for twenty years. Going into a presentation unprepared or ill prepared is one of the most nerve-wracking things I can think of. So a big thing for me has always been to be very prepared, to make sure that when I'm working a lot that I'm warming up my voice, that I'm practicing my guitar. That I'm rear-ranging the songs so that they're interesting to me, and just doing the work—everything I need to do to get into the zone. Also, I'm not going to be hampered by any technical stuff. That's obviously another big part for me.

MB: Last question: Do you have any other advice to give to people on getting over stage fright?

BH: The biggest thing is that you can't give up. You can't let stage fright stop you. And obviously the more you perform, the less it [stage fright] will matter. I think that's really the central thing.

Dan Hicks

Dan Hicks is one of the defining figures in American music. The original Dan Hicks and the Hot Licks recorded five Billboard-charting records, putting Dan on the cover of *Rolling Stone* magazine three times. The newest incarnation of DH & HL released the wildly successful "Beatin' the Heat." *USA Today* called it "one of the blessings of the new millenium." Other releases include *Alive & Lickin*, and the CD/DVD *Dan Hicks and The Hot Licks Featuring An All Star Cast of Friends*. Both *Mojo* and *Downbeat* magazines rated it "Four Stars . . . one of the best CDs of '04." 2005 brought *Selected Shorts*. The *New Yorker* remarked that it's "as great as his early masterpiece *Where's the Money? . . .* truly superb." 2009 brings Dan Hicks and the Hot Licks' tenth studio CD. To quote *Daily Variety*, "Dan Hicks is at the top of his game . . . [A] new studio album from Dan Hicks is like a new painting from Picasso . . . STAY TUNED!"

MB: How long have you been performing?

DH: I was playing drums in a little Dixieland band in junior high school. Then I picked up the guitar when I was about twenty and started singing in front of people.

MB: When you started out, did you get nervous performing?

DH: I think so. I'm going to count performing as when I played the guitar and started singing, because that was more pressure. Playing the drums is one thing—you're back there; you're in a band. Security in numbers helps.

As far as being up on the stage and in front of people, I started singing in hootenannies and stuff around San Francisco, going to these folk clubs, stepping up to the mikes and doing my three or four tunes. The first time I remember performing like that I wore finger picks, and I was sweating so much they fell off. So from the get-go that nervousness was there. But being nervous, that got better later.

MB: And what do you think made you more confident?

DH: I would just practice more. I could just do it and do it, and I was confident in what I could do. In other words, I knew I was gonna keep the beat, I was gonna finish the song, I was gonna remember the words. I was gonna get through the thing. I was gonna sing pretty much on key, in tune. In a way, I'm kind of surprised in myself that I was able to get up there.

MB: Why are you surprised?

MB: Because I was an introvert. I was a shy kind of guy, which I think may still be the case.

MB: What do you mean by "shy"?

DH: Not totally comfortable with people. Reluctant to speak or nervous in the presence of people. But when I get up on stage now, it's different, and it's been that way for the last—oh, let's say since 1970, or the '60s, when I started fronting the Hot Licks and all that. I knew the songs, I always had a kind of humor. I could rely on that. I always said that I could think faster up on stage.

MB: What do you focus on when you're on stage?

DH: It's not that I want people to like me, especially; it's that I want them to like the show, the music. I'm not thinking, "Do they like me?"—I can't think about that.

I think the time I have the least stage fright is when I'm in a comfortable room, among a comfortable crowd, and the crowd knows me. When I've got the band with me, I'm not by myself, and I know my material, I'm confident. And the rest is frosting on the cake. It's really the opposite of stage fright. It's really more like "stage comfort." But I would say stage fright does come for me in a couple of ways.

MB: So it occasionally happens even now?

DH: Yeah. There is the element of the unknown. The element of "how's it going to go over?" With us, the sound is different every night. We depend on the house stage guy. But I think what brings on stage fright with me would be the unknown stuff.

MB: So when you have stage fright now, how do you deal with it?

DH: The only way is to plod on through. Perhaps, after ten minutes or a half-hour up there on stage you might realize that things are getting better. Things are feeling better. It's like the audience is getting it. The only way, I think, is just to do it. Just do it. There are no tricks.

MB: There's nothing you tell yourself?

DH: There's nothing except that I've gotta proceed. One of the times that I feel the most stage fright is when I'm on television. Television has always frightened me.

MB: Is there anything you've done to make it less scary?

DH: No. I just go through it. The fear—it's there. There's nothing I can say or do [to lessen it.] Once I was going to be interviewed on CNN. And in the cab I was thinking of all the worst scenarios: "Oh man," I thought, "the studio with these guys with the cameras, the whole thing" . . . And I wanted to jump out of the cab. I did. I did.

MB: You jumped out of the cab?

DH: No! [Laughs] I thought, "If I jump out of the cab, man, I can kiss my career goodbye. I can kiss everything goodbye. If I jump out of the cab, I'd better disappear."

So I got there, and there were these remote cameras, these robot cameras. It was really only one guy and me, and it went okay.

Radio interviews I don't mind. I'm pretty good with those; I'm comfortable. I majored in radio and TV. So I kind of like broadcast studios and the radio set-up. I like the medium.

MB: So familiarity makes you comfortable?

DH: Maybe. Another way I get stage fright is if I know there are celebrities in the audience. I'd certainly . . . *certainly* . . . rather not know they're there. I just start thinking about them. And I don't dig it. But sometimes it works the opposite, and I perform even better if I know there's some singer out there.

One night I heard that Bruce Willis was coming in. On the first song a couple came in and sat down, and I thought the guy was Bruce Willis. So the whole night I was nervous that it was Bruce Willis. And it turned out it wasn't even him! I went through all this trouble for nothing.

So I guess you'd call it stage fright, or people fright. I had this saying for a while: "All the world is a stage, and I've got stage fright." You can put that in. [Both laugh]

MB: You say your main concern is, "How's it going to go over?" Now there must be some times, though I imagine they're infrequent, where you feel it didn't go over. How do you deal with that?

DH: Oh, man . . . I might have a short list of the worst gigs I've ever played. And it usually doesn't have anything to do with audience acceptance.

I did the Bammies [Bay Area Music Awards] one time. It was back in the day when the Bammies were a big deal. It was at the Bill Graham Memorial Auditorium. Dick Bright was the band leader. The idea was that I was going to do a tune with the big band, which was cool.

So they arranged this tune, "Up, Up, Up"—one of my songs. First of all, I'm not really the Bammie crowd's most well-known person.

MB: No?

DH: No. It was all rock n' roll. Sammy Hagar would be the guy they would be clapping for and and wanting to see. Not me.

So I was out there by myself singing, and it was like a throwaway. As far as the audience was concerned, I thought, "They'll be glad when this is over." In a way, this was a form of stage fright because I was thinking, "What am I doing here?"

[Finally] I got off stage; nobody was there to say, "Cool." Nobody was there in the wings. So I just went out the back door, and right over to where the homeless people were, and I sat down on a bench. And I thought, "Oh, man. Was that horrible."

MB: When did you start to feel better? While you were sitting there with homeless people?

DH: [Laughs] I don't know. I just waited until the next day, man. I just decided that sucked. That sucked. And there it was. [Both laugh]

MB: I don't know of anybody that doesn't get a little nervous before they go on stage. What's your take? Do you know anybody who claims they don't get nervous?

DH: I don't think so. There's no way [performing gives] the same feeling as just walking across the street and putting something in the post box. No way.

MB: And being nervous doesn't bother you, then?

DH: Right. It's part of the territory; it's like, "Okay people, it's show time."

MB: Is there any other advice you'd give to people who want to get over stage fright, other than "Plod through it!"?

DH: Plod through it!

JeROME

One name. One Man. One Mission. That's to entertain! JeROME is a Los Angeles based entertainer who has primarily worked as a stand-up comedian for more than 20 years. Born in Jamaica, Queens, New York, JeROME's and his family later moved to Oakland, California. After doing college talent shows, JeROME was bitten by the show biz bug and pursued it as a career after graduating from North Carolina Central University. He has performed world wide at clubs, casinos, colleges, corporate and political events, cruise ships and USO/military shows, and has even opened for legendary comedian Richard Pryor. JeROME does both "clean family" and "adults only" shows. Television network appearances include NBC, CBS, A&E and Comedy Central. His acting work includes commercial, film, and stage productions. JeROME is also an R&B vocalist who performs solo and with bands and orchestras. He's done recording sessions with artists including H.B. Barnum, Aretha Franklins' musical director.

MB: How long have you been performing?

JK: Since I was a kid, singin' and acting silly in front of friends in New York and Oakland. I even formed a singing group called the Funkadelic Five with me and my buddies on our block in Jamaica, Queens. We patterned ourselves after the Jackson Five. They weren't really serious though, so we only rehearsed like about three times. Later on I even sang in a band called Rhythm Section my senior year at Oakland High School. The band leader wasn't too serious then either, 'cause we only had two gigs.

Comedy-wise I did play one of the comics in our high school take-off of the old game show called "Make Me Laugh." I guess the time when I really said, "Okay, I'll start doing comedy," was around '86, when I graduated from college. I did a couple of talent shows at my college, North Carolina Central University.

MB: Were the talent shows your first public performances?

JK: Yeah, other than the high school band stint. In college I hosted the talent show called "Eagles Night Live" (North Carolina Central University Eagles). It was supposed to be like NBC's "Saturday Night Live." I hosted, sang a few tunes and told some Redd Foxx and Bill Cosby jokes. I figured that maybe nobody would catch it. I also did some original material about the school's fraternities and sororities. It went pretty well, especially the stuff I had written about the frats and sororities—it killed. So I was like, "Well, all right!" And then people were saying, "Hey man, I think you got a knack for this."

MB: Were you telling yourself anything about the performance?

JK: No, I really don't do all that. Some people feel they have to motivate themselves by sayin', "You can do it, man. You know you're funny." I don't do that because I'm pretty confident in my talent. I know I'm capable. My fear in the early stages of my career was about forgetting what I'm gonna say. Most of the nervousness was about the delivery. I'd be thinking, "Am I going to forget this stuff? Am I gonna deliver it correctly and in the right order?" I went through the lines over and over again in my head. I also was apprehensive about getting the names correct on the acts that I was bringin' up when I was emceeing.

MB: So there was some fear connected with that?

JK: Yes. The fear would be of not having a person's name, not remembering what the hell I'm supposed to say as their intro.

MB: What were you afraid of happening if you didn't remember?

JK: If that would happen, I feared I was going to look like a damn fool and these folks were going to rake me over the coals—that the crowd was going to rear its ugly head and I'd have to face these motherfuckers for the rest of the year at school.

MB: So how did you deal with that thought?

JK: My thing was, "Hey, I gotta get this shit down pat. I've got to keep repeating it, make sure this delivery's going to come out right!" And then you bounce out there and do it! While you're out there doing it, you're kind of pumped up on adrenaline and nervous energy.

MB: As you continued to perform, how did your nervousness change?

JK: What happens is, the more familiar you are with your material, the more ingrained it is, whether it's comedy or singing. And the more automatic it is, the more you flow smoothly and fluidly. If you know a joke is always going to work, or you know a song is going to work, then over time you gain a greater amount of confidence.

There's always a little bit of fear wondering if things are gonna go well, especially with comedy, because sometimes the crowds don't pick up your vibe. Most of the fear comes in the first few minutes before and into the set.

MB: So what do you tell yourself to deal with that fear?

JK: The main thing is, "Here are my first three or four jokes. So bang, bang, bang, let me get out and deliver these." Sometimes I'll think, "What else is going on in the room that I can riff some lines off of?" If the first few minutes really get 'em, then the rest is cool, 'cause they're on your side.

Once the crowd is convinced that you're good, they're with you. The audience's energy is like an ocean wave. Once you kick it up to a high crest you stand up on your surfboard and ride it on in.

MB: How do you deal with it when things don't go the way you want?

JK: Well, I pull out every trick in the book: go to Plan B, C, and D. Sometimes it still doesn't go. Sometimes the crowd doesn't get you. And as weird as it sounds, even though these people are strangers and you'll probably never see them again, you still feel kinda fucked up, 'cause you wanted to rock and you didn't. But it's not as bad as if you're performing a family reunion, and your act dies. You can never get away from them.

But the times when I really bombed big . . . it was a weird feeling—you're getting booed and heckled but you kind of get comfortable in that space. Then it's okay. It's like, "Okay, I'm bombing. Fuck it! This is where I'm at. We (the audience and I) are both present and in this together so let us all ride this shitty toilet wave!"

There's always a certain amount of sadism in people, some more than others, so once this energy is tapped people actually can find entertainment in it. It's the "Train Wreck" syndrome. You know it's terrible but you keep watchin' the news clips over and over anyway.

You can even feel comfortable in bombing. I performed at this one club in Miami called Miami Nights, where they would notoriously boo you. The crowd was all drug dealers, strippers and pimps. Half of 'em were regulars, and they knew how to time a comic's jokes and heckle his ass. The run ran Sunday through Tuesday, with Tuesday being their traditional night to boo the hell out of at least one of the comics. My shows went just half-assed on Sunday and Monday, so come Tuesday, they were just layin' to plow into my ass. I was the bloody meat thrown in the starving lion's cage. I was about three-and-a-half minutes into my set when the stampede went full throttle. The rest of my set was me and the crowd goin' toe to toe talkin' shit and slammin' each other for about twenty minutes. I finally got off the stage when the booker gave me the light [show biz signal to finish your set]. Do you know the main dudes heckling me were havin' so much fun that they even paid me fifty extra bucks so I would go back up there so they could boo me some more! [Laughs] They wanted that. I understood and it was cool, not a negative thing. . . . So I got back on the board and we all surfed that wave of comedy chaos!"

When it's all said and done, no matter how bad your show goes, it's only one set in a lifetime so it really ain't all that serious. It's like the old ghetto saying, "Three Tears In A Bucket! MuthaFuckit!"

MB: So what do you tell yourself in order to be comfortable with the bombing?

JK: At the time you're bombing, you have to either leave the stage or get comfortable. It's just like people that live in Siberia or Barrow, Alaska. Human beings can get comfortable living in whatever the situation. Either you get comfortable living in forty below, or you leave.

I don't leave the stage. At a certain point, you realize, no matter what straw you reach for, they're all short. Your regular material is just not working, so you gotta go ahead and say, "Well, let me just ramble on or slam that heckler. Maybe I can kick up a spark." And if you kick up enough of a spark, then you can start a flame and you can get the crowd back on your side.

For years, I would always be a little nervous before a show. But after doing it year in and year out, it's very rare that I'm nervous, because I know I'm going to rock, and I know the environment.

You get to the point where you know your act so well that you can allow it to just flow. With comedy, you're using whatever material fits the situation, because you've got material for almost any occasion. And even if you don't, you're so comfortable with performing that you're able to ad lib, make up material on the spot. It's like riffs by Coltrane or Ella Fitzgerald in Jazz. It's like the freestyling rapper who's just makin' up the lines on the spot. That only comes when you've mastered your craft. Experts say that it takes about 10,000 hours at something to be a master at it. The faster you get to that 10,000 hours the less nervous you should be.

Usually when you start out as a comic, you're playing any and every type of crowd in any and every type of situation. Some people are not there for comedy. For example you may be doin' a set during an intermission in the middle of a gangsta rap concert, where they just don't wanna hear no fuckin' jokes. Of course you're gonna shit bricks 'cause you're about to be thrown to the wolves. But over time you just perform in the venues that you do the best in. You find your niche. You and the audience are on the same page, especially if you have fans and a following. I don't think Barbara Streisand is gonna get many hecklers. Then again, who knows, she may be booked this weekend at Miami Nights.

MB: You feared bombing, but you were able to get comfortable with it. What was it that you told yourself that allowed you to get comfortable?

JK: In my case, I really don't tell myself much of anything. I just talk. I'm looking at the people, and they're looking at me, and I just talk. Fuck it. I don't feel that there's any safety issue—I don't feel like I'm going to get beat up or shot, so there's no fear of that. No fear of personal harm.

Unless the manager or club owner tells you to get off the stage, you just keep rattling on and trying to think of something to try. You always have to let the audience know that you know what's goin' on. You can't act like your not bombin' or that it's not goin' well. You can even address the fact that you're bombing. Most humor stems from truth and just exaggerates it. When you point out that you're bombin', the audience will agree on that truth and your exaggeration of that will be funny in itself. Before you know it, you can get 'em on a roll . . . and it's surf time once more.

MB: So you're able to keep yourself from panicking?

JK: Yeah, there's no panic involved. A certain amount of it is controlled apathy. A dichotomy. I care, but in some instances I don't give a shit. What's the worst that can happen? And later on in my career, the thought was, "Well I know I'm good; it's just not working now, so fuck it! I just hope they don't remember my name."

MB: You said you don't get nervous very often now, but the times you've been up at a rap show, or whatever—and they're throwing you to the dogs—you say you could still get nervous under those circumstances?

JK: Yeah. The adrenaline is flowing a little more, and my brain is clicking really fast. It's the same as [I described] before—I'm just thinking about my first few minutes of executing. I feel like, "Okay, I gotta really execute these first things. If they don't work, then . . . fuck! [Laughs] As I said before that becomes very rare once you been in the game awhile because you don't choose rough gigs to perform anyway. You know, a Rabbi ain't gonna book a sermon at an Al-Qaeda pep rally. Hey, does Al-Qeada even have pep rallies? [Laughs] . . . No . . . maybe just barbecues. [Laughs again]

MB: So when it does start going rough, how do you deal with that?

JK: My thoughts are on just doing my material or song really well—as opposed to: "Okay, my God, what am I doing?" As a comic, if you start thinking about how you're going to bail out of this, then you're really lost. You have to feel the vibe so you know how to flow into the next joke or the next topic. The best direction to go may not be your written material. It may be the ad lib. You wanna be at a Zen level of performing where your performance is like water. You're goin' with the flow.

MB: And why are you lost there if you start thinking about how to get out of it?

JK: Because if you think too long then the crowd can see it. They'll sense your fear and will feel you're not in control and scared. With comedy, the audience has to accept you and allow you in as their pilot. No one wants to get on a plane with a scared, out-of-control pilot who doesn't know where he's goin'.

MB: One of the thoughts you mentioned was, "Nobody's going to shoot me."

JK: Right. You figure, "What's the worst that can happen?" And the worst that can happen is you just don't do well. You're still getting paid. [Laughs] You get in your car. You go home. You sit on the couch. You watch TV. You put a gun to your head! [Laughs]

You just feel bad because you didn't do well, and if you see those people in the crowd afterwards, they might look at you kind of funny. But usually you get to leave the situation quickly—after it's over, you're gone. You don't have to see those people ever again, unless you live in the same town. Then it's worse. But if you're on the road, it's like, "Hell, it just didn't work this night. Gotta figure out what I did wrong and do it better next time."

MB: So if you see the people in the audience again—or let's say you bomb at a family reunion—how would you feel?

JK: Well, if you see somebody again, and the last time they saw you you didn't do well, you feel kind of weird. You wonder if they're thinking, "Damn! You're the one that bombed!"

MB: So what do you tell yourself so you don't get bummed out when that happens?

JK: Either they bring it up, or I bring it up: "Last time you saw me, that shit was rough." I talk it out that way. We just go over the fact that I ate it. "Other times I rock, and you just gotta see me then. There's a new thing I'm working on. Blah, blah, blah." I'll address the situation.

MB: Can you remember the worst case of stage fright you've ever experienced?

JK: I guess one of the toughest was when I was running for sophomore class vice president in college and had to give a speech. I remember all those people looking at me, especially the girls. The girls would make me the most nervous, I remember, because they all were so beautiful to me. Nobody wants to look stupid in front a beautiful girl. I'm going, "Oh my God. They're picking me apart. They're seeing how my hair's fucked up. They don't like my teeth. They think I'm ugly."

All this shit was going through my head—all this self-esteem shit—and I was trying to remember my speech, and it was coming off as monotone! I'm thinking, "Damn, I'm monotone! I'm monotone! I'm monotone! Damn it!"

And then I tried to speak up with a little more comfort and spark, but it was obviously forced, and I thought, "They know that it's forced! They know that it's forced! They know that it's forced!" I was nervous as hell—my fuckin' hands were trembling, my palms were sweating. I was looking at the people like, "Oh shit, I'm losing 'em." I didn't know what they were thinking, but in my mind, it was, "Damn! They know I'm terrible. They know I look stupid. They think I'm a fool."

And then I made the stupid statement: "In conclusion, PEOPLE, WHAT WE NEED IS . . ."—and I had to look at my paper for three seconds—A STRONG STUDENT GOVERNMENT." [Laughs] I got about three claps and half-stunned silence. I know they were thinking, "This is just one goddamned idiot!" They didn't boo me. But it's almost worse if they don't say anything. If they're booing you, fuck it. At least you know you're getting booed. [Both laugh]

MB: Okay. So what did you tell yourself to get through that situation?

JK: "Keep going." I remember that vividly. "Keep talking. Keep letting it flow."

MB: So how do you get past that, then? A lot of people at that point would hang it up or panic. How do you keep that from happening? How do you keep from slitting your wrists?

JK: Are you talking about afterwards or during it? [Laughs] At the time, you just panic or whatever and get through it.

MB: What are your thoughts if you're happy while you perform?

JK: It's a great feeling. I used to say, "Yeah! I got 'em in the palm of my hands!" As I matured, I realized that this is slightly narcissistic. It's not "Me The Ego" that has 'em. They allow me to be the catalyst for emotional energy. For example, fourteen-year-old girls just wanna scream and emote at concerts, whether it's Elvis, Michael Jackson, Justin Timberlake, or Kanye West.

Sometimes before you hit the stage, comics or entertainers use a negative phrase for good luck, like "Hey, break a leg!" Or somebody—maybe the emcee—says, "Hey, the crowd is good." And you'll make the statement, "Well, I'll ruin that."

MB: And what does that do?

JK: That's just being humble. You're making a quick joke. You don't want to come across that you're too arrogant and everything is perfect. At least I don't want to come across like that. But in my mind, I feel like I'm King Kong.

MB: Okay. But what do you mean by arrogant?

JK: You don't want to make it look like you know everything and they know nothing.

Some people feel a certain amount of nervousness is good, 'cause you can use that nervous energy. And I agree with that to a certain extent. Sometimes you can be so comfortable that you're almost too comfortable, and you come out being a little bit lazy.

MB: When things go well and you're not too relaxed, how do you feel?

JK: I just feel that what I'm going to give the audience is something they're going to really enjoy. And I try to go for the yin and yang, try to find what we all have in common, the common denominator. We're all basically about the same. We go through the same feelings and thoughts. And I do show that through my humor.

MB: Last question: Do you have any other advice for performers who get nervous?

JK: Just repeat to yourself: "Three tears in a bucket. Mothafuckit!" [Laughs]

MB: What the hell do you mean by that?

JK: You've never heard that?

MB: No.

JK. Hey, man. Shed the tears and don't worry about it. It ain't that bad. The main thing to really remember is the more prepared you are, the better it'll go. And the more you do it, the more it becomes automatic.

MB: But if somebody's still afraid of it not going well after rehearsing eighty-five times in a week, what would you tell them?

JK: Just remember that the audience is really there to see you do well. They want you to do well. They're on your side. Most of the fear is you thinking you're not going to do well, and that they're not going to like you. But they are going to like you—that's why they're there.

MB: And if they don't like you—what advice would you have for people who experience that?

JK: At least finish the performance. Then think of why they didn't like you. You have to look at your act and say, "What can I improve?"

MB: But in terms of not putting yourself down . . .

JK: It's not so much you. It's just your performance that night. It's not you at the core. It's not you as a being. Don't say, "I'm fucked up. I'm no damn good." Just say, "My show just didn't reach 'em tonight." Still give it your all and don't quit. To paraphrase the great Sammy Davis Jr., "When you give it your all the people may not like your show that night, but they will walk away saying, 'That cat performed for me, man!'"

Mickey Joseph

Mickey Joseph was born to an Italian immigrant jazz musician and a Croatian seamstress. Raised in San Francisco, he developed his comedy by attending Catholic School to incorporate bobbing, weaving, and pleading for mercy.

He attended the Academy of Dramatic Arts in Pasadena, and waited on tables at an Italian Restaurant. His boss, observing Mickey doing impressions and juggling dinner rolls, quickly suggested he dive into show business, or any business other than his restaurant.

Mickey moved to Hollywood, joined an improv group, and began writing and performing. He then got married, fathered two children, and divorced, all in one sentence.

Upon returning to the San Francisco Bay Area, he quickly became a favorite in some of the most well known comedy clubs in the country. He continues to perform standp-up and act, with recent credits including the Plaza in Las Vegas and playing Joey Bishop in *The Rat Pack Is Back.*

MB: When you first started performing stand-up, what were the circumstances?

MJ: When I was in acting school, I was doing impressions for friends. We'd go out to the beer gardens, have a few beers, and, I would do Sydney Portier ordering breakfast, and Brando, and stuff like that. I'd really be getting laughs from them with that.

When I got to L.A., I wrote a little act, doing Ricky Ricardo as president and a few other impressions. And I went down to the Laugh Factory, which was a teeny little brick oven at the time—with maybe ten people in the audience—and I got on stage, and that was the start of it. But I did write before I got on stage. I did plan my first set.

MB: Were you nervous when you started doing stand-up?

MJ: I had some gigs early in my career that were too big for me. Some big crowds, big events. It was KSJO's twenty-fifth anniversary, and I felt nervous. It was a rowdy crowd; there was no reason, really, to have a comedian there. People weren't seated; they were standing. They'd been watching bands, and it was rough.

MB: So what were you telling yourself?

MJ: Just, "I hope it goes well." But also, "I really don't have the experience to be stepping out on this stage and doing my act." I'd only been doing comedy for less than a year.

MB: Were there any other thoughts in your mind?

MJ: Absolutely. Just that it might not go so well. Or I might not have everybody's attention in the room. I might get heckled. I might get embarrassed. I might embarrass myself. And a friend of mine was there to film it, so that's always an added pressure.

MB: How did you handle the thought that you might embarrass yourself?

MJ: Well, you have to accept the feeling. You're in a situation where you gotta go on, so you throw caution to the wind and just go for it.

MB: As you continued performing, how did your nervousness change?

MJ: Well, it changed from nervousness to anxiety. Not anxiety in a bad sense—anxiety in the sense of, "I want to get on stage. I want to feel the crowd. I want to get it over with."

MB: You've done the San Francisco Comedy Competition. What was that like?

MJ: There was anxiety there. But, you know what? If you're having a good set, and you're in the Comedy Competition, there's no better feeling. It has to happen within the first few jokes. You have to have the audience within the first two jokes in order to relax and say, "Okay, here we go." If you don't get 'em going, then you're having all kinds of thoughts, like, "Oh shit! I should speed up, I should slow down. I should go here. I should go there." And the next thing you know your time is up.

MB: How did you feel at the Comedy Competition?

MJ: Well, it was all of that: anxiety, and nervousness, and hoping for a good audience. And on top of all that, I was also hoping for a fair score from the judges.

MB: What was it like when a set didn't go well in the competition?

MJ: Well, at the time it was very important for me to do well, so I'd immediately start figuring the math and looking at the scores. After it got to the third or fourth day, the score looked a little more confusing. And all of a sudden people were separated by a tenth of a point and then a hundredth of a point. It just became a maze of mathematical gobbledygook.

So if you have a shitty set you go right back to the score, and you're picking your lip and saying, "I wonder what this is going to do to me." And you're hoping that other people suck. It's a terrible thing. It's everything that's wrong in stand-up comedy.

However, I will say, performing after the competition, when nobody's got a score pad or pencil and nobody's there to point a finger at you, or judge you in any way—that next set is the best set you're going to have all year. So the competition has its value in that respect for young comedians, 'cause it teaches them that nervousness is there; you're going to have to deal with the pressure. Then when it's not there, you can really feel like, "Okay, this is what I'm doing. This is what it is."

MB: How does the pressure feel?

MJ: Like I said, it depends on where you sit. Guys that are coming in first or second or third every night, after the second or third night, they're feeling pretty damned loose. The guys that are sixth, seventh, and eighth every night are really uptight. They want to make it into the next round. So it has a lot to do with how it's going.

MB: Do you ever get nervous now?

MJ: There's a Woody Allen film called *Broadway Danny Rose*. The booking agent's got all these fucked-up acts—bird acts, a xylophone player with one arm. And he says to them, every time he talks to them, "Did you say your three S's?" And the three S's were "star," "smile" and "strong." Those are the words that he wanted you to vocalize before you went on stage. That's something that I use to this day. Because when an audience sees me walk on stage with a smile, I've immediately won over eighty-five percent of them. They want to know what I have to say. They like what they see already.

A comedy audience is really there to laugh. They don't go to a comedy show, buy tickets, sit back and say, "Okay. Make me laugh." They sit up in their chairs and they're ready to go, they're ready to roll. They want their money's worth. So remembering "smile," "star," and "strong" is a great advantage to me.

MB: When do you get nervous now?

MJ: I might get nervous if I see the act in front of me struggling with a heckler, or people that are talking or disrupting him. But even then I don't worry because my act—I hate to gloat about it—but my act is so strong now that, seriously, people will rarely stop me to heckle me, unless they're very drunk.

MB: So how is it if you do get nervous—how does that feel? What thoughts contribute to your feeling less secure?

MJ: A thought like, "Oh, I should have gone to pee one more time. I'm going to be up there for forty-five minutes. What if I become incontinent during my set?" Which has never happened during a set or in my life. But these are things you think about. All of a sudden the faucet could open up, and you're standing there pissing in your pants on stage. You'd better be able to improvise.

You know what? I really don't get that nervous, man. You have two choices as a headliner: You can pace back and forth, and look at the guy ahead of you and say, "Oh God, how am I going to follow this guy? He's killing!" Or you can stand there and appreciate it and laugh your ass off. I read about Jack Benny—they said that he would stand in the back of the room and laugh and laugh and laugh, and he would take that attitude right on stage. Relaxed and ready.

MB: What do you think he was thinking?

MJ: "I have no reason to worry. I can follow anybody." I think that's what he was thinking.

MB: And what about the guys that would worry and pace and let it get to them? What do you think they'd be telling themselves?

MJ: "I can't follow this guy. I can't follow this guy. I can't follow this guy." I've been in some situations like that. I followed a guy who was being featured at Harvey's, which is a big live club. And he was funny, very funny, very dirty, and very handsome. The girls loved him. And he talked about nothing other than fucking and eating pussy, and getting his butthole licked. He was hysterical.

I tried to stand there and take it. And I was saying, "Oh my God. This guy's killing. He's absolutely destroying this place. What am I gonna do?" Or I could have said to myself: "He's great. I'm great. We do different things. I just gotta ride that energy out."

MB: Do you have any other advice on dealing with stage fright?

MJ: Smile. That's it, man. Smile at the audience. I've told people all over the place to smile when they get on stage. It just changes the audience. Let them know that you're having a good time, that you're not afraid. They smell fear.

And I always make jokes when I'm waiting to go on. I'll say, "Look how nervous I am." And I'll hold my hand out and it's perfectly steady. Or often times, as I'm going to the stage while being introduced, I'll stop at a table and ask people, "How's my hair look?" [Mickey is completely bald.]

And if I can get that one laugh from them before I even start the set, the audience notices: "Hey, he said something to those people to make them laugh." It's just that fast—walking by them, saying that one little joke, and having them laugh.

Kevin Kataoka

You may have seen Kevin performing standup on Comedy Central's "Premium Blend" or acting on "Cheap Seats" on ESPN Classic. Originally from the San Francisco Bay Area, but now living in Los Angeles, Kevin has also graced the stage at the Just For Laughs Comedy Festival in Montreal and appeared in animated form on Comedy Central's "Dr. Katz," which spawned a nationally syndicated comic strip he helped write. In addition to performing stand-up across North America, Kevin has also written for Fox's "Mad TV" and "Blind Date," and ABC's "America's Funniest Home Videos."

MB: Do you ever get nervous when you perform?

KK: I always get nervous. There are different levels to my nervousness. It obviously depends on what kind of gig it is.

MB: At what kind of gig are you the most nervous?

KK: I'd say any time I'm in a situation where I have to be at my best because somebody [from the industry] in the crowd is watching me, or because I need to make a tape that's important to give to somebody else. When I'm performing for a week at a club, I can do anywhere from six to nine shows in that week, so if one show doesn't go well, I can always worry about the next show—which is twenty-four hours later. That's not as big of a deal, so I wouldn't be very nervous. But if it's just a one-shot deal, like a set for a comedy festival or a TV appearance, then yeah, you gotta bring it for that particular show. When the stakes are higher, that's when I get a little more nervous.

MB: How do you deal with being nervous?

KK: I think the number-one thing for me is preparation. You have to be so prepared and confident in what you're doing that you're almost sick of doing the material.

MB: Is there anything you tell yourself to calm yourself down?

KK: I think everybody has their own tricks. A lot of times, I'll just tell myself out loud to have fun, because I think that's what it really comes down to—having fun and not really caring that much. Obviously you do care, but you also need to know that it's not the end of the world if you fail. It's one performance, so you shouldn't care that much.

The other thing I do is listen to music on an iPod. That will relax me. Strangely enough, I always think about the 1964 Beatles. [Laughs] I think about when they came over to the states. If you watch any documentary footage of them, you can see they're having so much fun—they don't look nervous at all. It could have been the most nerve-wracking thing, but they're just having so much fun, and their eyes are wide open to anything and they're just taking it all in. That's the kind of energy I'd like to have all the time.

MB: You mentioned "not caring that much." What do you mean by that?

KK: You shouldn't care to the point where you believe that if you fail in a performance it's going to ruin your life. You know it's important, and you want to think it's special because it's one performance only, but if it doesn't go well it's not going to ruin your life; you'll have another shot at it. It's a strange line—to care and not to care at the same time.

MB: Could you describe how you care so it's helpful and not hurtful?

KK: Well, you don't want to be so relaxed that you're not focusing. You want to keep your focus. And you want to have a belief in your abilities when you walk out there. So you want to care to that point.

When you perform, there are so many factors that are out of your control, and I think performers need to accept that—whether it's an unruly crowd, technical problems with the mike, or a bad stage set-up. Or you could be booked on a show that's not really a good bill for you and your particular style. There are a lot of other factors that are not in your control, so that's why you can't always take the blame for things.

MB: Have you ever had a show that was important where you failed, and if so, how did you deal with that?

KK: For me, I find that failing hurts generally for the rest of the evening. But I honestly believe that if anyone feels lousy after a performance, they should go out and have something nice to eat. Or go home, relax, and go to bed. And the next day, they should have a better grasp on it.

Occasionally, if the feeling does last for more than a day, I think time eventually will solve it. Eventually another opportunity will come around and you'll seize it and something good will happen. I think the main thing to remember is that it's not your last shot. There always will be another chance.

MB: How did you deal with being nervous when you first started out?

KK: I don't recall any tricks that I did. Like I said, I think the key is repetition, just practicing and performing as much as you can to the point where it's second nature. When you perform enough on stage that it's just not that big of a deal to be on stage anymore, then you find the nervousness goes away.

MB: When you don't get nervous, is it always because it's a less important performance? Or are there some times when you get less nervous under circumstances in which you'd normally be very nervous?

KK: There are a lot of factors that go along with not being nervous. It could be familiarity with the room, with the type of crowd. A knowledge that your material will work, and confidence in your abilities. It could be something as simple as the fact that you ate at the right time and you didn't have coffee.

I know people who get nervous and don't understand why, and it's not something mental—it's physical, like they just drank a double espresso. They wake up and they're just too amped. You have to look at those things as well. Think to yourself: Did I get the right amount of sleep? Was I stressed out before I went to do this set? Have I had any coffee? These are all things to consider when you're nervous. Sometimes that's all it is, just a physical reaction to the situation.

Not being nervous could also happen because things are going so well in your life in other areas that you just exude self-confidence, and the next thing you know you're performing and it's carrying over to your performance. Suddenly, what seemed to be important isn't as important.

I'll tell you a story. I worked with a comic named Nick Wilty. He's a British comic. He fought in the Falklands. He told me this story of how he went to basic training with another soldier he had met at boot camp, and they ended up being stationed together at the same place. They were shipped off together on the same ship to the Falklands. They landed on the beach and they ran onto it, and shots were fired immediately. Everyone hit the dirt, and then their orders were to commence the attack. So everyone got up and started running. And Nick noticed that his friend didn't get up. He turned him over and he realized that he had been shot in the face. And he started running anyway. Then he told me: "And that's why I don't get nervous doing comedy."

And that's what I think: When there are other aspects of your life that can put it all into perspective, sometimes that's all it takes. Not everyone has those kinds of things to draw upon.

MB: I asked if you get nervous and you said, "Yeah, I always get nervous." I'm guessing, from what you've said, that you have no shame at all about being nervous.

KK: I think the thing people have to realize is that most performers—I would say over ninety-five percent—get nervous. It's just a matter of not letting it show. I think a lot of great performers are able to keep it buried, and utilize other skills that they've learned to not let it show. But I do think, underlying it all, there is a certain nervous energy. Maybe it's not to the point where you're shaking, your voice is cracking, and you're getting cotton mouth, but I think we all have a certain amount of nervous energy. If you lose that, I think it's not a good thing. If you don't have it, what's the thrill?

MB: What if you're not getting laughs? If you can, think back to one of your worst experiences in bombing. How did you deal with that?

KK: I think you have to believe that your material has worked before, and that this is just something that doesn't happen every time. You have to believe that you're funny or talented, that this is just something that occasionally happens. I think most comics don't automatically think, "Oh, I'm terrible"; I think their first thought is, "How come this isn't working?" [Both laugh] It's almost more confusion than a loss of self-esteem. I think most comics' first response—which is not necessarily the smart response—is "What's wrong with these people?" [Both laugh]

MB: What do you think a smarter response would be?

KK: I think a smarter response is to ask yourself, "What's going on? How can I adjust to make this work?" I think in comedy the thing is, if it's not working, you have to change your pace a little bit, you slow it down, or you try different material. And I think half the time shifting gears will make it better. Of course, sometimes that makes it worse. [Laughs] I think as more and more of these situations arise, you have more and more tricks to fall upon to get you out of each jam.

MB: Have you seen anybody who wasn't able to get over being nervous, to the point where it would just paralyze them?

KK: Yeah, I know a number of comedians who are like that, people who I think are hilarious, great writers. The thing is, in almost every case that I've noticed this happening, they stop performing for a long period of time. They'll come back six months later and do it one more time, and they'll get nervous again, and then they get frustrated and they stop again. You can never get over it if you just do it once every six months. Of course you're going to be nervous because, once again, you're building all this pressure around this one set. You can't do that. You can't put that kind of pressure on yourself.

You have to keep performing over and over and over and over again so it's just second nature. And that's the only way I think you can get over being nervous.

Richard Lewis

Richard Lewis has carved his lifelong therapy fodder into a compelling art form. Comedy Central has recognized Mr. Lewis as one of the top 50 stand-up comedians of all time, and he was charted on *GQ* magazine's list of the 20th Century's Most Influential Humorists. He's working on his seventh season of "Curb Your Enthusiasm," and is on his "Misery Loves Company Stand-Up Tour." The Screen Actors Guild nominated Lewis for his work in the ensemble category for his recurring guest star role, playing true-to-life, as one of Larry David's closest friends in "Curb," the "Seinfeld" co-creator's hit HBO series. His memoir, *The Other Great Depression*, has found a new audience in reprint with a new, passionate afterword; it is also now available as an audio book.

MB: How long have you been performing?

RL: I hit the stage with reckless abandon a few months before my twenty-fourth birthday in 1971 in Greenwich Village.

MB: Tell me about the first time you were anxious or nervous. What were the circumstances?

RL: My dad died in April of 1971. It was a huge shocker for me and the family. Although I was headed toward stand-up, I was mostly dabbling in comedy writing. Somehow, even with a degree in marketing from Ohio State University and some success in advertising, I was basically biding my time until it was the right moment to hit the stage.

It was far from a coincidence that most of the good material I submitted to comics was rejected for more commercial stuff. My personal stuff didn't make the cut, which made sense to me down the line. Some two months after my dad passed away I became a comedian, going on stage, and with the attitude that this was it for me and there would be no turning back, as full of fear as I was.

MB: How did you feel?

RL: I was both scared and emboldened by the sheer audacity of believing that I could make it in such a tough field. There were moments when I wished my father could swoop down like some huge hawk and pick me up, grab me by the collar and place me on stage already a success. But that fantasy quickly turned into thinking about my craft 24/7 with total determination.

MB: What were you telling yourself? What were your thoughts?

RL: Not a thing was going through my mind but the fact that I was actually going to be a real comedian, and I was trippin' on that big time. I was in a "zone" and at a club that no longer exists in the Village, but it was a great place to start because the acts were diverse, ranging from someone like me, who was "on a mission," to others with equal passion but who were jugglers or singers that would have the cockroaches heckle them. In other words, the pressure was off because it wasn't a showcase as much as a place to really begin with zero experience.

MB: Were you anxious?

RL: At the very first show, my anxiety level—if there was any—was somewhat mystically non-existent because of my excitement and blind determination to never give up, no matter what.

MB: As you continued performing, did your amount of nervousness change? If so, what were the circumstances?

RL: The circumstances were endless. Clearly, the more accepted I was as one of the new, hot comedians in New York, the more that gave me both a streak of confidence and anxiety that much more was being expected from me at every set. If I had a bad set, I wore it like a cloak until the next show, when hopefully I would "kill" the audience.

MB: How did you feel?

RL: I felt with experience that each show, with its different set of people [in the audience], would bring different responses to the same material. So I was mostly thinking about making sure that my material was really strong and proven. Then it took many years to develop a persona that I felt was fearless and authentic.

MB: What did you tell yourself? What were your thoughts?

RL: Again, all these circumstances made some shows easier than others and less stressful than those with more consequences. For example, auditioning for talk shows filled me with angst, but, fortunately for me, I used anxiety as the essence of my persona.

In fact, early in my career, my older brother—who had done some acting—mentioned to me after a set that if I felt nervous, maybe I should be honest with the audience and somehow express it. That was a great tip, and I didn't even know it would mushroom into my entire style of confessional humor.

MB: Do you get nervous now?

RL: I get anxious that I won't come through, because I don't have a set act and I also improv a great deal. So every show is a high-wire act.

MB: How do you feel when you're performing, when you're doing that high wire act?

RL: I usually work myself up into a negative lather, but I think that's more of a way to turn the anxiety into some weird form of energy. It's like I get down on myself sometimes unconsciously; I feel like I have to overcome my entire childhood—the bad parts—and get into an "I'll show them" attitude. And as childish as that technique sounds, it seems to have worked okay.

MB: What's the worst case of stage fright you've ever had?

RL: I've always been more nervous off stage than on. It's not unusual for many artists to find sanctuary from the madness of life on stage.

MB: So when don't you get nervous?

RL: I usually don't get nervous when I don't have to answer questions about nervousness and when I'm cumming.

MB: Can you be a bit more specific about the circumstances when you aren't nervous?

RL: When I'm isolating and usually masturbating.

MB: How do you feel then?

RL: Isolated and free from fear of intimacy.

MB: What do you tell yourself about that?

RL: Therapy failed.

MB: Could you elaborate on what's going on in your mind when you're not nervous?

RL: I'm usually in some state of gratitude and acceptance.

MB: What advice would you have for performers who experience stage fright or nervousness?

RL: Use it creatively or get over it.

Paul Lyons

Paul Lyons has been performing stand-up comedy for over 25 years. He has headlined in every state in the United States, and overseas in London, England and Sydney, Australia. His more than two dozen TV appearances include "Everybody Loves Raymond" and Showtime's "Love at Stake."

As an essayist Paul's inspiring, peculiar pieces appear regularly in *Playgirl, TV Guide,* and *Details* magazines.

His philosophy of life is "If you take yourself lightly you can learn to fly." Paul plans to adopt it as soon as he gets over his fear of heights.

MB: How long have you been performing?

PL: Since college, in 1978. My first set was in front of a classroom. A teacher said to me, "Lyons, you're funny. Do you want to get up in front of the class tomorrow and do some material?"

And I said, "Sure." I did it the next day. I came in with fifteen minutes. At that point I was coming up with jokes, one-liners. I had about ten decent jokes, and then I just started doing the observation-type humor that George Carlin did.

My first ten jokes went over very well, and then I had about six minutes of awkward silence. [Laughs] But it felt good that the first ten jokes went over well.

MB: How did the six minutes of awkward silence feel?

PL: Well, I knew that I was just trying it out, so I wasn't devastated. I was still very happy that the beginning jokes worked.

MB: Why do you think you weren't devastated?

PL: Well, because my initial fear was "What if they don't laugh at all?" So the fact that they laughed at my first ten jokes made me feel relaxed, I felt vindicated, like, "At least I always have that."

MB: You said your fear was "What if they don't laugh at all?" What were you telling yourself that made that idea so fearful?

PL: Unlike a regular crowd that you don't have to see for the rest of your life, these would be people that I'd have to see for the rest of the year.

MB: And so why was that scary to you?

PL: Well, it was scary because, first of all, it's something I'm passionate about, something that's important to me. Particularly at that point, and probably for many years after, my whole self-worth was tied into how funny I could be.

MB: Could you elaborate on what you mean by saying your self-worth was tied into how funny you were?

PL: Yeah. That was kind of my identity. And it's one of the main reasons I wanted to go into stand-up: This is something I've always succeeded at; this is something that makes me worthwhile. So underneath, I was feeling that "I'm not okay. But this will make me okay." [Laughs]

MB: So you did overcome that thinking?

PL: Yeah. But it's amazing how tied in comedy still is to my self-worth, my self-esteem. And it's really amazing how much better I feel after I do it. It feels great. But certainly I see the big picture. It's not like my whole life is wrapped around this. I see it for what it is: one moment in life.

MB: When you're doubting yourself, do you know what you're telling yourself?

PL: Generally what's happening is I'm taking myself for granted. Since I know what I'm going to say [when I perform], I'm not necessarily as entertained by myself as I am by watching somebody else.

What's great about an audience, particularly with comedy, is that a lot of times you'll go up there on stage with stuff that's infuriating to you, and you'll express it, and all of a sudden, since they have a distance from it, they see the humor of it, whereas I'm only seeing the pain of it; I want to make it funny, but I'm still so close to it.

One of the things that I've come up with is "Express, don't impress." But I'll want to look good—which is a real trap—instead of just being myself, letting myself make a mistake. You know? Who cares how well you do? Just have as much fun as you can.

MB: What are the circumstances when you get nervous now?

PL: One of the worst times when I was nervous was back when I did a cruise ship. I don't think I'd been that nervous in my whole career. And part of it was "This is gonna be my ticket! I'll do well on these cruise ships from now on. I can make a good living, and I won't have to put up with all the crap from all the sleazy club owners and all that stuff. I need to do it, because if I don't do this I can't see myself going back to what I was doing before."

MB: So how did you get out of that thinking trap?

PL: Well, the way I do it now is to be much more realistic. No one event is ever so important that it causes success. To me, success has to do with where you're coming from—it's not something you attain. I'm coming from being successful, not "if I do well, this will make me successful." So, I make sure to never put all of my eggs in one basket. I make sure I have a lot of things going on. So that one event isn't so important.

MB: What role do your thoughts play in getting nervous?

PL: They're a big part of it. One of the things I've learned to do is focus on my breathing. Rather than connect with my thoughts, I'm just focused on my body and my breathing. I'm not caught up in the thought. I realized if I'm in an insecure mood, my thinking can be a treadmill of negative thoughts.

MB: And the negative thoughts would be?

PL: "If I screw this up I'm a loser. I don't deserve this. I don't belong here. I'm not worthy. It'll never work out."

MB: How do you counter that?

PL: I go back to "You know what? I'm only going to do this if it's fun. The reason I'm doing this isn't because of all those other things—the ego-oriented things about how good I am, how great I am. You know what? You know, fuck it! I'm doing this because it's fun. I'm doing this because it's a great thing to do. And I'm only going to do it as long as I feel that way. All these other things aren't important—like what it gets me, what I look like. I'm doing this because it's something I really want to do and it's something I really have fun at."

MB: Can you think of the worst case of stage fright you've seen in somebody else?

PL: Yeah, I just saw an open miker not too long ago. And he didn't seem to be himself at all. He was petrified. He was internalizing what he thought the audience was thinking. He was being so harsh on himself. Your heart just went out to the guy. It was like, nobody could be that cruel. [Laughs] But you could see the guy was just condemning himself for a joke not working.

His whole self-image was involved in it. He was telling himself that these people wanted more, they expected more, they were incredibly disappointed in him. Almost that he looked like a complete fool. And the thing was, if he had looked like a complete fool, it would have been funny [both laugh]—if he was really in touch with that. But he was frozen stiff. It was that whole thing of thinking, "I'm making a mistake. I don't want to make a mistake."

MB: Lastly, what advice would you have for performers who experience stage fright?

PL: Welcome mistakes. Maybe even seek them out. You're going to make mistakes. So don't fight it. Mistakes can be the funniest thing in a routine. They can be the most interesting thing. Mistakes are the most spontaneous, interesting things in life. Hell, I was a mistake.

Maria Mason

Maria Mason is an actor, teacher, wife and mom—not necessarily in that order. A "journeyman," she's done summerstock, NYC showcases, regional theatre (in Boston, New Orleans) and camera gigs (TV pilots, films, and commercials)—playing romantic leads, dizzy dames, leaders, nurturers and rebels—even touring to Budapest and to Tbilisi, Republic of Georgia. Her favorite stage roles include Irish rebel Meg in "The Hostage," love-struck Olivia in "Twelfth Night," gamine Belinda in "The Public Eye," tap-dancing Dulcy in "The BoyFriend," Annie Sullivan in "The Miracle Worker" ("Big Easy" Award for Best Actress), Lynn Fontanne of the legendary Lunt theatrical team in "The Celestials," Agnes, the knitter, in "Dancing at Lughnasa" ("Big Easy" Best Ensemble), and Sonya in "Uncle Vanya." She recently played Burt Reynolds' wife in the feature film *Deal*. During her 16 years in New Orleans, she taught acting at Tulane University and the Southern Rep Theatre. After surviving Hurricane Katrina, she and her family now live in North Carolina.

MM: What kind of questions do you want to ask me so I can be brilliant here?

MB: [Laughs] You're already brilliant. You can start by telling me how long you've been performing.

MM: Hmmm . . . First time? Fourth grade. Mrs. Pace's class! In a little review. And this darling gal, Nancy Green, and I played twins. It was a 1920s Charleston little variety show. I knew that something had kicked in when Nancy and I flopped on the floor on our bellies, and paged through a picture book. We were supposed to be low focused—what a director would say now is "continuing the life." I was reading through the catalogue, having inner monologue in character, wishing for my Christmas gifts, but I was very subtle, because I somehow knew that I wasn't supposed to steal the scene. And it felt so real, my imagination was "*on*."

My next performance that I recall, beyond a few dance recitals, was in the seventh grade when we were dramatizing our book reports, and Annie Sullivan or Helen Keller—one of them—was absent that day. So instead of just being the director of my project, I had to jump in and do Helen Keller. I had a great time: I was absolutely in the moment for the "water"/word miracle at the pump. That's when my teacher, Patty Jones, said, "Maria, I think you've found your calling."

But acting professionally? When I got that Equity card, two years after my MFA in Acting at UNC-Chapel Hill/PlayMakers Rep. Twenty-plus years of doing it.

MB: So can you tell me the first time you can remember being nervous?

MM: Oh, gosh, it was probably right back in fourth grade. I also remember one time in high school. I had the most brilliant high school English and Drama Club teacher, Tom Orr, who I'm still in touch with. And who is still brilliant. It's not just me remembering him very fondly—he's still cutting edge, super visionary.

We were doing an early autumn high school assembly about joining clubs. I was a little queen. I was super-involved, a super volunteer, doing all these award-winning one-acts and stuff. I had made up all this poetry about the Drama Club, which—this was in the pre-rap days—was pretty much rap. It was only me on the stage at that moment, directly addressing the audience, and I went totally blank—a good twenty-five seconds. It was awful.

That's the worst case of nervousness I've ever had. Where the whole freakin' audience knew.

MB: Do you know what you were telling yourself at the time?

MM: No. Yes! I remember I kept berating myself in the panic attack. I kept saying "You forgot???! Get back! Where am I? THINK! CONCENTRATE!" It was an endless litany of yelling at myself. In my mind's eye, I kept seeing the piece of lined notebook paper with my pencil-scribbled rap/rhymes. I kept trying to find a pickup place. Finally I just jumped to the conclusion. And drat! I had some good stuff that no one would ever hear. But I had to get offstage!

I would see this panic in other people later, if anything would start to happen in a scene study class in New York, or in performance when other people have gotten that "Oh my God" look in their eyes.

Actually, it's very easy to deal with: you just take a deep breath, look down at the table or the floor or whatever your character is doing, and just continue. And you calm down—you pour the tea, or you put the phone receiver down, and your imagination will certainly save you. But you've got to breathe. You are "filling in, in character" as you recover. Hopefully the audience can sense the wonderful energy. It's nothing to be afraid of.

MB: Is there anything you can think when you're in character that diminishes the nervousness?

MM: I think it's a two-step process. You have to acknowledge that the *actor* part of you is a small percentage of your brain . . . because, hopefully, the larger percentage engaged in performance is the *character*. You're going, "Oh my God! I've screwed up," or "So and so has yet to enter," or whatever. So you don't try to fight that. You breathe. The actor part of you then steps back, and you allow yourself to think in character. You go into an activity as the character, and something interesting will happen.

Here's an example: in the Scottish play [Macbeth], I was playing Lady McDuff, and there's a beautiful scene, where she's tending to her children. That's the set-up. Then a dear friend comes in to warn her: "They're coming; they're coming!" And she starts to rally her little chicks.

And the murderers don't come on. And they don't come on. And they don't come on. It was intense, because the adrenaline was flying. You're going to get killed! You know that they're out to get your husband; he's probably already dead. So you're trying to flee. And in those days, I guess like in Iraq today—all wars, frankly—the marauders raped and pillaged and impregnated. And if you were a woman, you were in really bad shape. You would have almost rather died than be a victim. And you've got to save the children first! Anyway, the adrenalin from the character was flying.

And then the adrenalin from me as the actor, is going: "Oh my God, where are the murderers? This is the plot point. This is a scene closer. An act closer." So I just screwed around. I gathered my two young sons to me, hugged and hussled them out, away! I clung to my baby [a doll], then hid her in the trunk. I would stall the men. But when they hadn't come yet, I thought, I'll hide in the trunk with her.

That's when the men came in. One had to drag me away from the trunk, because then I was frantically trying to put the lid on to hide her! It was horror—the audience jumped too! Later, of course, you have the most brilliant solutions. I know an absolutely gorgeous Celtic lullaby from 500 A.D. or something. Later, I thought, "Oh my God! If I had just spent that crazy time to softly sing my baby to sleep, and then hid her in the trunk. . . what an interesting, intense two-stanza vamp!"

I mean, there's always a way that you can make situations work. But I think the short answer . . . Sorry I'm so loquacious . . . The short answer is take a breath as the actor, just acknowledge the shit and carry on as the character.

MB: Could you elaborate on what you mean by "acknowledge" it?

MM: #1: You just acknowledge that something isn't happening that's supposed to happen. #2: You take a breath. You tell yourself to breathe. Because when you're panicked, your shallow breathing kicks in. And you sure can't think or create then! So you say, "Breathe!" And then #3, you just find something to do in character. You fill the time until the problem can be fixed—either you remember the line, or the tech team jumps to the climactic shot, or the lighting or sound cue, or whatever. Or your fellow actor gets his little butt on stage.

You just have to give your imagination time to kick in. So you do a creative, character-appropriate activity, and it becomes a beautiful moment. Usually, that becomes a moment the audience talks to you about later. Because you're very alive. They don't know the panic, but they know the energy, the *realness*.

In fact, that's a great question you asked. One director I worked with, Joe Warfield—four times I was blessed to work with him—he called these [problem] situations "happy accidents," and what he meant by that was that they're not anything that's going to be a safety issue—like water on the floor that could make somebody fall. But something happens that absolutely kicks you into focus and character work—and you really listen to each other. And I tell you, I've been a witness to that resulting in beautiful moments.

MB: Could you elaborate on what "happy accidents" mean to you?

MM: A "happy accident" is something unexpected that's happened, whether it's technical or actor-related. It's an improv with yourself, your creativity, and hopefully your fellow players.

I have two examples from Southern Rep days. As Sonya in "Uncle Vanya" I was climbing on a chair to get a bottle for Dr. Astrov and me to share for our late night visit. Well, the chair tipped, crashed and I was falling. Guess who caught me? Dr. Astrov! That made for a beautiful cascade of reactions and feelings and recovery for us both!

Another was when I was playing Annie Sullivan and during the famous food fight Helen's hair got caught in two of my shirtfront buttons. We were absolutely attached—no unraveling it. Well, I cradled/dragged her upstage with me to the sideboard, opened a drawer stocked with silverware, got a serrated knife and sawed her hair off my buttons—carefully of course! But we had to separate. My castmate, Soline McLain, was brilliant in trusting me. God love her, she just went with it.

I can think of lots of other moments in other productions. As an actor, you come to love those "happy accidents."

MB: So by viewing the accident as "happy," you're not denying it, or you're not feeling bad about it, or you're not telling yourself that it shouldn't be happening.

MM: Yeah! Exactly. In fact, there's no judgment about it at all. You might in your mind say, "Oh, fuck! So and so hasn't come in!" or "Oh, fuck! This phone isn't working." But there's no judgment about it; it just is. Things happen. So who cares? You don't sit there and blame yourself and judge yourself as you're trying to remember that line on the top of the page that you can visually see but you can't get to. There's no judgment. You just acknowledge it quickly, and you breathe, and you do something as the character. It's great. It's great.

MB: Okay. Cool. Do you ever get nervous now?

MM: All the time. That's a question that college students ask, and that little kids ask. I say to them, "Honey, don't even start to worry about that. Nervousness is a form of energy." And I say, "I've been doing this for X number of years, and I'm nervous every time I have to audition—every time I have to walk into a casting director's office. Every time I'm being introduced to somebody important. Every time that I go on stage or I'm doing a take on film. Or a commercial. Every time, I'm nervous! But I'm not afraid of it. It's energy."

Now, I think there are two types of nervousness. And I think your psyche is so intelligent you can't really trick it. One type of nervousness is when you think, "Oh my God. I am not prepared at all. And I should have been." Like, you've been given the script, and you never read it, or it isn't properly memorized, or you didn't do what was asked of you. And you're there trying to fool people. That's a very guilty type of nervousness. And it's really hard to trick yourself out of it. Basically your psyche is mad at you and you know you screwed up. So you've gotta focus extra well.

The other kind of nervousness, I think, is when something is new and the outcome is very important to you. Maybe you want somebody to like you. Or it's an important job opportunity: you're thinking, "Oh my God! This counts so much. I've got to make this work." You're putting pressure on yourself to be perfect or scintillating. But you are as prepared as you're going to be—it's the unknown that makes you nervous. So I try to turn it into: "It's just energy. Let me focus on one or two character things" or "What's my goal here?" or "What's the layer I will explore in this particular rehearsal or take?" Dare yourself to honestly explore and react to whatever comes up! The improvisation energy of that is a fabulous gift!

MB: So what role would you say your thinking—what you're telling yourself—plays in your nervousness and how you deal with it?

MM: My mentor in NYC, Terry Schreiber, would probably say that it is just part of your personal inventory, part of being in the present, then you push onwards to the work.

I think I'll have to elaborate on something I told you earlier. To me, when you perform, there is a percentage of your brain that is very much rooted in the present moment as you, the actor, on this particular stage in this particular time. But the larger percentage of your brain is immersed as your character. You accept this. So I tell kids for rehearsal and performance, "Don't try to brainwash yourself to 'be the character,' where there's no percentage of you left—that's insanity. That's not cool. Don't try to chase away your present actor self. Just invite your creativity to be a higher percentage of your being. Hopefully you're really inspired and you the actor are in the background.

So that's how I deal with nerves. The nervous energy is part of being fired up, ready, alive. It might be a bit unfocussed at first, but hopefully you can focus it.

MB: Are there any circumstances in which you don't get nervous?

MM: I think that there might have been one in filming my last project! I was so awed with Charles Durning that I thought, "I am in the hands of such a great actor here; I'm just going to lean back and play ball." And I think I needed some of that nervous juice.

The bottom line: There is a way to make the nervousness positive. And it is absolutely a tool. And if glitches occur, that is an opportunity for beautiful moments.

MB: So you don't freak out about getting nervous.

MM: No. You just have to channel it.

MB: Is there any other advice you'd give to people with stage fright?

MM: You have to honest with yourself. If you aren't prepared, you've got to acknowledge that. But in the moment of performing, you still have to get back on character track with, "How do I solve this problem?"

MB: So it's really helpful to view problems not as obstacles but as opportunities?

MM: Yeah! Obstacles are your friend! "Problems," "obstacles," are a door. Go through that door. A lot of times these horrifying "problems" are kicks in the butt that get our characters onto a more interesting, quirky, insightful path! Dare to discover!

Meehan Brothers

Growing up in the mayhem of the Meehan home was divine preparation for San Francisco's thriving comedy scene. Chris along with his brothers Mike and Howard turned the chaos into comedy and formed the sketch comedy group "The Meehan Brothers" in 1999. Their combined stage experience exceeds 40 years. Michael began his professional stand-up career in 1984. An international headliner, he has been on the "Craig Ferguson Show," "Dennis Miller," PBS "Comedy Tonight" with Whoopi Goldberg and most recently the semi-finals of "The Last Comic Standing" with his brothers Howard and Chris. Howard, an accomplished playwright, has 12 years experience as a stand-up comic and as an actor. His sense of structure and story has been the spine of the Meehan Brothers' narrative. Christopher, although most recognizable from his 60+ commercials, was trained in the Meisner technique at New York's Neighborhood Playhouse and has been performing professionally for the last 10 years. Their two most successful shows, "Meehan, Myself and I" and "Mommas Boyz— One Man's Journey to Move Out of His Mother's House" have been performed to critical acclaim throughout North America.

MB: Were any of you nervous when you started?

HM: I was terrified. Twice I walked off stage in the middle of a show at Cobb's Comedy Club. One time Mike followed me with a microphone, and one time both he and Chris lectured me about how "You can't leave the stage. Or if you do leave the stage, make sure to do it before the show, rather than in the middle of it. That way we can avoid you altogether."

MM: I was more frustrated trying to get these guys on the same page: "Come on. We need more; it's gotta be funnier. It's gotta be funnier. I wasn't nervous as much as I was frustrated with the lack of familial talent.

CM: I was nervous, but I knew where I needed to go. I always had something to do on stage. And a lot of that was just looking like a deer in headlights.

HM: My nervousness came from trying to memorize lines instead of realizing what I was saying and why I was saying it. And it took a long time to realize that why I'm saying something, or just being emotionally present on stage, is absolutely the key, and that I don't need to worry about the exact wording. The wording will come.

MB: What do you mean by "being emotionally present on stage"?

HM: Not freaking out. Let's say we're doing a bit that we end up memorizing by working it out on stage. It's easy to get stuck on words instead of just being in the flow.

MM: We needed to hire a security guard to keep Howard on stage.

CM: One of our first bits was a pretty funny rapid fire word bit, and Howard had the first part of it. And he got up there and started speaking gibberish. It sounded a little bit like Japanese. And then he saluted. Remember Howard?

HM: Right. Because I didn't want to leave, I just tried to stay and make something up.

MB: How did you deal with that?

MM: Through lots of derision. Making fun of him. That's how we deal with anything. If anybody drops the ball, we make fun of them and we try to crush their spirit.

CM: I was determined that no matter what Howard did, I was going to look good. To hell with him.

HM: It's based on the chicks at the petting zoo in San Francisco. They all peck each other until one bleeds. And then once one bleeds they go bananas until it's dead. It makes the Rodney King beating look like a group hug.

MB: Do the three of you ever get nervous now when you perform?

HM: I got worried, because for about two years I wasn't nervous at all. And I started tripping on it. And I realize now that's okay. But it's also good to feel nervous because that's energy that helps you get ready. Now I look forward to feeling nervous. It helps.

MM: I like a little anxiety. As a solo performer, you have that. But with these guys I feel that we all have each other's backs. We can always do something.

HM: It was amazing: When we started I would be freaking out, and Mike would literally be talking to somebody right as he was going on stage. And I couldn't believe it. He could just do that.

MM: Seconds before I went on stage.

HM: And now he's even correcting me while I'm complimenting him. Do you see what I have to deal with here?

CM: I'm more nervous now than ever. I get very anxious and I go, "Why in the hell am I doing this?" The other things that make me nervous are like Mike, ten minutes before curtain, saying, "Hey, I'm going to get a cup of coffee." And then Howard—this is a true story—I was looking for Howard at a gig and I couldn't find him, and he was sleeping under the accountant's desk.

MB: What role does your thinking play in your nervousness?

MM: If you start thinking, and worrying, and doubting, you're obviously going to build nervousness. But if you just go through the set, you won't get really nervous. You may have a little bit of nervousness just to give you that scoot on stage that you need to sharpen your senses. But especially when we're doing a full scripted show, it's "Alright, let's go. We're ready to roll."

HM: I think paralysis of analysis is always going to hurt your performance. If you look at boxing, or any sport, you never see them jump from nothing to being on stage. They're always warming up and working up a sweat before they go perform. And I think that's the key. To have that going.

CM: You know, I write it into the equation. I say, "I'm nervous now. Why the hell am I nervous?" And then I think, "Wait a second. I wrote this into the equation. Bring props, know your lines, three microphones. Sound cues. And be nervous." So then I say, "Oh. Okay, I'm nervous. That's right. I planned this. I'm happy; I'm sad; I'm nervous."

HM: I think that's true. Acknowledging how you're feeling in the moment before you go on stage will dissipate fifty percent of your fear immediately.

MB: What's the worst case of stage fright you've ever experienced?

HM: I did solo stand-up, and I bombed so horribly that I had good reason to be terrified. I couldn't afford acting class, and I kept going up. My body carried me on stage. And I bombed. And it was horrifying. I think Mike and a couple other people have seen me have such bad sets that hecklers wouldn't heckle me because they felt so bad for me. And that's the truth. I don't know why I kept doing it because it was horrifying. It didn't get better for a long time. And it left me finally because I quit going on stage for a while.

MB: How do you think you could have viewed things differently?

HM: Well I think working on the set offstage helped. Not memorizing stuff, but connecting with why I was up there. Also dealing with my huge amount of personal shame helped. I think performers are driven to the stage somehow to think to themselves, "Hey, look at me. Make me feel better. Give me attention." And you're asking this from a bunch of people who are drunk that you don't really care about.

MB: What were you thinking that created the shame?

HM: Hold on Mick, my mom's here; I can't talk about . . . But no, it's me. I've changed my perspective on the world a lot. But truthfully, why do people go perform? "Look at me! Look at me! Look at me!" That's part of it. But it's also the desire to share something about yourself.

MM: Howard would always do crazy things. He was always a loose cannon. So Chris and I would always be wondering, "What is Howard going to do?" So it did add a nice element: "How are we going to deal with *this*?"

HM: Other people have told me that they want to hire Federal Express to deliver my lines. I've got the timing of a sundial. That does not help.

CM: Well, performing as a group, you rise with the tide. So we get to share the joy of performing well. But what's even better than that is that when you stink up the place and bomb, you have two other guys to run a distraction while you get out of the club.

Also, Howard on stage became the whipping boy. He was so nervous that it actually alleviated all of my nervousness, because he took all the energy there was to be nervous.

MM: He wasn't the scapegoat. He was the sweat goat.

CM: He was so nervous, there was nothing left. He monopolized it. He hogged every ounce of nervousness. And I would think, "He's got it all; there's nothing left."

MM: Careful what you say about Howard, Chris; mom's within earshot.

CM: She is? Okay! I've been experimenting, facing my fears. And I've realized that a man's big furry bushy mustache tickles when you kiss him. But at least I conducted the experiment.

MM: Well, let me tell you, Chris: A woman's big furry mustache tickles, too. I know. I'm married to an Italian woman.

MB: What's the worst stage fright you've experienced performing with each other?

HM: Well, as I said, I left the stage.

MB: What was going on in your mind?

HM: At that point, I had no mind for any thought to be in.

MB: Who's the least consistent of the three of you?

MM: I would say that I am. Even with twenty-four years of experience.

HM: Michael doesn't always show up at gigs.

MM: Well, that's true, Howard. But let's observe the details, shall we? There was that gig in Marin where you didn't show up.

HM: How about the sketch fest when you stayed away and we haven't been asked back since.

MM: Funny thing Howard, they asked Chris and me back, and told us to exclude you.

CM: This is the resentment part of the interview: Chapter 14: Resentment.

MB: You seem really relaxed with your performing. What do you attribute that to?

HM: Here's the thing: Beyond interacting with each other, thinking about what we're doing, hitting our marks—above all that, being open to whatever's going to happen.
    But it's mainly accepting the fact that the worst thing that can happen has already happened: bombing completely.

MB: So how do you deal with that?

HM: Accepting it, and then going on from there. If the audience senses that you're really really scared, they can't laugh.

MM: It's the terror in the eyes that really throws 'em off: "Hey, I just paid twenty-seven bucks for these tickets! This guy looks like he's caught in Dick Cheney's cross hairs!"

CM: Howard was performing solo recently at San Francisco Comedy College, and he went up there, got a couple of jokes out, and then he started going downhill very quickly. So he sat down on the stage and said, "Listen. You want the truth? I live at my mom's house. I'm forty-six years old. It's not been a good day." And immediately the audience started laughing. Howard just talked to them about his life, and it was hysterical.

MB: Really? You got laughs from that?

MM: It's hard to believe, Mick, but suddenly you tell the truth, and they see what a nimrod you actually are.

HM: I think if you get in touch with who you really are, and tell the truth, there's definitely a lot of humor in that.

MB: Michael, what else were you going to say about telling the truth?

MM: I forget, Mick. There are so many lies, I can't keep them all straight.

CM: Working as a team you get to share the excitement and the victories. But also when you eat it you can spread that around a little bit: "It's my brother's fault."

HM: It's like the [acting teacher Sanford] Meisner training: Staying in the moment, working off of each other. If on a certain night, someone's really on, you can compete with them and make it fun. But you also want to feed it. They are connected to the audience, and the ultimate goal is to entertain the audience.

CM: There are some performers who get upset and say "Fuck you" to the audience. But I think the trick is instead of staying "Fuck you!" say "Fuck it! I don't have complete control over this. Let's just have a good time. It really doesn't matter anyway."

MM: We can be replaced by some guy with a boom box. We actually have been.

MB: What would be the first piece of advice you'd give to somebody with stage fright?

HM: Don't take it personally. You go up and eat it—you're in flames. And you're thinking, "Oh my God. They've rejected every ounce of my history." You can't take it seriously. Most people don't remember your name in comedy anyway, even when you're good. Just go up and do it. But now with Facebook they can track you down.

MM: They do. That's why I'm coming up with a new one called "Ass book." It's from behind, so no one can really tell.

CM: Unless you're in a San Francisco public restroom.

MM: You know how to whistle in San Francisco, don't you? Go to the men's room and blow!

HM: It's really helpful to get away from "I'm either going to kill or I'm going to die." If you perform long enough, somewhere in between is the truth.

CM: If you bomb, it works a lot better if you make a joke about it. Even if you were horrible, own it, accept it, but don't let it affect your acceptance of yourself. But often you just want to get away and crawl under a rock. One time, we did a gig at San Quentin . . . No, it was Marin County Jail.

MB: Are you serious?

CM: Yes. We had to go through several doors that locked. Then we had to sign a no-hostage policy.

MB: A what?!

CM: If you become a hostage, you can't sue the prison.

MB: You can't be serious.

HM: That's absolutely true.

MM: And what's more, I signed one of those no-hostage policies in my prenuptial agreements.

CM: So we got into our act and we were doing well. But we were very uncomfortable because we were in a prison, and we wanted to get out; but there was no place to go. So we finished our show, and Howard grabs the door, but it wouldn't open. The only reason Howard did it was because he got to it before I did. And it got a big laugh because all the prisoners were thinking, "Where do you think you're going?" Thank God we didn't bomb. But anyway, they were the nicest guys.

HM: Yeah, they were great. They were sectioned off into the 16-inch-bicep and the 17-inch-bicep sections.

MB: Are there any admirable traits you've seen in other performers when they deal with pressure?

HM: Really good comics are authentic in their acts. In contrast to that, it's really bad when comics say, "It's the audience's fault." It's never the audience's fault. Even when it is, it's never the audience's fault.

MM: The comics who overreact to their success also overreact to their failures. Vanity and insecurity are two sides of the same coin: lack of self-confidence.

CM: There's something that's been very helpful to me: The twenty-forty-sixty rule: At 20 years old, you worry about what everybody's thinking about you. At 40 you don't care what people are thinking about you. And at 60 you realize that nobody's been thinking about you at all; they're too busy thinking about themselves.

MB: How do you deal with disappointment about where you're at? You've been doing this for years and years, and you haven't made it nationally.

HM: I had to work through what was bugging me, how it was bugging me, and what my part was in it. I'm not kidding around now.

MB: I believe you. Tell me about it.

HM: Well, that's pretty personal.

MB: I know. That's what the interview's about. Do we want depth here, or do we want fluff?

HM: Well . . . Michael is a genius performer. A lot of comics have been very inspired by Michael Meehan; Michael is a very generous person. But what happened at a certain point in the Meehan Brothers, in my opinion, besides my craziness, is that Michael started getting really upset at Chris. And I felt they were at each other's throats a lot. Michael started getting picky, but Chris can stand up for himself. And he did. But I think that sometimes Michael didn't respect Chris's comedy. Chris is usually the funniest, and he usually gets the most laughs.

CM: That's right. I usually get the most laughs saying Michael's lines and Howard's lines. Being the youngest brother, I get to cherry pick the material.

HM: I don't want to give this one dimension though, because when we started doing comedy as a team Michael's experience and connections bumped us up far past where we would have been had we been starting out together rather than riding his coattails, riding all the years he did stand-up. He taught us what was hack and what was original. A lot of times I'd write something hack that I thought was original and Michael set me straight. And he would switch it around so it would work. So we do owe a great debt to Michael.

MM: And don't you forget it Howard. You owe me your first born.

HM: How about my third born, Michael? He's twenty years old, and he can kick the shit out of all three of us.

MM: Yeah, well if he's so tough, how did you raise him?

HM: I didn't. He's raising me. Every weekend I ask him for approval of the women I date.
   But getting back to being serous, one of the big things that's held us up is the reality of making money as a three-man group.

MM: Yes. Making money as a three-man group was always rough in the clubs, so then we had to do the big theaters, which we weren't geared up for. But as a trio we did have a lot of animosity, and I had a lot of discontent. In the beginning I was really frustrated because I felt like I was carrying these two motherfuckers—

HM: (interrupting) Michael, mom can still hear us. Make sure not to call us sons of a bitch.

MM: But then as we started to grow as a group and these guys started to feel that they had something to give, then I backed off. But then I got very picky about stuff.

HM: Michael also has a self-sabotaging attitude of not wanting to be successful. And I'm not taking anything away from you Michael. You have a great wife, a great son, a great daughter.

MM: I have a great ex-wife.

MB: Okay, so how do you improve on what you do?

MM: Preparation. Having a routine. I remember one time we did a thing with Brian Setzer. Before he went out he had this little altar that he centered on; it was very Buddhist. And then he went out and gave a terrific show. That's basically what we do: Rehearse and say a prayer. That's going to help you every time.

MB: What if you don't pray?

MM: Well, if you don't pray you have another routine. And that's rehearsal. Sometimes it's going to go great; sometimes it isn't.

But your routine allows you to center yourself. But if you churn around going, "Are they gonna like me?" then you'll show up on stage with all this anxiety.

HM: It's all about you instead of them. And thats what I've learned: The basis of stage fright, in a very condensed way, is self-obsession. And I'm talking extreme and in the moment.

CM: But where it's funny is that if you actually admit to yourself, "I'm completely self-obsessed," it actually helps take the problem away. It's hysterical if you look at yourself as if what you are doing actually matters more than the audience's personal lives. Like that time you were bombing Howard, and you just said to the audience, "You know what, I'm having an awful day. I'm going through a divorce. I'm sleep deprived." And everybody appreciated it.

HM: And I'm not saying that stage fright is about self-obsession in some shaming way. I'm just saying that ultimately when you boil it down and you really want to give a gift to the audience, then it's not about you.

CM: If you have extreme stage fright, don't do it. Don't perform. Be ordinary. Be like everybody else. And there's nothing wrong with being ordinary. Or say to yourself, "I'm scared shitless." Admit it. "I'm choosing to take a leap here." And it's not going to kill you.

HM: There is a moat between the front row and the stage and it's full of crocodiles. And I think it should be that way.

MB: Is there anything besides stage fright that you've ever been afraid of, and how did you get over that? Or did you?

HM: Life. Taking the bus. Going to school. Working.

MM: I had stage fright when I was born. I actually lodged myself in the birth canal for twenty minutes. There was a whole bright room full of people out there.

HM: I think that's when you get stage fright. You go from the dark to the light. It's all about you. You're in pain. And you bomb. Right from the beginning.

MM: Then they hose you off and love you.

MB: You guys are so much fun you make me want to be part of your family.

HM: Mick, that's a really good place to be: wanting to be part of our family while not having to actually be in the family. It's like a tofu turkey: You get a makeshift facsimile of the experience but get to avoid all the steroids that they pump into the bird. Because if you're actually part of our family you have to participate in our family rituals: Just as you walk in the front door, right on top of the banister, is that Prozac salt lick . . .

MM: But Mick, it's nice when you come over to our house and you're sporting that visitor's pass.

HM: You know how people say if you have eight relationships and you don't get along with anybody, the problem is you? In my family, that's not true.

MB: Thanks. This has been fucking great.

(MM's one-year-old crawls into the room.)

MM: Mick, take it easy! Remember what Kinky Friedman said: "Don't say "fuck" in front of the k-i-d!"

Larry Miller

One of Hollywood's most recognizable faces, Larry Miller has appeared in over 50 films, including *Pretty Woman*, *Best in Show*, *Waiting for Guffman*, *10 Things I Hate About You*, *The Princess Diaries I & II*, *The Nutty Professor I & II*, *For Your Consideration*, *Keeping Up with the Steins*, *Kiss Kiss Bang Bang*, with Robert Downey Jr. and Val Kilmer, *The Aristocrats*, and most recently as a featured character in the animated Jerry Seinfeld film, *Bee Movie*.

Television credits include "Medium,""Desperate Housewives," "Dirt," "Law & Order," "Seinfeld," "Boston Legal," "8 Simple Rules," "Mad About You," "Real Time with Bill Maher," "The Tonight Show with Jay Leno," and "The Late Show with David Letterman." Mr. Miller has also starred in several of his own HBO comedy specials and on Broadway in Neil Simon's play, "The Dinner Party."

Mr. Miller also wrote the best-selling book *Spoiled Rotten America* and is a contributing humorist to the *The Huffington Post* and *The Weekly Standard*.

MB: How long have you been performing?

LM: That would be since '78. Stand-up comedy. It was at The Comic Strip in New York. It was great. I loved it from the start.

MB: Were you nervous at all?

LM: Rather than nervous, I would say not very good, and perhaps unabashed. I really did feel that the first time I went on stage I wasn't very good. But even then, I had the idea that if you want to look like Schwarzenegger you should start doing push-ups. And that image came into my head: "Well, I think I just did my first push-up."

MB: Did you find yourself getting nervous at all when you started performing?

LM. No. There were a couple of jobs where I was somewhat ill at ease. But not as a syndrome relating to comedy. Not at all.

MB: What were the circumstances when you were ill at ease?

LM: [That happened with] two jobs out of what, eleven thousand?

MB: Well, I'm interested in how you dealt with those two situations.

LM: Okay, I can tell you about one situation, because it does touch on that. I was at the Iowa Stage Police Association Convention—oh, fifteen years ago. And it was this big, domed ballroom.

I'm standing in the back. And there's a trooper who's going to walk me to the front—like the trooper from that Norman Rockwell print, with the giant shoulders and the big, deep chest. So he's standing there and I'm standing there. And they have a couple of hours of awards and speeches, which is fine. Then one of the speakers said, "All right, as you know, last week young Danny McPhan was shot and killed in the line of duty." And I kind of blinked. I turned to the trooper and said, "What did he say?" And he said, "We're going to have a little memorial service." And I said, "You know, I'm a comic." And he said, "Shhhh!"

They bring on the guy's partner, who breaks down, can't finish. They bring up . . . God bless them . . . they bring up the guy's widow and kids, and they give 'em a check.

MB: You're not making this up?

LM. Oh, no. I'm not making this up. . . . They have to carry the widow off stage. And they unfurl a portrait of the guy, next to an American flag. Everyone stands and sings a hymn. And then, as if it had been scripted, this trooper says, "And now, here to make you laugh . . ."

I looked at the trooper next to me, and he looked at me, and I went up there. Because it didn't occur to me for a fiftieth of a second to not go up. Not because I have such a manic need to perform. But I think there is something about comics . . .

It didn't occur to me for a second not to go up. In fact, the audience was terrific. Not right away. I mean, for long chunks of time—five minutes—nothing. There was no bond there. Those poor folks had just been in a very different place in their hearts. But then you know what? My performance went fine. And afterwards, I went off with some of the folks into one of the hospitality suites, and chatted about this or that. Just had a grand time.

MB: When this situation was going on, how did you feel?

LM: Well, on a conscious level, I was certainly saying, "Well, this is wild!"

Here's another one that may be easier to relate to. There's a club called Nick's in Boston; it's a tough place. I was in there on a Saturday night and a fight broke out. And I mean a fight. It was the only time in my life I've seen an "F Troop" type fight—chairs flying, an empty pitcher thrown at a guy's head. The police came and broke it up.

Now, I was on stage, so I didn't need anyone to tell me to move. I tippy-toed off and darted into the office, which functioned as the green room. At any rate, the police took them off, and the owner turned to me and said, "Okay, go ahead. You can go up and finish." And I looked at him and said, "What?" He said, "Yeah, go up and finish." I said, "What do you mean, finish? It's finished. There's no show." And he said to me, "Go up. You'll be fine."

I think I said, "I have these delicate word pictures; that's really about it. I think my stuff is good. And I think I'm a pretty good comic. But I don't think this is the right moment for it." And he said, "I want you to go up. We're going to finish the show." And that's another moment where I just went up. I didn't say no. I didn't say, "But I can't." And sure enough, I had a fine set, for whatever time was remaining in it.

I'm not talking about laughs; I'm talking about the bond between performer and audience—the sincerity between performer and audience. Because audiences always know. Lenny Bruce said about audiences: "Individually they're idiots, but together they're a genius." And that sounds a little harsh. But together they know everything.

Anyway, I didn't complain. I didn't say, "But what do I do?" And I wasn't even nervous, really. I just thought, "Okay. I guess I'm going up." There's some kind of hard bark on comics. As I said, I don't think it's bravado; I don't think it's need; and I don't think it's anything manic. I think it's some kind of easing thought, like, "This is a place and a moment in the universe where I belong."

Maybe it's an extreme form of being in present time. The sun stops spinning at that second. And the mountains just fly right off into space. And life on earth ends. That would be the right moment for the comic to have gone back on stage. And then the world ends. But the comic went on stage.

MB: So even under these incredibly undesirable circumstances of the memorial service, and the fight breaking out, it sounds like you still felt okay, and you weren't telling yourself this was a horrible situation.

LM:. No, I wasn't. I wasn't saying, "This is the worst ever." And I wasn't saying, "Oh, this is gonna be bad." If I had any thought at all, on a couple of those bad jobs, I do remember thinking, "I can't wait to tell the fellas about this one"; I'm a comic and they're comics, and they're the ones I can talk to. Sort of like cops hanging out with cops—or doctors with doctors, or teachers with teachers. Because only another teacher or cop would understand.

MB: What role would you say your thinking or what you're telling yourself has in affecting your nervousness or lack of it?

LM: I don't know. That's a very hard question.

One of our kids is pretty good at golf. But he just gets up there and hits the thing. He gets up there and doesn't know that he's not supposed to be doing or not doing anything. He just hits the ball.

I think in a way that's a good metaphor for stand-up. I've always had an image that the stage is a rocket, and that the first stage just blasts the rocket off—and that's exuberance, talent, youth, innocence and joy. But that first stage burns off. And the second stage is knowledge, maturity, craft and professionalism. And those are just as wonderful. Then after that stage burns off, the third stage kicks in, and that stage is respect, virtue, faith, pleasure, ease, and affection. They can all blend together.

So I think in that first stage, I don't think I put a pen to paper for four years. I just thought, "Wow, I'm saying these things. That's a more honest way of doing it."

Well, you know what? That's not so. Not in my opinion. Because craft is wonderful. And vital. Maybe the greatest word in show business. And no, no—write things, if you like the audience, if you want to be good. Prepare things. I know there was a big trend over the last twenty years of saying, "No, it's false somehow to prepare." I never thought that was true. It's disrespectful to yourself and the audience to not prepare.

MB: I remember there was an interview with Chris Rock in which he said he doesn't have much respect for comics who don't put in a lot of time preparing to go on stage.

LM: I agree with him. And I care so much about that moment. The gift a performer brings. A literal gift. A nice wrapped gift. And you say, "Here. I've made this for you, Because I care about this relationship."

It's not negotiating treaties. And it's not saving lives. And it's not dragging people out of burning buildings or being in a war or operating on someone's heart. But it's a very good and important thing in all of human relations: the gift of performer to audience. And especially in the very American form of stand-up. (It is American, by the way. Stand-up is as American as the banjo.)

MB: Lastly, is there any advice you'd have for anybody who has a lot of stage fright?

LM: I'm not sure there's anything that would help. You'll either get good or you'll get out.

David A. Moss

After receiving a scholarship to attend The School of Performing Arts in San Diego, David worked as a stand-up comic for several years before returning to theater and film. He received a Critics Choice award for his role in the independent film *Street Music*; his performance was hailed as a "stand-out" by *New York Times* reviewer Vincent Camby. His portrayal of the "brilliantly mad" Malvolio in the College of Marin's production of "Twelfth Night" earned him performance of the year recognition from the *Marin Independent Journal*. David recently played the title role in "Othello," which one reviewer described as "elecrifying." He is the recipient of a Marin Arts Council grant for Outstanding Solo Performance and he just completed a short film, *Shadows*, which he wrote and directed.

MB: Were you ever nervous when you went on stage?

DAM: Yes. I still get nervous. I still get very nervous.

MB: I can never sense that. Driving here, I was thinking to myself, "I'm writing a book on performance anxiety and I'm asking David to share his insights; I don't know if David ever gets nervous."

DAM: I get a lot less nervous now than I used to. I think what I've learned —and I'm still learning—is to take the nervousness, the anxiety, and channel that into the performance. Instead of spending a lot of time worrying if the people are going to like me, or whether I'm going to be funny, I've learned to focus that [energy] into the performance.

MB: So how do you channel it into the performance?

DAM: Without sounding too airy-fairy or esoteric, I'm at a point now in my life and my performing where I don't really care whether the people like me. I'm up there for the art form, I want to be true to the art form. And so one of the things that helps me is not being perfect—not being perfect and not wanting to be the best. Because we're taught that we have to be the best, not only in performance—[which you'll understand] if you've gone to any kind of performing school—but in life in general, starting with our parents: "You do the best that you can. And you be the best that you can be."

Me, I just want to be average. And that sounds really simple. But telling myself that takes so much pressure off of me. I don't want to be the best. For instance, if I'm doing a showcase like I'm doing tonight, and there are fourteen comics, all of whom I'll follow, I don't sit there and say, "I'm going to be the best of all." I just want to be average. To just be David.

MB: Have you ever found that anger got in the way of your performing?

DAM: It did in the past. That's what fueled me. Having so many demons and not dealing with them—or dealing with them through the use of cocaine and alcohol—just really fueled the anger. I was funny, but very angry, and very scary.

MB: What are your ideas about perfectionism?

DAM: What I've learned about perfectionism in comedy is that, at least for me, comedy should be a very spontaneous art form. There was a time where if I didn't get the words exactly right I'd consider it a lousy set. Now that's neurotic. All week I would've been doing a piece a certain way, and if this one particular night I switched it around or used another word, in my mind that was failure. That wasn't perfect. And this is comedy. That ties into being way too serious, missing the point.

MB: How is it that you're able to keep going after eighteen years? A lot of folks that never got a big break have stopped performing.

DAM: When I first started doing comedy, the scene was getting ready to move into its heyday, its peak. And I really didn't know anything about it, because I'd been an actor all my life, so I did comedy to see if I could do it.

I started getting paid all this money. And I started doing drugs, and there were all these gigs available. When I got sober, the landscape of comedy had changed because of cable television, and there aren't as many gigs anymore. But I do it because I love the art form.

MB: When a set goes really terrifically, do you ever overreact?

DAM: I think what happens when you're having one of those phenomenal sets is you start out really extraordinary, and you suddenly realize that it is one of those sets. And then your mind starts thinking about all the things that you could cram into it to try to make it even more extraordinary. And you start interfering with the natural process of what was already happening. There's this connection. The audience is loving everything that you do. And the room is just full of laughter—it's hitting you, and bouncing back. Then you start thinking, "Well I could do this; I could do that." And then you get off. Because you start thinking about it. You're not allowing the process to happen. You're going through the Rolodex and thinking, "Okay, what are the big guns I can bring out? Then they'll *really* love me."

One of the fun things for me is that I'm at a point where I'm not up there for adulation, to get a pat on the back. I love it when someone tells me they enjoyed my set, but that's not why I'm up there. And that's an extraordinary power to have. I'm up there for me."

MB: Are you ever hard on yourself as a performer?

DAM: Yes, all the time. The solution ties back into not taking yourself so seriously, learning to lighten up. One of the ways that I'm not so hard on myself now is by not expecting that I should be at a certain point, on a television series, or in movies. I've accepted the way my life has gone.

And I have choices. And I can still attempt to do those things. But I'm comfortable with where my life is right now. The thing that I really love about comedy, or even a play, is that you do a set, and it's okay if it doesn't go quite like you wanted it to. It's not celluloid, it's not a movie. It's one set. It comes and goes. You can always come back tomorrow.

MB: What do you do when you have a special performance where the stakes are high, like an audition for a national TV show?

DAM: When you have a set that could lead to Letterman or one of the other shows, or when you have an agency that could be interested in you, you approach that showcase or that show the way you would any other show. If there are people in the front row talking, you go after them. You don't stand there stiff, pretending like it's not happening. If I dress in a sweater and jeans for a regular show, that's the way I'm gonna dress for a special show. You go and you do what you do. My philosophy regarding the audience is, "I didn't make you come here. You paid your money to come here. And I'm gonna be me." I owe that to myself.

MB: Why are you happier doing comedy now than you used to be?

DAM: I do it because I want to. And I'm not up there because I want people—strangers, no less—to approve of me and give me my self-worth.

I enjoy it. That's very empowering because I do the kind of material I want, and I do it for me. It doesn't mean that I'm like Miles [Davis] and turn my back on the audience and riff to the wall. But I'm not up there asking a room full of strangers, "Please love me." And that used to be the case. Comedy was the only way I could get any love, because I didn't love myself. Now, I don't have to use comedy that way. I have this wonderful wife, who is an absolute gem. The three best things that have happened to me are sobriety, my healthy children, and this wonderful woman that I met.

MB: How would you describe the progress you've made with your own performance anxiety?

DAM: My anxiety came from, "I hope they like me." Now, I like myself. I'm not gonna drive all the way to a gig and not have fun. I don't think, "I hope I'm funny." I know I'm funny.

Frank Oz

Earlier in his career Frank Oz was known for his creative collaborations with the famed Jim Henson, performing many Muppet characters, including Miss Piggy, Fozzie Bear, and Animal, as well as Bert, Grover, and Cookie Monster. Some of the projects Henson and Oz worked on together included "Sesame Street," "Saturday Night Live," and "The Muppet Show. For his work in television, Oz has received four Emmy Awards. He has also performed the unforgettable Jedi Master, Yoda, in all of the Star Wars films.

Oz has directed *The Dark Crystal* (With Jim Henson), *The Muppets Take Manhattan, Little Shop of Horrors, Dirty Rotten Scoundrels, Housesitter, What About Bob, Indian in the Cupboard, In and Out, The Score, Bowfinger, Stepford Wives*, and his latest, *Death at a Funeral*.

Among his many honors, Oz has been awarded two George Foster Peabody awards, The American Comedy Awards' Creative Achievement Award, The Art Director's Guild award, and three gold and two platinum records.

MB: How long have you been performing?

FO: Since I was eleven years old. I think the first professional show I had lasted for twenty minutes, and I was paid twenty-five bucks. It happened in front of a supermarket.

MB: Were you very nervous?

FO: I only remember that I felt as I did most times before a performance—that I wanted to do it right. I wasn't scared. I just wanted to make sure that I did a good job.

MB: As you continued to perform, did you ever become nervous?

FO: No, I was never scared or frightened of the audience. I was nervous when things went wrong—I was embarrassed. But I've never been really frightened of an audience, partly because as a performer, a puppeteer, you're behind the character. When I was a kid, I had low self-esteem and I think that's one of the reasons I became what I am. My feelings could be safe behind the character. The idea of being frightened of the audience never even came up because it wasn't really me in front of the audience. There was something buffering me—as opposed to how it is with an actor, who's out there naked.

That doesn't mean that there are only unhealthy ways to be a puppeteer. There are also healthy ways. There are performers who do puppets who don't do it for the same reason I did. They do it because it's a means of self-expression. I'm just saying that in my own instance I used it as a safe way to express myself without feeling rejection.

MB: Have you ever felt rejection? I'm sure you've made appearances as Frank Oz and not as someone operating a puppet or a Muppet.

FO: Oh, that stuff is easy. I love doing that stuff. I've done talk shows, I've gone to Cal Arts and to Harvard and to—God, I don't know how many places I've been to and done question-and-answer sessions. Those are easy. Those are a piece of cake. I love doing those.

I love them because I love talking about the craft. I tried to mix things up and make it less about the fluff of it all, and more about the craft. And I challenge the audience. It's exciting.

As an adult, I think I did it [performing] for a more healthy purpose. Now, after many, many years, I'm not hiding. I've found out more about who I am, and it's too late to hide now. The audience sees who I am, and that's the way it is. They can take me or not take me.

I don't feel rejected if people don't like my movies. I even challenge them. I say, "Is there any movie you didn't like?" And I hope they say that they didn't like a movie I did, or a performance, so I can pick it apart. I say, "Why? Let's talk about it." That excites me.

MB: What do you think you're telling yourself that enables you to do that? A lot of people wouldn't be able to face criticism so easily.

FO: I don't know. I guess it's because I know when I do good work and when I don't do good work, and if others disagree with me, that's fair.

There was a time in my life when I was rejected as an actor. I tried to be an actor in New York in my twenties for about six months. I went from audition to audition, and I finally gave up. I couldn't take the rejection, or the stupid directors. [Laughs] I couldn't take that kind of rejection because it made no sense. It had nothing to do with the craft or how good one is; it just had to do with what they wanted. But I felt very rejected at that time, like I'd just been humiliated, and I said, "Fuck this!"

MB: So how did you feel humiliated?

FO: Well, the last thing I auditioned for was a Bird's Eye commercial. When you do that, everybody looks like you: bald with glasses and a mustache. And you're told to go into the casting director's assistant's office, and you're supposed to sit on the floor and pretend you're in the Arctic, fishing through the ice. When I did that, I had an out-of-body experience, thinking, "What the fuck am I doing here?"

There are other times when people are stupid. Once, a director for an off-Broadway show I was auditioning for told me to laugh like Jack Lemmon.

And then just being turned down on auditions is rejection. I can't deal with that as well as other people. Actors are very brave that way.

MB: What do you think aids them in being brave?

FO: I think it's the need for the job. I'm serious. The need for the job is what makes them brave.

There's an actress friend of mine who goes in with the right attitude, which is, "They want me for this job. They're looking for somebody." And she's right. As soon as the directors find somebody, they can stop looking and do other work. Her attitude is "You know, I'm going in there, and they're hoping it's me." Then if she doesn't get the job, she doesn't feel rejected because she doesn't think she did a bad job; she thinks she wasn't what they were looking for.

MB: So since you haven't had much of a problem with being afraid in front of an audience, can you think of at least one bad case?

FO: It's odd. I always enjoyed performing, so when I saw an audience I always saw it as an amorphous, friendly thing. Whenever I approached an audience, innately I believed they were on my side. I believed they were friendly, and the only person who could screw it up was me. So I didn't go out there saying, "I'm scared to death of this audience." I'm out there about to enjoy myself.

As to the stage fright thing, I think I did have it once. [Laughs] I was actually an actor, I think when I was about fifteen doing the role of Gepetto.

MB: Well, that's appropriate.

FO: [Laughs] Yeah. It was a performance for the Oakland Parks Department. I was doing it outside for forty or fifty people—it was just rinky dink. But I totally forgot my lines. I just blanked out. And the kid who played Pinocchio was helpful. He whispered very loudly, "You forgot your line." [Laughs] Thanks a lot, kid!

I was scared at that point. I was scared shitless then.

MB: Do you remember what you were telling yourself?

FO: I was just blank. I was wiped out.

MB: What would be a better way of dealing with that kind of situation?

When there's a mistake in a live situation, you use it. You don't say, "Oh my God, it's a mistake. What am I going to do now?" It's like with any actor—you use it. If there's a fly buzzing around, and you know the fly's buzzing around, and the audience knows the fly's buzzing around, you can't go on with the piece, because the audience is looking at that fly. So you'd better acknowledge that fly and make it part of the piece. Then the fly's not a mistake.

But if there is a mistake in the dialogue, then the person who's supposed to have the next line can't just say the next line. That person has to acknowledge that you fucked up. And then you have a little fun with that, and then you go on. You have to let the audience know that there was a screw-up, and then you can all be in on the joke and move on.

MB: Can people tell themselves anything to diminish stage fright?

FO: Yeah. I think you could say, "What have you got to lose?" And there's the old adage, "If you can't be good, be loud." I think that's a good adage to have. I mean, go balls to the wall.

And you have to ask yourself what you're doing there. What's the intent? If the intent is touching the audience, then what's the fucking worst thing that can happen to you? If you loosen up and make a mistake, then the audience will see you're human. And they'll like you.

I remember doing an "Ed Sullivan Show" once, and a singer was on—I forget his name—and he started singing and made a mistake, and he stopped. This is live on "The Ed Sullivan Show." And he said, "Could I start over again?" Sullivan came on and said yes. And from that point on, the audience was with the singer. There were pulling for him, because they saw in his mistake their humanity.

One thing that's happened with taped TV that didn't happen with live TV is that when tape came around you could make things perfect. And that's the very thing the audience doesn't want. Nobody is perfect. The audience wants to be touched by somebody who is like them. If you're perfect, then the audience is not going to enjoy it. They love seeing mistakes. They love seeing the humanity of things. If you're too scared, that means you're going to try to do everything absolutely, perfectly right. And that's the very thing they don't want to see.

Ron Paul

Congressman Ron Paul of Texas enjoys a national reputation as the premier advocate for liberty in politics today. Dr. Paul is the leading spokesman in Washington for limited constitutional government, low taxes, free markets, and a return to sound monetary policies based on commodity-backed currency. He is known among both his colleagues in Congress and his constituents for his consistent voting record in the House of Representatives: Dr. Paul never votes for legislation unless the proposed measure is expressly authorized by the Constitution. In the words of former Treasury Secretary William Simon, Dr. Paul is the "one exception to the Gang of 535" on Capitol Hill.

Dr. Paul is the author of several books: *Challenge to Liberty*; *The Case for Gold*; *A Republic, If You Can Keep It*; and *The Revolution: A Manifesto*. He has received many awards and honors from numerous organizations A fellow congressman commented, "Ron Paul personifies the Founding Fathers' ideal of the citizen-statesman."

MB: How long have you been speaking in public?

RP: Since 1974. That was the first time I ran for Congress. I didn't do it before that.

MB: Were you anxious or nervous at all when you began to do public speaking?

RP: I don't remember being nervous about it. I think the anticipation of getting started, even today, is the same as it was back then. But I always felt more comfortable if I knew my subject. On occasion, I might be stuck in a situation where I'm not well informed [about the topic under discussion]. That would tend to make me more tense.

MB: Are you telling yourself anything that helps you be less tense?

RP: Yes. I usually tell myself a few things. One is not to be antagonistic, and to come across as sincere. That's easier when you're knowledgeable. [Laughs] But I always make an effort not to offend the opposition, which I think not only helps me, but it helps the message, too.

MB: So to help yourself not be nervous, you're telling yourself not to be antagonistic?

RP: That's what I'm thinking about: "How do I present this without getting overly excited, or accusatory?" And that sets the stage for me.

MB: You said that you tend to be more nervous when discussing matters on which you aren't well informed. Are you telling yourself anything there that could be contributing to your nervousness?

RP: I don't want to look like I'm not doing a good job.

MB: Can you tell me about the worst case of stage fright that you've experienced?

RP: Well, the most annoying thing is not having adequate time to answer a question. If I'm doing a TV interview, which I do a lot of, it's a matter of: "How long is it going to be until they interrupt me? Do I have thirty seconds or forty seconds?" And I might speed up in order to get information in before they cut me off. That's a big nuisance, and I don't like it at all. So that makes me tense, or a little bit angry, at times. I hardly get a chance to answer the question.

MB: Obviously, you're able to deal with that situation. What do you think you're telling yourself that helps you do it?

RP: I just try to summarize in two or three sentences what I might say in five minutes. I try to formulate the most important thing that I can say, and it's not always the easiest thing to do. Because the shorter the speech, the tougher it is.

MB: What are the circumstances that allow you to be the least nervous?

RP: If I'm in my district, and I'm talking to any group—whether it's a Republican group, or a business group, or a group that philosophically supports me. And if I'm not told precisely how much time I have, and I'm given an opportunity to present my case and motivate, that's when I'm the most comfortable.

MB: What's the worst case of nervousness you've seen in somebody else?

RP: Well, I don't know if it was the worst, but there's something I remember from a long time ago. In '74, it was the very first time I ran for office, and we were going to Republican houses for small meetings. There were two or three candidates at different levels: I was running for Congress and somebody else was running for state office. There was a gentleman there that gave the same speech to the first two houses. I didn't pay a lot of attention to it—if you talk to three audiences in three hours, the speeches are going to be similar. When we went to the third house, he got all tensed up and just couldn't get going. And here he was reciting words that he had memorized, not giving a speech from his heart, so to speak. And he just couldn't get going. The whole audience was embarrassed. Finally, somebody in the audience helped him out and asked him a question. The impression it left on me . . . I never was tempted to memorize speeches. I was going to know the subject and speak spontaneously.

MB: Is there any advice you could have given that might have helped him out?

RP: I'd have told him, "Don't memorize speeches." A lot of people do. Some people are more capable of memorization and delivering. But I never liked that. I feel much more comfortable speaking spontaneously, knowing the issue, and just remembering to make the several points that I've decided are important.

MB: Is there any other advice you'd give to anybody who does any sort of public appearances or performing in terms of staying calm?

RP: Know your subject. Be excited about your subject. And really believe in the program you're presenting. If you know the subject and you're comfortable with it, and if you have an intense belief and conviction in it, I think you'll be a good speaker.

MB: How do you get excited about your subject?

RP: Well, I don't know how I get excited about it. It's just that the subject for me is promoting the cause of freedom. I am so utterly convinced that the world would be better off if we had more freedom and less government. Not only would the rich benefit, but the poor would benefit, and there would be more peace in the world. I so intensely believe that, that it's my driving force.

Simon Phillips

Simon Phillips is one of the world's most renowned drummers. He has worked with Mick Jagger, The Who, Jeff Beck, Jack Bruce, Peter Gabriel, Joe Satriani, Tears for Fears, Judas Priest, Roxy Music, Al DiMeola, Pete Townshend, Russ Ballard, Robert Palmer, Stanley Clarke, The Pretenders, Jon Anderson, Whitesnake, and Dave Gilmore.

His solo albums include "Protocol" (1988), "Force Majeure" (1992), "Symbiosis" (1995), "Another Lifetime" (1997) "Out of the Blue" (1998) and "Vantage Point" (1999).

Simon is also involved in producing and engineering, working with Mike Oldfield while also co-producing Toto's "Tambu" (1995) and "Mindfields" (1998), and engineering "Through the Looking Glass" 2001/02.

On Toto's "Falling In Between" (2005), Simon played, engineered, composed, and shared production duties. He then went on Toto's "Falling In Between" world tour, playing 177 shows in 31 countries. Simon is now concentrating on his sixth solo album, running his studio, Phantom Recordings, and traveling the world playing drum clinics.

MB: You say you've never had stage fright?

SP: Not what I would call stage fright. I've been nervous, sure. Nervousness and stage fright—those are two totally different things.

MB: How would you distinguish between them?

SP: Well, with stage fright, people get sick. They really get quite, quite sick. I've only come across it a few times. Stage fright doesn't really go away. It's a little bit deeper than just being nervous.

Being nervous is something you start with, and you go out there, and once the gig gets going, it subsides and you're okay.

MB: Can you tell me about some of the worst cases of stage fright you've seen, without telling me who the people are?

SP: I've seen people getting sick, having to throw up and stuff. But like I said, it's very rare. I haven't seen a lot of it, and when I have worked with people who have suffered from it, they've concealed it very well, because if you're a professional musician, you have to cope with it. You have to learn a way of getting around it.

In terms of nerves, I can only really speak from personal experience. I suffer from nervousness maybe at the first show of a tour, in a major town, or a town where a lot of my friends are. That's when I get a little bit more edgy. Nervousness manifests itself in different ways—some people get more irritable; some people get a little bit tense and start panicking. I tend to just go along with it, because these days I kind of welcome it. When I've got a few nerves, I go, "Wow, that's fantastic; I haven't felt that for a while."

Most of the time, when you're playing on the road, gig after gig, it's great to be excited to play. And there are other gigs where you're not excited to play—you're tired, you've done a lot of traveling, you haven't had a decent meal, and maybe you're jet lagged and you've got constipation. [Both laugh] The last thing you really want to do is play.

On the other hand, you know that by playing the gig you're going to get lots of exercise, and it's the best thing to get you over your jet lag. So it's a double-edged sword. But I love it when I get a feeling of nervousness before a gig; I think, "Oh, this is great. It's going to be a good gig."

MB: When you've been nervous, have you ever had to calm yourself down? Do you do anything to keep yourself calm?

SP: No. When I'm nervous, I still remain pretty calm. You probably wouldn't even know that I'm nervous. And, like I said, my kind is a healthy form of nervousness. It's just like sports. I used to race cars. And boy—when you're on the grid ready to go—you've never felt nerves like that before in your life. There could be an almighty start line accident. But just the whole fact that you've got the car, the engine is revving at seven thousand revs, and you've got a clutch that's biting under your foot—with twenty-five other cars around you—that's nervousness. [Laughs]

And then you drive the first lap in a bunch of about ten or fifteen cars, which are very close to each other, and which could touch each other at any time—that's nervousness. But you have to remain calm. And it really focuses you. There's nothing like a bit of nerves to get the old adrenaline going. And that's why I said it's positive, as long as you're the sort of person that can focus and channel that energy, 'cause that's what it is: energy. I get the feeling that stage fright is the same kind of nervousness channeled in a very bad way.

MB: So, you've never had to work on being nervous?

SP: No. If we get out there and start playing, and I feel a bit jumpy, I just tell myself, "C'mon, relax. It's just a gig. You can only play as well as you can play."

MB: Have you ever had the experience of not playing as well as you wanted to? Let's say to a regrettable degree. [SP laughs] Like, "Wow, it just wasn't as good as I wanted it to be last night."

SP: You know what? The thing that you come to realize is that if it's not recorded or videoed, or bootlegged somewhere, it's just a gig. And maybe a thousand, maybe seven thousand, maybe twenty thousand people saw it. You know what? You're not the center of the whole gig. You're just one part of a band. It didn't spoil the whole gig. Often, when you don't play so well, people come up to you and say, "That was really cool." And often, when you think you've played the best you possibly can, nobody says anything. So again, the view from where you sit is very different from what it is for people who sit outside.

But you get over it, because by the time you wake up the next day, you'll be en route to the next town. It's not being cynical about it. It's just thinking, "It's a gig. It's a tour. C'mon, get on with it. They loved it."

Also, don't take it out on the audience, just 'cause you're having a bad time. You go out, get over it, and entertain them. Know what I mean? Sometimes there's a little too much self-importance placed on one's own area, and not the big picture. That's not to say you shouldn't play as well as you can. But you gotta kind of balance that up a little bit. By the way, remember that there's a lot of other stuff going on. There are lots of other gigs in town going on. It's not the end of the world. [Both laugh]

Yeah, sometimes you have meltdowns and it's like, "Ooh, I hope nobody recorded that, 'cause that's a real giveaway." Sometimes you just spaz out. For a split second you cannot play the drums. The same with guitarists. Sometimes they totally spaz their tunings, and they're like a quarter-tone out. I've heard some great players and they just went, "Whoa, I just could not hit it." Singers, I've heard them sing totally out, sometimes a semi-tone out, for a whole line. Playing night after night with all the ridiculous differences of sound, shit happens.

What you've also got to remind yourself is how fast it's history: "Move on, don't dwell on it." It's the same with racing. If you miss a gear and two people overtake you, you can't spend the rest of your race thinking about it. Move on, because it'll mess you up for the next corner. I guess that's something that racing actually taught me about playing music.

MB: Do you have any advice for performers about nerves?

SP: The classic example is you go out and play the first song, and it's really fast and really stiff. The important thing to do is concentrate on the tempo of the opening song—getting the tempo right. You know what? The last set list that we've been playing, I start the show. I go out and I play a tom tom groove. And it's not the simplest of grooves. The only time the bass drum plays is the second sixteenth note of the first two gong drum hits. So it ain't on one and three [the normal beats that a bass drum plays in most styles of popular music].

Before I go out, I have a little metronome, which my drum tech holds, and I just zone into that tempo. When I walk out onstage and step up onto the drum riser anything thing could happen, so I keep that tempo in my head, sit down, pick up the sticks, and I am ready to start the song at the correct tempo.

That's the most important thing—to concentrate on the time and make the band sound comfortable. Make the first song sound like it's the sixth song of the set. A lot of young bands throw away that first song because everybody's pumped up. Everybody's nervous. They've got a lot of energy, they haven't settled in, and that first song suffers. You really spend that first song just kind of checking it out. But you can't really do that. You've got to nail the groove and the time first, 'cause if you're there, the rest of the band will know, "Okay, that's where it is." And they can settle down, too. That's very important.

Mark Pitta

Mark Pitta is a national headliner coming from the effervescent San Francisco comedy scene of the 1980s. He has appeared on "The Tonight Show" with Johnny Carson and Jay Leno, hosted "Totally Hidden Video" for the FOX network and "Friday Night Videos" for NBC, made guest appearances on "Mad About You," "Third Rock from the Sun," Comedy Central's "Premium Blend," "The A-List," "Dr. Katz," and "Make Me Laugh." A favorite on the comedy club, college and corporate circuit, Mark has opened for Chris Issak, Celine Dion, Vanessa Williams, Paul Anka, Kenny Rogers, Olivia Newton-John, Smokey Robinson, Big Bad Voodoo Daddy, and Rick Springfield. He has performed as master of ceremonies five times for the prestigious Elan Awards, and has enlivened Anthony Robbin's financial seminars. Every Tuesday in Mill Valley, California he runs a comedy showcase at the 142 Throckmorton Theatre, giving new comics a chance to develop as seasoned veterans drop in.

MB: Do you remember the first time you were nervous on stage?

MP: It was at the Punchline [in San Francisco], the place was packed and I was on third. It was only my second time on stage. I remember, during this one joke, I was pointing, my arm was outstretched, and I noticed that my hand was shaking slightly. Had I not seen my hand shake I think my memory would have been that I wasn't nervous at all. Apparently I was.

MB: Do you think there was anything you were telling yourself that was causing your hand to shake?

MP: Maybe it was the excitement and anticipation. The time before there were only twelve people in the audience. You almost have to be blasé about it, the fact that there's a full house, because the audience can sense if you're nervous. If that happens, it can become uncomfortable for you.

I think the audience already gives you points for going up there, because they know they couldn't do it. They're not thinking, "I wonder if this guy is nervous." They're just thinking, "This guy goes on stage and tells jokes." You have a little bit of a gap there between being legitimately nervous and showing that you're nervous.

Whether you're in front of a thousand people, like at Comedy Day, twelve people at a club, or millions of people on "The Tonight Show," you almost have to treat it like it's no big deal.

MB: As you continued performing, how did the pressure change?

MP: Each night is a different experience, so it's hard to say. When I was auditioning for parts in sitcoms, that's what made me nervous. It was getting the job that made me nervous.

MB: What do you think you were telling yourself that contributed to making you nervous about that?

MP: I had a manager who was horrible. She would put pressure on me by saying, "It would be really great if you got this." Well thanks. Duh!

And the other thing that adds pressure: You're in a room or a hallway with people that you admire, or people you know are funnier than you—or they're at least your equal—and you can't help but think that they're going to get the part you're all auditioning for, because they're funny.

The reputation of the person you're auditioning for comes into it, too. There was this one audition where I knew that the person I was auditioning for was a tough casting director. There she was, sitting behind a desk as I read my lines. After my last line she said, "Keep in touch." And I thought, "How rude. 'Keep in touch'? She's dismissing me with that?" I walked out the door—just nodded and walked out the door. I went to my next audition, which was an improv audition, so I didn't have to prepare, and I took out my script from the previous audition. I thought, "Where did I make a mistake?" I looked, and my final cue was: "Keep in touch"—that was HER line! She was just cuing me. I wonder what she thought of me leaving the audition so abruptly.

MB: What were you telling yourself about her that made you so nervous that you left rather than respond to the line?

MP: It was the fear of rejection. And walking into a room where her reputation said that she was going to reject me.

MB: And if she did reject you, how would you have felt about that?

MP: I would have said, "Yeah, she's tough. I hate her." The key, always, after an audition, is never to think about it again. If you get a call to go back, that's great. If not, chalk it up.

MP: What role does your thinking—what you're telling yourself—play in your nervousness or composure when you're performing?

MP: That probably pays the biggest role, because if you give yourself too much time to think about something, you'll come up with reasons why you're going to fail. That used to happen a lot. Like, "I'm on 'The Tonight Show,' I'm going to forget all my jokes."

MB: How often were you on "The Tonight Show"?

MP: I did it once with Johnny Carson. Then when I did it with Jay Leno, it was less nerve wracking, because I know Jay Leno, and I don't look up to Jay Leno like I did with Johnny Carson, growing up watching Carson.

Before the Johnny Carson "Tonight Show" taping, I actually prepared my set, and I went to "The Tonight Show" the day before [I was to appear], and after that show I said, "Can I stand where I'm going to stand tomorrow night?" And they let me, while the band was wrapping up their instruments and putting them away. And I was mumbling to myself my whole act. Then I saw some band member and I said, "Is this bothering you?" He said, "Nope; seen it before."

MB: Did going to "The Tonight Show" set the day before help diminish the strangeness?

MP: Yeah. Not to say it wasn't surreal when it happened, because it was.

MB: What could you tell yourself about an adverse environment that would make performing easier?

MP: You know how you put somebody on a pedestal? You have to demote these people in your mind. Like you could be performing for the president, but you'd think to yourself this guy is like any other person. Again, it's just pretending.

MB: Do you remember the worst case of stage fright you've ever had?

MP: Here's one: I got an audition for "Third Rock from the Sun." And I was the last person cast for this guest-starring role. So I get the part, in which, incidentally, I play a comedian. And I'm very excited. Then they say, "The table read is in about an hour. So you're going to read the script with the cast in an hour." That's how late this thing was cast.

So I'm sitting in a room, waiting for the cast for "Third Rock from the Sun" to come in. That was a little nerve wracking. John Lithgow walks in, Jane Curtin—all the people on that show come in. And I have to convince myself I'm one of them. I already passed the hard part, so I am one of them. And I had to look at these people: Jane Curtin—having grown up watching "Saturday Night Live"—John Lithgow. . . . And we open the script for the table read; and I'm the first.

What helps with the nerves is when you get your first laugh. So I look for spots to loosen everybody up. The producer says, "All right, ladies and gentlemen, we finally cast our comedian for the show; the character for the show is Joe, and it's Mark Pitta." Then they all applaud and I just pretend to take a very theatrical bow. It's what I do to make any nerve-wracking situation less nerve wracking.

MB: What do you tell yourself to get yourself a little more energized?

MP: What do I tell myself? Well, it's pretty simple. If I'm telling the same jokes I've always told, and I know I'm going to get laughs in the proper places, I always put new jokes throughout my act so I look forward to those jokes. Yeah, I'm opening the same way, but the twentieth joke is going to be the new joke. So I'm looking forward to the new stuff as I'm doing it. That's what motivates me.

MB: And it motivates you because it's unknown?

MP: Yeah, because the whole thing about comedians is getting the laugh. But if you do this joke and you've written it and rewritten it and now it gets a laugh every time, you're done. You can put that one to bed. It's the new joke that you're excited about.

MB: Can you think of any instance where somebody went down in flames and it was primarily due to their nerves?

MP: Yeah, without naming names, there was a female comedian I was giving stage time to (at the theatre I run on Tuesdays in Mill Valley) and she was supposed to do ten minutes, and I said, "Okay, I'll give you the light at eight minutes." And she was doing so badly that in six minutes she just said goodnight.

MB: Is there anything you think she was doing that contributed to her not doing well?

MP: Yeah: thinking that what she was saying was funny. She literally didn't have jokes. And when she ended a sentence, you were going, "That can't be the joke. That's the set-up to a joke, but it's not a joke." And there is nothing worse than silence if you're a comedian.

You can make one joke and say, "Oh, that sucked." And they laugh at that. But you can only use that once. And then when you get, like, five jokes in and you're not getting laughs and you're just talking, there's nothing worse than that. Then the nerves turn into . . . sweat. You're just a puddle of sweat at that point.

MB: I remember once I was working with a guy who asked me, "Who's the comedian who's able to bomb better than anybody and come out smelling like a rose?" I said, "Johnny Carson," and he said, "Exactly." Do you remember his monologues when they would just not work? The guy was able to come through with no problem at all. Can you speculate on how he was able to do that?

MP: Survival. There's a survival instinct where you think, "If I don't acknowledge this bad joke, I'm going to look worse off."

I remember Carson one time doing the desk humor. And he just burned the script right there at the desk. When a joke didn't work, he would make fun of it. I remember one time he pulled the boom mike down and said, "Is this on? Is this on? K-mart shoppers, we have a special on aisle nine."

MB: Is there any other advice you have for performers in dealing with stage fright? Anything you haven't said, yet?

MP: Well, nerves can also be construed as excitement. You can be excited about something, and the excitement is causing the same physiological feeling in your body that nerves would.

MB: Is there anything else about stage fright?

MP: I remember now: The last time I was really nervous nervous was when I was interviewing somebody I really admired for the TV show "Mornings on Two" that I hosted for five years. When I walked into the room with someone who had a reputation, I got a little nervous. I'd think, "Oh great, I'm going to talk to one of my heroes and they're going to be an asshole. And I'm going to hate them now."

Kevin Rooney

An Emmy Award-winning television writer, Kevin was also a stand-up comedian, appearing five times on "The Tonight Show with Johnny Carson." Kevin has written for many variety shows, including Dennis Miller's syndicated and HBO shows and "Politically Incorrect with Bill Maher." He co-wrote and guest-starred in Jay Leno's Showtime special, "Jay Leno and The American Dream." Kevin also wrote for a number of sitcoms, including three seasons as co-executive producer on "My Wife And Kids," starring Damon Wayans. Kevin lives in Los Angeles, California and Nice, France with his wife, the actress and author Carole Raphaelle Davis, and their three rescued dogs, Lamby, Finley and Jinky.

MB: Can you tell me about the first time you were anxious or nervous when you were on stage?

KR: I'm almost always anxious and nervous when I go on stage because you don't know exactly what the animal is that you're facing; you can't really tell what the crowd's going to be like. You can get a sense of them, but you really can't tell what you're dealing with until you're talking to them. So you've got to be on your toes. I guess it's like jumping out of a plane; you check all the equipment and the weather, but until the chute opens . . .

MB: So the first time you experienced anxiousness or nervousness on stage, what were the circumstances then?

KR: When I did "The Tonight Show" for the first time, I was very aware of being anxious because I was sitting around for an hour waiting to do a five-minute set. A five-minute set on national television makes for a very short, intense period of time.

MB: How did you feel?

KR: Very zoned out. You're not paying attention to a lot of things around you, and you get focused on what you're doing. You cling to specific stuff, like, "Are my shoes tied? Is my zipper up?"

MB: Could you be a little more specific about what your feelings were? Were you nervous? Were you calm? Somewhere in between?

KR: I was a little nervous. But it's not like you're going to be shot. It wasn't like I was walking past a snake pit.

MB: Why do you think you weren't nervous in the same way you would be if you were walking over a snake pit?

KR: Well, because it wasn't a life-or-death situation. I wanted it to go well and I wanted to get laughs. But there was nothing much I could do about it. I just had to keep going forward, have faith in the material.

MB: So, what were you telling yourself the first time you went on "The Tonight Show"?

KR: There's a point where you just say to yourself: "I've tried the jokes, I know the jokes work. Take a breath. Hit your mark. And just enjoy yourself as best you can." Still, it was a really big moment in my life and I was anxious. Then I saw this stagehand just standing there with his hand on the curtain waiting for a signal from the stage manager to pull it back and let me out. Like a horse out of a chute. I looked at him, and I thought, "This guy's done this thousands of times for thousands of comics—he couldn't care less. Who knows how many comics have gone out there [through that curtain]? None of them blew up or got killed."

Walking out onto the stage that night was a huge adrenaline rush. I did my material and it worked. As I started to get laughs, I started to feel confident. See, that's really where the nervousness comes from—the nagging doubt that maybe on this night, with this audience, it won't be the way you want it to be. It's the same way when you get married. You'd like it to be great. But you have no idea if it will be great or a nightmare.

MB: [Laughs] You're the first guy who's equated performing to getting married.

KR: It's a big commitment. You step on stage, face the audience and say to yourself, "Oh my God!" And you hope for the best.

MB: Could you elaborate on what's going on in your mind as you're getting more relaxed, when you've broken the ice and things are flowing?

KR: Just relief. I think getting laughs in that situation probably felt like landing on the beach on D-Day and finding out the Germans were gone.

MB: How about audience rejection? How bad can it feel?

KR: Well, you can obsess on rejection for weeks. You start to think you shouldn't be out in public.

Once I was on a cruise ship, going from New York to London, where the majority of the audience didn't like what I did. The average audience member was seventy-five years old and spoke English as a second language. I did a fairly political act, and they didn't like it. I was tired, they were nearly dead, the show was late, and it was terrible. So for the rest of the cruise, five or six days, I didn't want to come out of the cabin, 'cause the minute I did I'd overhear people saying: "What was that comedian's name? I never want to see him again. What he said about Dan Quayle was disgusting!" I had a small group of people on the ship who liked what I did, and they would tell me in private, like in the movie theater, they'd whisper in my ear in the dark, "I liked what you did." But nobody wanted to be associated with me in public.

MB: So how did you feel under those circumstances?

KR: Terrible! It felt like the entire ship hated me. And that was just a bad show on a boat. If you bomb in front of a national TV audience, you think the whole country hates you.

MB: So that's your biggest fear: "The whole country hates me"?

KR: Right. You're hated. You're a laughing stock. It's like puking on the bus on the first day of school. You gotta go to another school.

MB: But you did say that it's not like being over a snake pit.

KR: You have to tell yourself that. "Material things don't matter"—that's what you hear after somebody's house burned down. Not before.

MB: If you're telling yourself, "Hey, it doesn't matter," you're almost going to the extreme of saying, "It isn't important," when it is important.

KR: In fact, your doing "The Tonight Show" is not that important to other people. If you do well, it's a great thing for you. But if you don't do that well, then you just didn't do that well. But you do want to do well, and that can make it seem more important than it is. Telling yourself it doesn't really matter is a lie you tell yourself to keep from freaking out.

MB: If you tell yourself it's not the end of the world, to me that's not a lie, that's the truth.

KR: It is the truth, sure, but it is also true that you want it to matter a lot. You want everybody to recognize that you're a comedic genius, and it'll be the start of something big for you, a life changing event. And anything that has the power to change your life seems also to have the power to end it.

MB: What was going through your mind the first time you really bombed?

KR: I think I did what every comedian instinctively does, which is lay as much of the blame as possible on the audience. If I bomb, I'm going to call them stupid. I'm going to say they were drunk and mean spirited, they were put in a bad mood by the performers in front of me, that they were poisoned, that they were tired . . . Anything to keep from saying to myself, "Well, you're just not very funny."

MB: Because that's the biggest fear, right?

KR: For a comedian? Who *are* you if you're not funny? If I had bombed the first night I did stand-up, I probably never would have done it again, because at that point I thought the audience was a monolith. I would have thought, "Well, if these people don't like it, why would anybody else?" But then as you perform more, you realize the same audience will be different at different times of the week and different times of the evening. And beyond that, the audience isn't a monolith. There are groups of people who won't like you—they just won't. And you know what? That's fine, 'cause I don't like them. But you try not to take it personally.

MB: And by "taking it personally," you mean?

KR: That their assessment of you as unfunny is actually correct. That, no, you're not funny. The truth is that you're just not funny to them. And that's okay.

MB: Have you ever left the stage?

KR: I have. I was in a situation in Pleasant Hill [a wealthy, conservative sub-urb in Contra Costa County, to the east of San Francisco], with just a nasty group of people, who were making comments like, "Hey, you a Jew?" I said, "Well, what if I was?" And they said, "We'd throw you in an oven. Heh, heh." And I said, "You're just a nasty group. They're paying me to be up here for forty-five minutes, but I'm not saying anything else." I sat down on the stage and just stared at them for twenty minutes. Then they said, "No, come on back." And I said, "You don't have to apologize to me. I don't like you. You don't like me." "No, come on," they said, "We're sorry."

So I took the mic again and a woman said, "Show us your dick." And I snapped. I said, "What's wrong with you people? You think I got on 'The Tonight Show' by showing Carson my dick? Look at you. You're married, don't you have a dick of your own around the house you can look at? I'm done talking to you people. You can get out." I threw them out. The whole audience. Actually kicked them out of the room. The woman said, "We paid to get in!" I wadded up a twenty and bounced it off her forehead, "There's your money. Put it toward your G.E.D." It was a horrible, angry night, but I didn't care much, because I bombed in front of a group of people I didn't like.

MB: If you bomb in front of a group of people you respect, how do you feel then?

KR: I feel terrible about it. I ask myself, "What did I do? Did I have a few drinks before the show? Was I just not prepared? Was I too tired? Didn't I do it right? Did I offend them? How can I avoid this in the future?" It's a tough thing, bombing. You feel like you've let people down.

Eventually I got out of stand-up. I didn't want to go around the country annoying people anymore. I was doing what I thought was a good grade of politically aware stand-up, but I felt the audiences had gotten just generally less interested in that, and they were annoyed with my politics. So, when I got an opportunity to do something else, I did it.

MB: You said you failed at times. What were your thoughts when you had to deal with that?

KR: The worst way I dealt with it was self-pity, thinking, "I'm not funny. I should get out of this business. I should be a hermit."

But usually I had another gig coming up, and so I'd say, "Well, I'll go do this last gig, and I'll save the money. And then I'll get out of the business, 'cause I'm terrible." But then I'd go do that gig and it would turn out to be, "Hey, that was fun. That was great. That's why I do stand-up." Once you've gone through that a couple of times, you realize there's always another audience. After bombing, you just have to get to that next audience.

MB: Last question: Do you have any other advice on stage fright?

KR: Well, stage fright is an illusion. It's made up. It is in your head. Your sense of where you are, what you want out of that crowd, how you're going to get it—it's all in your head. You should think of a performance just as something that you do, like in the Zen notion: before success, chop wood, carry water; after success, chop wood, carry water.

MB: Something you do, as opposed to?

KR: Something you want. Most of the nervousness comes from your wanting something. The reason men get nervous when they meet pretty girls is because they want to fuck them. And that's really all it is. If you could just meet someone, without expectations, you could forget about the fabulous body and you wouldn't be nervous. The same with stage fright. When people start to shake and their palms get sweaty, it's because they want something and they are afraid they won't get it. That's what stage fright is: the fear you won't get what you want, and that not getting it will ruin your life.

MB: What do you think these people are telling themselves?

KR: Well, they're telling themselves, "I need this girl to like me, I need this audience to like me so that I can be successful and get what I want."

But the only way you can guarantee that you get what you want out of that moment, really, is to want what you get. And that means you just have to be who you are. You have to be comfortable with yourself. Do the work. Prepare. And then relax and just trust the moment.

MB: What are the thoughts that help you relax?

KR: One thing I try to remember is that the audience wants to like you. No matter who they are, they want to like you. They might not; it depends on who they are and who you are and what you have to say to them. But they want to like you. So, relax. It's amazing how much funnier things are if the audience knows the performer is relaxed and confident. The audience gets nervous if you're nervous. They can feel it. They think, "Oh my God, this person really needs us to laugh." And that's the hardest time for them to laugh, because they are worried about you instead of enjoying themselves.

When you go on stage, stop thinking about yourself and what you want. It is hard to do, maybe even counterintuitive, but it is the key to success. Paradoxically, and this is probably true for most endeavors in life, you are never more likely to fail than when all you are thinking about is succeeding.

Bob Sarlatte

Bob Sarlatte is a San Francisco-based, nationally known commercial actor, radio and television personality, comedian and speaker. His extensive credits include announcer, writer and regular comedy contributor on the first "David Letterman Show" for NBC in 1980, over twenty appearances on the Late Night version of that program, with guest spots on "The Late Show" as well. He has been the co-host and features reported on the Bay Area's "AM San Francisco," national humor reporter for "Entertainment Tonight," and has done comedy/commentary for the Fox Sports Network. He has done voice-over work in over 5000 radio and television commercials and cartoons, been a guest on NBC's "Night Court," ABC's "Match Game," co-hosted PBS's "Comedy Tonight," as well as acted in *Star Trek IV*, *So I Married an Ax Murderer*, *EDTV* and *Flubber*. Careerwise, he currently remains as active as possible for one individual human being.

MB: Can you tell me about the first time you were nervous performing?

BS: When I first started doing stand-up, I wasn't that nervous initially . . . I look at performing in a methodical way. There usually are two types of comics: the people who are great working the room and the people who write good stuff. But you gotta be able to do both. I had a bunch of stuff initially, so I just kind of wanted to get the words out of my mouth. To me, that's sort of it. If you're scripted, only you know the script and you're producing your own show, so that can cut the nervousness a little bit. As opposed to approaching it like, "Oh, I'll just try doing this." And if you just do that you're working without a net, and that's the time when your nervousness is just out there. Because if you don't know where you're going, that's what will really freak you out. But then the art of stand-up, as you know, is the art of over-learning material so it looks second nature.

MB: So when you're feeling nervous, what are your thoughts?

BS: Well, it makes me nervous talking about it. [Laughs] You almost have this feeling of impending doom, like, "You know what? I'm dead!"

I did Letterman in the '80s, and I was doing a joke about Duran Duran. The joke was, "Hey, I see Duran Duran just broke up. That just goes to show you can't misplace an eyebrow pencil and not expect repercussions." That's the joke. So when I got on stage, here's what I did. I went, "Hey, I see Duran Duran just broke up. That just goes to show you can't misplace an eyebrow pencil." And I forgot the rest of it. And I went to myself, "YEOW! What's the next [part of the joke]? Now I'm ruined."

So I forgot the [end of the] line: "and not expect repercussions." I couldn't remember that. But, as you well know, jokes on television can be more glib and smarter than jokes in a club. In a club that joke would not work, but that joke would work on TV. So I'm going, "Oh Man! I've never really done this joke like that before." But I'm smiling at the crowd and I end up getting applause like I thought I was going to at the end of the joke.

MB: Do you remember what was going on in your mind?

BS: I can tell you exactly. I was going, "I'm screwed! I'm finished." You know what it was like in my mind? I was thinking like a spiral notebook that a reporter has, you know?—with the pages being flipped. I was Rolodexing in my head, going, "What's the next joke in the set?" Because I'm trying to remember the end of the joke, and I can't remember the real joke. "What's the next damn joke?"

MB: So if you're telling yourself, "I'm screwed," how do you deal with that?

BS: Well, you're smiling at the crowd and going, "I hope . . ." and it looked like I was frozen; I'm telling you, it seemed like an hour. I was going, "Oh Boy! I'm sunk. This is live." Because Letterman goes live to tape; they don't screw around with anything. So I kind of shook it off and I got a little applause, so it gave me time to gather my thoughts for five or ten seconds to get to the next part of the set.

MB: How did you gather your thoughts rather than continue to panic?

BS: There were two things: I was thinking in my mind's eye, going down the page: "What's the next joke?" And my face was trying to exude, "Hey, that's the end of the joke, c'mon!" I was trying to bluff my way through the ending that I didn't remember.

And that's what I did. It was kind of like being in control of two things at once—being in control of what I outwardly looked like, and what was going through my mind. That was pretty harrowing. I kept thinking, "Oh, I don't want to watch this!" But I had to. It was like pressing a bruise. And then when I watched it on TV, later in the hotel room, it looked pretty seamless.

MB: You mentioned giving up on the idea of being Mr. Perfect.

BS: Yeah. You know, let your real personality show through. Dave has that luxury because he's on for an hour. He can let his own personality show through very easily.

That's one of the things that I talk about now. I try to demystify show business and say it's different than other businesses, but there are a lot of similarities. The building blocks and the preparation—having the weapons in the arsenal—are very similar to a lot of other things.

MB: Do you get nervous now?

BS: Sure. In fact, you know what? I keep digressing, but it's the same point: I call it "the thrill of being nervous."

MB: And by "thrill," you mean it's a real rush, or exhilarating?

BS: Well, it's exhilarating in the prep because you hope the fruition will be that you're going to do well. But even that . . . In what other profession can you still have the thrill of being nervous? [Laughs] And I think that thrill adds to people's ability to overcome things.

MB: Were more nervous in the beginning when you started stand-up, and then you became less nervous? If so, how did that happen?

BS: I think, overall, my nervousness probably isn't that much different except that I now have these sort of building blocks, this material that I know works. That's really the difference. The difference is I can get up there on stage now and screw around and get away with it in the end. Certain elements never change. For example, I'm getting ready to do Letterman again; the preparation to do Letterman never gets easier. And that's because of two things: One is the nervousness; the other is the question, "Do I have enough areas of conversation that I can talk about?"

MB: How do you feel about going on Letterman again?

BS: It's kind of a cumulative feeling that never goes away. For example, I'm going to New York to do the Letterman show. So the whole preparation of going and flying and being there and coming home—that's all part of it. And for seven minutes, you're investing a couple of weeks. So I think it's a cumulative effect. I think the nervousness gets flattened out more through preparation than just by virtue of having a lot of experience.

Here's another interesting point that no one talks about, really. And this is more of a youth thing, like "the problem with these kids today . . ." But it's true. No one has much of the fear of failure any more. And I think that's a huge, huge deal. I teach speech at a Catholic grammar school, and the best kids have the fear of failure. But most of them don't have it anymore. And I think it's a very big point: fear of not doing well; fear of not looking good. And it isn't just in the performance situation—it's anything.

It's like, "Hey, Mick, you know you didn't do your homework. Stand up in front of the class and tell everybody what a loser you are." Because you deserve it because you didn't do the work. But now, people don't care about that. They'll just say, "Hey, I didn't do it." Well, you know what? Don't you have any pride? I think the fear of not doing well, the fear of not looking good, is a very big thing.

MB: So the kids have no fear of failure because they're not concerned about the results?

BS: Well, they're not so concerned about what's happening next. I think the good people do. A guy like Chris Rock cares if he doesn't do well. Obviously, people who have made it care. But I'm talking about people on the way up. I mean, I see guys working in clubs now who may have nice presence but they've got no jokes, and they don't seem to give a damn. But it's not that they don't give a damn; it's just that the prep, the work ethic isn't there—the idea of knowing more of what you're going to say than what you're not going to say. Don't you see that a little bit yourself?

MB: Well, I remember Erin O'Connor in, like 1987 . . . She went and did a set at the Improv—I think it was in Santa Monica, which was a really great club. But she came back saying, "I can't believe these people are getting on stage. They get on stage and they have nothing prepared. They think this stuff is just going to fall down like manna from heaven or something."

BS: That's right. Then again, it sounds like an old school versus new school sort of thing. But I remember that when I was starting up, everybody had written things.

MB: Yeah. Even the worst guys had five minutes prepared and ready to go.

BS: That's right. I think a lot of people work without prep because of the culture. If you look at stuff on TV, it's like all of it's based on that now. All the reality stuff, it's based on people just living their lives, which to me isn't good enough.

MB: What role does your thinking—what you're telling yourself—play in your nervousness?

BS: You know, I don't get that introspective about it. I'll know when it's right. I can get nervous about an event. But I'm generally not nervous from the standpoint of having the hay in the barn and being ready to go.

MB: What's the worst case of stage fright or nervousness you've seen in somebody else?

BS: Those are things that you really try not to remember. I can't really think of anybody who choked, because you're rooting for anybody you're watching.

MB: Where do you think nervousness in others comes from?

BS: Well, I think in general that nervousness can come in any situation where you're not prepared. Most nervousness—I would say eighty percent — can be dissipated by preparation.

MB: Going back to what we were talking about earlier, what's with the Duran Duran joke? You ended up getting a laugh out of it. You said it seemed seamless when you played it back. What was it you did that somebody else might not have done? Because we know people do go down in flames on national television; it does happen.

BS: Again, it's over-learning something so much that it's second nature to you. Again, here's an athletic allusion. Everybody says, Geez, Michael Jordan's so great." But why did he average eighteen points in college and thirty in the pros? He got better.

The point I'm making is that you should do things so often that they're second nature. So, I think when I forgot the last part of the Duran Duran joke, I was hoping that it would come to me by just kind of looking [at the audience] in a bluffing manner—"Hey everybody, this is where you're supposed to laugh."

MB: Did anything keep you from panicking?

BS: I started to [panic]. It was like those old Dristan ads where the lightning bolts are coming. "Bam/Yeow!" It was like getting hit by lightning: "Bam/Yeow!" [Laughs] Boy, this is bringing back some memories here, pal. [Laughs again]

MB: I've had people tell me they don't get nervous at all. Do you buy that?

BS: That's pure bunk. If you talk to most athletes or most performers, if they say they don't get a little nervous before they're going on, then they're blowing hot air.

Did you read about this? This is pretty interesting. I never did "The Tonight Show," but I worked for Letterman at an NBC affiliates' convention one time about twenty-four years ago, and Johnny Carson was hosting; he was behind the stage. And he did that thing they mentioned in his obituaries: he would always take short jumps in the air to get himself jacked up to go on stage. So he was nervous. And that's how you dissipate nervousness. You have a ritual.

MB: Is there any other advice you'd have for performers dealing with stage fright?

BS: I would say that the preparation and the writing will dissipate the problem of nervousness. Not totally. But I think you've got to up your odds by being well rehearsed.

For example, everybody knows this: If you've got a good act and all of a sudden you're in the crowd doing something, sometimes an ad lib that you come up with will find its way into your act. It doesn't happen that often, but when it does, being prepared just means that you're ready to deal with it. You can go off book into the crowd and come back.

So it's all those building blocks. It's the same as coaching: If you have your starting five, and you have two-and-a-half kids that are good, just make sure the other two and a half don't hurt you. [Laughs] There's a theory that the [side that makes the] least mistakes wins.

Mark Schiff

Mark Schiff has been a comic for 30 years. He has been on "The Tonight Show" and "The David Letterman Show." Mark wrote a book called *I Killed,* published by Random House. He was a writer on many TV shows and is also a playwright. His play "The Comic" was performed before sell-out crowds and was optioned by HBO to be a film.

MB: I remember your telling me about your first "Tonight Show" appearance. You said you were so nervous that the room spun around for the whole seven minutes you were on. But you rehearsed your set a hundred times over the course of a month, so even though the room was spinning around the entire time, you were still able to do it.

MS: Right. Well, what I said was that I rehearsed it so much that if I'd had a stroke out there, I would still have kept talking until the set was finished. Oh yeah, I rehearsed it for months. Jimmy Brogan ["The Tonight Show" writer and talent coordinator] helped me. We went from club to club to club for months. And I was in a real state of panic the day of the show.

MB: It's neat that Jimmy helped you, giving you tips on your set.

MS: He's very good with that, helping out the comedians.

MB: Under what circumstances did you first start performing?

MS: I started auditioning at the small clubs—The Improv, a place called Al and Dick's Steak House in New York. I would just show up and do it.

Let me step back a second. . . . When I was eighteen years old, I did my first stand-up performance. And after that I had such stage fright that I didn't get up on stage for five more years. I went to acting school for the next five years, but I didn't perform stand-up, because I was too shell shocked.

MB: What would you attribute your "shell shock" to?

MS: Well, of course it goes back to childhood trauma.

MB: Was there anything that was going on in your head that was contributing to the nervousness?

MS: You mean up on stage?

MB: Or after the whole thing took place. You didn't perform for five years. Was there anything you were telling yourself about it that made it difficult to perform?

MS: Yeah, I was just too scared, I was too frightened, I was just afraid I was going to fail.

MB: And what were you telling yourself about failing?

MS: Well, it's the fear of humiliation. The fear of being humiliated kept me from getting back up on stage.

MB: And what changed that allowed you to get back up on stage?

MS: As silly as this sounds, I didn't want to have a regular job—ever. I was more afraid of working in an office than I was of going back up on stage.

Going on stage presented me with a tremendous amount of fear of humiliation. Getting a regular job presented me with the fear of suicide. So I would kill myself if I had to get a regular job, but I would only be humiliated in front of the entire world if I went up on stage.

[MB laughs]

It's true. I had regular jobs when I was eighteen or nineteen. They made me suicidal.

MB: So as you continued to perform, how did your nervousness or stage fright change?

MS: For the first five years of performing, I had stage fright probably every night. It was horrible. Absolutely horrible.

MB: What was going on in your mind?

MS: Well, I just didn't feel worthy enough to stand up in front of all these people. I would have choking attacks on stage, where I couldn't swallow. I would keep water on stage—I still do to this day, in case I start choking—and a couple of times I almost passed out.

MB: So for five years, you had stage fright every night?

MS: I would stand in the back of the room. My heart would be like a punching bag, beating away in my chest. And I would say to myself, "This is it. I'm never doing this again after tonight."

MB: Mark, this is just great—it's going to be so helpful for people to read.

MS: I told you this was my favorite subject.

MB: So you still carry water on stage? Do you still get nervous now?

MS: Yes. I'm nervous thirty percent of the time, at least. Sometimes I still choke.

MB: [Laughs] Sorry to laugh about this.

MS: No, no. You can laugh all you want. I'm completely open to it.

MB: How do you deal with the nervousness now?

MS: There's nothing I can tell myself that makes it better. And I've had seventeen years of therapy. Nothing works.

You know, the one thing that does work is . . . I say a prayer. And I realize that I have a talent, that was god given to me. And I say, "This is the deal. 'God, let me just entertain these people and make it a better day for them. Thank you for this talent.'" And then I go and do it.

So what I do is take the focus off of me. I'm making it a bigger issue than some little stupid Jewish guy telling some jokes. I make it into a service event. You know what I'm saying?

MB: Yeah. You shift your focus, and you're no longer self-absorbed.

MS: Yeah. I'm not self-obsessed. And it's not about me. It's a bigger issue. I say to myself, "You know, there are people out there who may have lost people, who are sick, who are depressed. And they need to laugh tonight. And I'm going to bring them some happiness." That usually helps me get through the show.

MB: What was the worst case of stage fright you've ever had?

MS: Well, certainly the "Tonight Shows" where I started choking. I would take a sip of water before I would go out from behind the curtain, and I would hold it in my mouth until I hit the mark and had to start talking. Luckily, my jokes are so strong that when the people laughed I could use that time to recover. That was really frightening. A couple of times I wanted to bolt from the middle of the stage of "The Tonight Show."

MB: How did you manage not to do that?

MS: I just stood my ground. And then, if I get through the first two or three minutes, I'm usually okay from then on. I have to get through an incredible period of anxiety. But once I get through it, it's free sailing. It's almost like I need to do that to build my confidence. I start with no confidence each time and I have to rebuild it every time I step out on stage.

MB: And so your "Tonight Show" sets were your most anxiety-ridden performances?

MS: Well, I was working with Diana Ross at Caesar's Palace once, and I went completely numb. My brain went dead. I got frozen, and I started hyperventilating. There were about eight hundred people there. And I almost bolted off stage.

MB: How did you keep from doing that?

MS: I had brought water there, and I just kept drinking. The problem, when I get really anxiety ridden, is that my hands start shaking. So when I pick up the water, I look like I have Parkinson's disease—my hand is shaking all over the place. It's really disgusting.

MB: [Laughs] You said—when you were doing "The Tonight Show" and you were really nervous—you stood your ground. Could you elaborate on that?

MS: I refuse to let this thing beat me. That's really it. I accept that I have stage fright. It's a very self-destructive tendency that I have. And I need, periodically, to get myself in a position where I can blow everything up.

MB: What do you mean by "blow everything up"?

MS: Take the microphone, throw it down on the floor, and walk off "The Tonight Show" stage. You chuck your entire career out the window.

MB: But obviously you haven't thrown down the microphone and walked off.

MS: Because there's a part of me that doesn't believe that "I'm worthless. I'm garbage. I don't belong here."

MB: So the part of you that doesn't believe you're worthless and you don't belong—could you elaborate on that?

MS: It's the part of me that believes in the talent, and the ability, and the truth.

MB: And by "truth," you mean?

MS: Well, there are two things: There's the truth and there's the lie. Sometimes the lie manifests itself so it looks like the truth: "What are you doing this for? Richard Pryor, Seinfeld, those guys are funnier than you'll ever be." And you start believing it. And from there, the next step is "Why do this at all?" That's the lie.

MB: So elaborate on the truth that counters that.

MS: Well, the truth is that I have talent, that I'm a funny guy. I may not be the greatest comedian that ever walked the planet, but I do a good job, and if I do the work, and I'm prepared, I will have a very good show. That's true.

MB: I remember the week we worked in Sacramento, every night it was fun to watch you.

MS: I bat ninety-five percent. I'm very good at it, and I do a great job. But what goes on inside my head, people can't believe.

MB: [Laughs] But that's what's so useful, because so many people think that because they have stage fright they can't perform. And that's not true in the least bit.

MS: Right.

MB: So when do you get nervous and when don't you get nervous now?

MS: You never know when it's gonna hit you. You never know. I just came off four shows with Seinfeld. I opened for him in Missouri and in San Diego. I didn't have any anxiety. Five weeks ago, I opened for him and I couldn't even breathe on stage for ten minutes. I never know when it's going to hit me. I'm shocked when it doesn't hit me. And I'm shocked when it does hit me.

MB: When you're calm, what's going on in your mind?

MS: In my mind, I'm having a great time. I can't believe I'm enjoying this. The audience and I are in harmony. I don't even want to get off stage.

MB: What do you observe about stage fright in other people?

MS: I've talked to a couple of people about it. You know, I've followed a lot of people who I think have it and don't admit it. I'm a big hand-shaker, and before they go on stage I'll say, "Good luck" and shake their hand, and I can feel if it's like it was in a refrigerator for a half-hour.

MB: Just one more question. Do you have any specific advice for performers who experience stage fright?

MS: Yeah. The only thing I can tell them, which I've learned through my experience, is, first of all, stage fright won't kill you—which is what you don't know when you're experiencing it. You know what I mean? It really feels like death. There's a chill in the air, like you'd think you'd feel a few minutes before you died. Your feet are cold, your hands are cold, your teeth are chattering, your heart's beating—like right before they take you for major surgery. It's the same sort of feeling. But you just gotta keep doing it and rally against the feeling. Because the feeling is not a fact.

Feelings aren't fact. They change. I know, because I experience it. One night, I'll go on stage and I'm nervous; the next night I'm not. So the feelings come and go. It's like, "I love my life; I hate my life."

And I'd like to meet the man that overcomes stage fright permanently. I don't think it can done. I think you gotta learn to live with it your entire life, and deal with it—or else get some shit job where it's not going to bother you.

Ben Sidran

Famous for writing Steve Miller's hit "Space Cowboy," Ben Sidran is most recognized for hosting NPR's "Jazz Alive" (Peabody Award), and VH-1's "New Visions" series (Ace Award, best music series). He has recorded 25 solo albums, including "Concert for Garcia Lorca" (Grammy Nomination), and produced recordings for Van Morrison, Diana Ross, Mose Allison, and Jon Hendricks. He composed the soundtrack for *Hoop Dreams*, and scored the documentary *Vietnam: Long Time Coming* (Aspen Film Festival audience award and an Emmy). He is the author of three books: *Black Talk*, *Talking Jazz*, and *A Life in the Music*. While he holds a PhD, Ben generally avoids the academic life to perform and produce. Recent recordings include Nardis Music's release of Ben's own "Nick's Bump" (2003), while in 2004 Ben composed, with Leo Sidran, the score for the award winning documentary *All Deliberate Speed*. Ben's most recent release is "Bumpin' At The Sunside," a live recording from famed Paris club, The Sunside.

MB: How long have you been performing?

BS: I started when I was a kid. My first gigs were when I was fifteen years old. I played in a little dance band when I was in high school. And then I went to playing in bands for fraternities and parties. By the time I was seventeen or eighteen, I was playing clubs.

MB: Can you tell me about the first time you were anxious or nervous while performing?

BS: Well, it was probably the first time I sat down to perform in front of an audience. I probably had this feeling of anticipation. I never had a terrible problem with stage fright, but I always had a certain amount of anxiety going into new situations, and I've kind of trained myself over the years so that if I do feel anxiety, I go toward it as opposed to away from it.

Like, if I'm playing with some great musicians that I've never played with before in front of people that I'm nervous about, I tend to lack focus and I recognize that as an emotional signal that I'm doing something that I haven't done before in some way, and that I should pay attention.

MB: Could you elaborate more on what your specific thoughts are when that's happening?

BS: Well, that's changed over the years. At one point in the early seventies I wound up in Los Angeles and I was trying to make a career in recording studios. They wanted me to play like Floyd Kramer or the other piano players at the time who were cutting pop records. And I couldn't do that. I kind of felt like . . . There's this famous Gary Larson cartoon of an elephant sitting at a piano on stage and he's saying to himself, "What am I doing here? I'm a flute player!" I kind of felt like that: "What am I doing here? I can't believe I'm trying to fool these people." I felt like I was going to get found out.

And then gradually, as I found my way and I got better at being myself and I understood the reasons why you should never not be yourself, I just accepted my shortcomings for what they are and went into it saying, "Well, they hired me, they wanted me; I'll just give it what I've got."

MB: Can you elaborate on "accepting your shortcomings"?

BS: Yeah. I think everybody starts out wanting to be their heroes, whoever they are. And you can never be your hero. And even the greatest musicians I've met have at some point in their careers tried to do something that they couldn't do based on some music that they fell in love with when they were young.

I think the hardest gig I ever played was . . . it must have been fifteen years ago . . . I was on a double bill at the Blue Note in New York. I was playing opposite Horace Silver; and when I was thirteen years old Horace was my hero. That whole week I traded sets with him, and every time I sat down at the piano I would hear everything I had musically taken from him. And I was just flummoxed to play something that came only from me and that wasn't a bad reference to him. It was really mind boggling. When I say "shortcomings," what I mean is that we all start out trying to be our heroes and then gradually . . . I think a musician's style comes more from what he can't do than what he can do, in some ways.

MB: Like Miles Davis?

BS: Exactly. He didn't have the facility of Dizzy [Gillespie], so he reinvented the sound of the horn. Or Bill Evans—he felt he didn't have the single-line fluidity of Bud Powell, so he wound up being this great inside harmonic player.

MB: When you found yourself playing on the same stage as Horace Silver and found yourself flummoxed, how did you deal with it?

BS: Well, I guess I did what I do every time this happens, and that is I try to shed all the unnecessary gestures that I carry along as baggage and just isolate the through line of my emotion at the moment. I try to get in touch with how I feel and try to let that feeling be the wave upon which the events take place, as opposed to focusing on anything else, on all the unnecessary gestures.

MB: So if you're feeling anxious or a little nervous, how would you go with it rather than away from it?

BS: Just by accepting the fact that that's how I feel. "I feel nervous. That's how I feel." I tell myself, "Here I am, sitting in this place. All my best efforts have gotten me here today. I'm on this path; I've been doing this for decades, and this is how I feel."

You just give it your best shot. Feel what you feel. I think the real problem with [doing] that is my memory—I'm old enough now that with any situation I go into, there's probably some reference to a situation I've been in before. So I'm not totally at sea anymore.

After a while, I accepted myself for who I am and just went with it. I think it comes with age: You realize you have what you have, you've worked really, really hard to secure it, you've created what you've created, and that's what you've got. You can't worry about what you don't have.

So if I find myself in a situation where I'm nervous, or I'm out of my element in some way, that's what I do. For example, if I'm in a situation where the musicians around me are playing something beyond what I feel comfortable playing, I just try to find some little thing in the midst of it that's me. I just try to go back to what I've got.

MB: When you get nervous now, what do you tell yourself?

BS: The things that used to make me nervous were mostly related to public acceptance. And I don't think that makes me nervous any more. But I'm still nervous sometimes dealing with acceptance from people who are my peers as opposed to the general public. I guess that means I would be nervous going up to sit in, maybe, and if they called a song I didn't know. How do you deal with that? What do I say to myself? Well, I'm just crazy enough now that when I get in a situation like that . . . call any tune in any key, and I'll do what I can. I will sit up there and play something I patently don't know, and just try to find three notes.

At this point, I'm sixty-one years old, and I have absolutely nothing to lose. So when I'm up there, what do I tell myself? "Okay, you've gone and done it this time. Now what are you going to do?" Really. I'm just interested to see what I can come out of the situation with. And I just hope to swing a little bit. Because I do believe that the great musicians recognize and value swing above everything else. Above great technical facility, above advanced harmonic concept. If somebody gets up there and swings with what they've got, ultimately that's what people respond to. And I find myself in situations where I've really played badly but I swung. It wasn't a total loss.

MB: What role does your thinking play in being nervous or calm?

BS: I'm not aware of telling myself anything. I'm aware of trying to feel what I'm feeling. I have the feeling that if you try to escape what you really feel at the moment, you're lost. You're not standing on anything solid. And if you just feel what you feel, and own that, and own the space you're in, and go into the event, whatever that event is, with your eyes and ears open, you've got a reasonable chance of surviving.

It's like rehearsing. At some point, you have to do it in public. The stuff you want to do won't happen in rehearsal. You gotta make your mistakes in public. You gotta feel what that feels like. That's the other thing—and I'm sure everybody else will say this to you too: You can't play differently when you're rehearsing than when you're on a gig. You can only play one way.

And you play that way whether you're playing at a daycare center or Lincoln Center. You only have one way to play. You don't have a separate switch that says, "Okay, I'm just kidding them." You gotta be just as serious in front of four year olds as you are in front of critics. [Laughs] And maybe even better than you are [in front of critics.] [Laughs]

MB: When don't you get nervous now?

BS: I guess when I'm at home playing with my friends. I still get nervous every time I walk on a stage, wondering if I can do it. I'm absolutely certain when I walk on a stage that there's a chance I'm going to be great and there's a chance I'm going to get lost. And I just go up there knowing that.

And that kind of not knowing what's going to happen, stepping into the unknown, gives the event the kind of tension that can really work for you and can make something happen.

When I'm hanging out at home with my pals and just playing with people I know real well and people I'm really comfortable with . . . every now and then I'm absolutely able to forget myself and it'll just be like shooting hoops or something.

MB: What's the worst case of stage fright you've seen in someone else?

BB: The worst case I ever saw was back when I was twenty-two, twenty-three years old, and I was living in England. I was there to go to graduate school—I was not a professional musician; I was studying history. But through a series of events, I was recording, and I had made a record with the Steve Miller Band. And these guys had come over from San Francisco. So I was plugged into this little recording scene in London. And I had a friend who was British and who was a really good piano player. And so I had arranged for this well-known British producer to come and hear him play, 'cause I thought I could hook him up and maybe he could get some work. But because [my friend] was British, he took the arrival of this producer much more seriously than I did. I just had met him on these sessions, and he seemed like a nice guy. He gave me some work, so I thought everything was okay. But I didn't realize [my friend] was as nervous as he was. So he pretended everything was fine, but he started drinking the afternoon of the day he was supposed to meet the producer, and you know where it went. He got totally sloshed by the time the producer showed up. It was awful.

242 • BEN SIDRAN

MB: So what do you think he was telling himself?

BS: I think that there's a very fine line between insecurity and the need for acceptance. The really insecure people sometimes become very famous rock n' roll stars. Because they have this gift. And the more success they have, the bigger their gift is, the more they become insecure. 'Cause they don't really feel like they've earned it on some level, and they're really afraid of being found out. So I think [my friend] was saying, "I don't deserve this."

What was he telling himself? I don't think he was telling himself anything . . . I think he was trying to blot out . . . I think when people get nervous, the first thing they try to do is blot out the annoying sensation that they're about to be exposed. They fear that they're going to be exposed; they don't want to be exposed.

Art Blakey once said, "When you're up there, on the other side of the lights, you're in your birthday suit. You're naked. You cannot hide." I think that's really just what it is. You gotta be ready to stand up there and have people say, "He's not as good looking as I thought he was," and say back, "That's right!" I think in that moment, it's just panic, man. I think the hormones have started rampaging and it's part of life.

MB: Could your friend have had a different attitude so that he wouldn't have been as nervous and reacted the way he did?

BS: Oh, absolutely. The deal is real simple: Go toward your fear. You have to train yourself to feel okay when you get that feeling of fear.

Say somebody calls you up and says, "I've got this gig for you. So-and-so wants to have you in the band. It'll pay you this much money." And your first reaction is, "Oh, I can't handle that. I'm not ready for that," or whatever. If you ever hear your voice in your head saying, "I can't," that's a sign that you have to. Literally. That's a sign that you have to do it. And you have to train yourself to say, "Okay, this is a good sign now." And go with it.

MB: Is there any other advice you'd have for performers who experience stage fright?

BS: Just clearly, nothing is as bad as your fear of it. There's nothing in life— or probably even death—that's as bad as your fear of it.

Robin Williams

Academy Award winner Robin Williams began his career as a stand-up comedian, creating a repertoire of indelible characters, first in the hit series "Mork & Mindy" and then in numerous film roles. In 1997, Williams received Academy and Screen Actors Guild awards for his performance in *Good Will Hunting*, having been previously nominated by the Academy for performances in *The Fisher King*, *Dead Poets Society*, and *Good Morning Vietnam*. Williams' blockbuster films include *Mrs. Doubtfire*, *The Birdcage*, *Jumanji*, *Hook*, *Night at the Museum*, and the animated films *Aladdin*, *Robots*, and *Happy Feet*. In 2009, he will star in *Night at the Museum 2: Battle of the Smithsonian*, opposite Ben Stiller, and the Thanksgiving comedy, *Old Dogs*, opposite John Travolta. Williams is currently in the middle of a sold-out comedy tour entitled "Weapons of Self-Destruction." His critically acclaimed 2002 comedy tour aired on HBO and earned five Emmy nominations. Best known philanthropically for his affiliation with Comic Relief, Williams supports numerous causes and recently returned from his fourth USO tour of the Middle East.

MB: First off, can you tell me how long you've been performing?

RW: Probably forty years. I was in high school—it was a play making fun of the teachers.

MB: Can you remember the first time you were nervous about performing?

RW: I think that was during a play in college. For the one in high school, I wasn't really nervous because it was the first time, and sometimes you don't really know what it'll be like. It went pretty well, and the moment I heard the laughs, that eased my tension about it.

MB: Can you describe how the nervousness felt?

RW: The first really hardcore nervousness I felt was focused on not know-ing if I'd remember my lines. If you're performing in a play, you go, "Wait a minute. Do I have it all? Do I know it?" It's about the question, "Can I do this?"—wondering whether all the things you've done to prepare are there and ready to go. You think, "It won't work. It won't work. I'll forget the lines. Oh no!" And the more people there are in the audience, the more intense the feeling is.

MB: Do you think there's a way you could have viewed it differently so that you would have been less nervous?

RW: I think that, especially in the beginning, nervousness is almost a natu-ral response. It's a bit like fight or flight. You go on stage and there's an adrenaline rush.

Could I have viewed it differently? Yeah, there's telling yourself, "It's going to be all right." But I think some of it's just to get you to think about preparation. What happens now with me is almost like a narcoleptic response—I start yawning, and I'm almost sleepy. I've heard other people say that happens to them, too.

MB: So as you continued performing, how did your nervousness change?

RW: There would be times when I'd be more relaxed, depending on the size of the hall and the type of audience. If you're performing for black tie affairs, it tends to be a little different than performing in a club, where it's much more loose.

Also, for me, being on live TV puts more pressure on. It's one of the few situations that still gets me going, "Oh jeez!" 'cause there's no going back; it's whatever you say. That puts a lot of pressure on the moment.

MB: So sometimes you still get nervous?

RW: Oh, totally. Whether it's the Academy Awards or the smallest club, you know there'll be people seeing your performance. If it's a paying gig, that puts a different pressure on. The expectation is, "These people paid. Let's do this." That's different than if you're just performing in a club, just trying something out, going on unannounced—which is what I like to do.

MB: So could you go into a bit more of detail on your thoughts, on what you're telling yourself when you get nervous?

RW: I don't really tell myself anything other than "I'm going on stage." It literally comes down to the fact that they've announced you and you say, "Okay. And we're off!" I think that what happens with nervousness, whether it's a play or stand-up, is you're trying to overcome the questions: "Do I know all this? Can I do this? Is it ready?"

I think the worst part of stage fright is that you're thinking, "Oh God, this isn't going to work. Oh no!" And then, "Okay. What could go wrong?" Once you get that out of the way, you're ready. But the worst is when the nervousness immobilizes you, the total terror of it. It's like: "I can't do this."

MB: Right. Has that ever happened to you?

RW: No. I've never had nervousness to the point where I couldn't perform. Not like, "Oh God, I can't speak."

MB: What's the worst case of stage fright you've ever had?

RW: The Academy Awards could be some of the worst. With the Academy Awards, it's a combination of viewing the audience—you look out and there's Olivier, and all these very famous people—and being seen by the world. There are a lot of people watching, combined with an audience of your very well-known peers who aren't having a wonderful time themselves. That gives you the best of all worlds in terms of things to get nervous about. If it doesn't go well, it gets written about. And there's also a time constraint—you usually only have two or three minutes. "Bang. Okay. Here we go."

MB: And what are your thoughts about that? What's going on in your head beforehand?

RW: In my head? Well, with me, there are also constraints with censorship —to the point of wondering, "What can I say?" It's the idea of sticking to what they want versus going off it a bit and making what I say funny. The biggest thought is, "Why am I doing this? What reason in hell do I have to be here for? Why did I sign up to do this shit again?" That alone is beyond stage fright. That's a point of existence.

And once again, it's live TV. But it's just the same whether it's a club or the Oscars. It's still the idea of "How will it go? How many people are watching this? Who is watching this?" And for awards ceremonies, the only thing that probably makes a difference is focusing on the people who you know are having a good time and not looking at the ones who've just lost. So you don't just do the lines, "And welcome now . . ."

MB: What role would you say that your thinking—what you're telling yourself—has in the anxiety or lack of it?

RW: I think it has a role in both. Obviously, thinking is what creates the anxiety. And also, thinking diminishes it. Simple breathing can diminish it. In the worst cases, when people hyperventilate, they're going into a fight-or-flight response. For a comic, it's thinking, "Oh God! What if I bomb!" The mind is working through that. The way to overcome it is probably to say, "So what?" or "You're not going to bomb. You know your stuff." A lot of it is just the initial process of getting ready for the arena—you can look at the performance as gladiatorial, except you don't have a sword, you have a pen. I think that will help you get through the initial "Oh fuck! What am I going to do?"

Then there's having faith in what you do: You know the lines, you know the place, you're prepared. True stage fright happens when people are caught totally off guard. If you haven't prepared, the idea of trying to bullshit your way through a performance is like the thoughts of a kid who didn't do his homework: "How am I going to walk my way through this?"

MB: What are the circumstances when you don't get nervous now? When is your nervousness at its lowest level?

RW: When it's casual. When I can just go on stage and do it. And when I don't have to prove anything—I'm already there, just to relax and explore. Versus a situation that makes me go, "Oh God, I have to prove myself. I have to do it. This is the big one."

MB: What's the worst case of stage fright you've seen in somebody else?

RW: It was on an awards show. Somebody I knew won an award and got up on stage and couldn't speak. That's because she had produced a movie she was very proud of, but she didn't want to speak—dreaded speaking—in front of people.

MB: That's really funny too, because she'd already been given approval by receiving the award.

RW: It wasn't about approval. It was about being afraid to speak, being in front of a large crowd of people, being televised. I ended up speaking for her. I had to say, "She can't speak right now. If she could, it would go something like this . . ."

MB: How nervous did she seem?

RW: Terrified. Almost like it was a firing squad, except it was cameras.

MB: How were you able to perceive that?

RW: By the shaking. It's perceptible if you're next to the person. When people really have stage fright, it's a full-blown fear. Stage fright is real for someone who does not like to be up in front of people. For people who are like you and me, performers, it's part of our existence. Some might say it's part of our drug, it's our milieu, it's what we do. And we kind of live for that. But the worst is bombing, which is a whole other thing. Then you get that "Oh God, it's really not going well" feeling. And performing at very elegant affairs can cause fear just because the more intelligent the audience is, sometimes the tougher it can be—although other times that can prove to be a total misperception.

There was a BBC live interview I did once where the technical stuff failed and I started fucking around with the audience. People thought, "What is going on?" But it was nothing about stage fright. It was more about taking the stage for other people, and it was actually a lot of fun. And it achieved the purpose: I did my thing for about fifteen minutes, and it was a group of very intelligent people having a good time, realizing that this was on the spot, nothing prepared. It helped sustain the momentum of the TV show till it went back on line.

They say that even though people are scared in moments of heroism—to compare stage performing to heroism, just making the decision to do it—they have to somehow overcome the fear and go, "I've got to do this. It's the right thing to do."

You have to ask, "How legitimate is my fear? What am I really afraid of? These people can't hurt me." It's like you said, that terrified woman at the awards show just got an award—what was she afraid of?

Look at all the circumstances. Sometimes, the audience paid to see you. Other times you'll be in a bar and they didn't pay to see you. And if they're crazy and loud, there's a legitimate fear.

Some nervousness is real and necessary to help you prepare for a situation. But when the percentage of fear inside you increases too much, you have to realize, "This is disabling me rather than motivating me."

MB: What thoughts contribute to disabling rather than motivating?

RW: Any thought that helps you explore the worst-case scenarios. You have to let those thoughts go. The simplest trick of all is to breathe. That will relieve a lot of anxiety. Breathe deeply and don't hyperventilate—because you can breathe too much and pass out. Also, realize you already got the gig. Rodney Dangerfield has a great quote: "I'm sweating. Why am I sweating? I own the club!"

MB: Well, obviously you've bombed less than most.

RW: I've bombed as much as other people. In different places, different clubs, all over the world. Some very elegant venues. Some not so elegant.

MB: How do you deal with bombing when it happens?

RW: Usually it's a great motivator to go, "Okay. You need to work more; you need to prepare more." Or sometimes you just think, "This is a group of people who did not get, or want to get, what I do." And, you know, that happens. Not everybody loves you—which is a hard thing for a performer to understand. You have to realize there are critics, and the world is not all in your court.

Another problem is that sometimes people with stage fright will try to compensate for it with an artificial means like alcohol or some medication. That's dangerous because it gives you a false sense of security.

MB: Right. Is there any other advice you'd have for people with stage fright?

RW: Breathe, and know where the exits are.

Bibliography

Burns, David. *Feeling Good: The New Mood Therapy*. New York: Harper, 1999.

Burns, David. *Feeling Good Handbook*. New York: Plume, 1999.

Burns, David. *Intimate Connection*. New York: Signet, 1984.

Burns, David. *When Panic Attacks: The New, Drug-Free Anxiety Therapy That Can Change Your Life*. New York: Broadway, 2007.

Edelstein, Michael R. "The ABC's of Rational-Emotive Therapy: Pitfalls of Going from D to E." *Rational Living*, 11: 1 (1976), pp. 12-13.

Edelstein, Michael R. and David Ramsay Steele. *Three Minute Therapy*. Aurora, CO: Glenbridge, Ltd, 1997.

Ellis, Albert. *Anger: How to Live With It and Without It*. Secaucus, NJ: Citadel Press, 1977.

Ellis, Albert. *.Better, Deeper, and More Enduring Brief Therapy: The Rational Emotive Behavior Therapy Approach*. New York: Brunner/Mazel, 1995.

Ellis, Albert. *How to Control Your Anxiety Before it Controls You*. Secaucus, NJ: Carol Publishing Group, 1998.

Ellis, Albert. *How to Make Yourself Happy and Remarkably Less Disturbable*. Atascadero, CA: Impact Publishers, Inc, 1999.

Ellis, Albert. *Rational Emotive Behavior Therapy: It Works for Me—It Can Work for You*. Amhert, NY: Prometheus Books, 2004.

Ellis, Albert and Robert A. Harper. *A New Guide to Rational Living*. North Hollywood, CA: Wilshire Books, 1997.

Ellis, Albert, and William J. Knaus. *Overcoming Procrastination*. New York: Signet, 1977.

Epictetus. *The Handbook of Epictetus*. Indianapolis: Hackett, 1983.

Frankl, Viktor E. *Man's Search for Meaning*. New York: Washington Square Press, 1966.

Knaus, William J. *The Cognitive Behavioral Workbook for Anxiety: A Step-by-Step Program*. New Harbinger Publications, 2008.